Also available at all good book stores

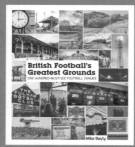

9781785316470

9781785313929

9781785315466

9781785314414

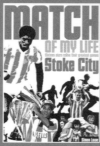

9781908051769

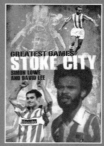

9781848182011

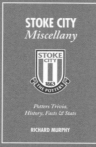

9781905411481

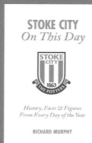

9781905411313

9781785317194

STOKE CITY
MINUTE
BY MINUTE

STOKE CITY
MINUTE
BY MINUTE

Covering More Than 500 Goals, Penalties, Red Cards and Other Intriguing Facts

SIMON LOWE

First published by Pitch Publishing, 2021

Pitch Publishing
A2 Yeoman Gate
Yeoman Way
Worthing
Sussex
BN13 3QZ
www.pitchpublishing.co.uk
info@pitchpublishing.co.uk

ISBN 978 1 78531 855 9

Typesetting and origination by Pitch Publishing
Printed and bound in India by Replika Press Pvt. Ltd

Contents

Dedicated to the memory
of every Stoke fan who
succumbed to the ravages
of Covid-19

Acknowledgements

Stoke City: Minute by Minute was one of those dream projects which came along and gripped me immediately. I loved the idea of working out which great events, like goals, penalty saves, sendings off, broken legs, fights, or even pitch invasions, happened in which minute of which Potters match.

It proved, though, to be a devilishly hard book to research, not least because I received the commission to write it during the 2020 to 2021 coronavirus lockdown period. Covid-19 meant that various archives which would have been go-to easy points of research were not available to me. So I had to come up with other methods to research the over 650 incidents from Stoke City history which feature in this book.

Enter Pete Smith of *The Sentinel* newspaper. Not only is Pete an intrepid reporter, who has covered Stoke City throughout the thick and thin of the last decade or so, but he has also donned a mask to enter venues up and down the country to bring us reports and interviews during the global pandemic. Thankfully, despite Covid-19 restrictions, Pete was able to plunder *The Sentinel*'s capacious Stoke City archive on my behalf to email me match reports, allowing me to put *Stoke City: Minute By Minute* together, and research some photographs for me to boot. Without him this book simply wouldn't have happened. Thanks, Pete. And thank you too to *The Sentinel*'s editor Rob Cotterill for giving permission.

I did manage to use other sources too. Mainly my own books such as *Stoke City: The Modern Era*, *Potters at War* and *Stoke*

City's Greatest Games, and then other authors' publications such as Tony Matthews's *Encyclopaedia of Stoke City,* Jeff Kent's *The Potteries Derbies,* Wade Martin's *A Potter's Tale* and David Lee's *Premier!,* plus a host of reference books such as the Rothmans/Sky Sports annuals.

Then there were various other assorted resources, such as BBC website match reports, *Match of the Day* and Sky Sports highlights, endless YouTube clips (and countless other newspaper clippings and old match reports that sometimes tested my eyesight to the limit when discovered in some murky area of the web). Eventually I could get the job done.

Thank you as well to all the many fellow Stokies who suggested their favourite goals to me on Twitter via @simonloweauthor and via the excellent @DUCKmagstoke. I've tried to include all of those beloved strikes within these pages – some of them were quite obscure – but there's always a story attached to each and every time the ball hits the back of the net, which is why we all love the beautiful game so much. These incidents often spark memories that go beyond what happened on the pitch.

Those coronavirus restrictions meant I could not gain access to archives to go back any further than the end of the Second World War, so this book is not able to feature Stoke matches such as the first in the Football League against West Brom in 1888; the games against Notts County and Aston Villa which helped shape the penalty-kick laws in 1891; the infamous Match With No Shots against Burnley in 1898; charismatic Stoke goalkeeper Leigh Richmond Roose being ducked in the River Trent when he foolishly took to the field for Port Vale in a reserve-team match in 1910; the winning of promotion in 1922, 1927 and 1933; Stan Matthews's 1932 debut and his famous four goals in an 8-1 thrashing of Leeds in 1934; the record 10-3 hammering of West Brom in February 1937 in which Freddie Steele scored five goals; and the 8-1 despatching of Derby seven months later in which Steele repeated the feat.

They are for another, non-Covid time.

ACKNOWLEDGEMENTS

Therefore, this book's earliest entries are from 1945 – 6-0 and 4-2 victories over local rivals Port Vale either side of VE Day in May 1945, and throughout the incredible 1946/47 season which saw manager Bob McGrory's Potters, featuring heroes such as Matthews, Steele, Franklin, Mountford, Ormston and Herod, come within one match of lifting the league title. The most recent of the goals featured in this book was scored in the 2020/21 campaign in which Michael O'Neill steered City to a mid-table position in the Championship, having miraculously saved Stoke from almost certain relegation the season before.

I'd also like to thank Potters legend Terry Conroy for very kindly providing the foreword for this book. TC scored one of the most important goals in the club's history in the fifth minute of the 1972 League Cup Final against Chelsea at Wembley, Stoke's first-ever goal at the national stadium. But that was one of 67 goals in his Potters career; he'll no doubt be too modest to mention scoring on his debut, his belting volley against Arsenal in September 1970, his winner in the epic League Cup semi-final tussle against West Ham which took us to Wembley or netting the club's first-ever goal in European competition against Kaiserslautern in September 1972. Terry also scored a magnificent brace against Liverpool on Easter Monday 1975, when it seemed as if the Potters could go on and lift a first league championship in their history. Sadly, it wasn't to be, but it has been wonderful bringing those goals and so many more incidents back to life for this book.

Finally, thanks to Paul and Jane Camillin – the tireless siblings who mastermind Pitch Publishing – for allowing me to write yet another book about Stoke City FC, alongside the editorial and production team who, despite the pandemic, have kept the quality and volume of books like this going to keep readers informed and entertained. I hope you all enjoy dipping in and out of it.

Introduction

What links Dennis Viollet, Jimmy Greenhoff, Wayne Biggins, Frank Bowyer, Carl Beeston, Arnar Gunnlaugsson, Peter Crouch, Jacob Brown and Asmir Begović? Well, as if you didn't know, that illustrious list of Potters have all scored goals in the first minute of games for Stoke City. A wonderful bit of trivia, made all the trickier by it including a goalkeeper!

There never was a clock of any kind on display to supporters at the Victoria Ground. But ever since the move to the new Britannia, now Bet365, Stadium, high up on the hill at Trentham Lakes, overlooking the old ground's site down by the D-Road and River Trent, time has been on show – an integral part of the game.

First there was a long, thin horizontal scoreboard with just the score and the time, displayed in an old-school digital 'square' with round corners, then that was replaced for the Premier League era by a full-colour digital screen, which showed teams, match highlights and, of course, the time, in the corner of the ground. When that corner – Gordon's Bank as it became known later, following the erection of the great goalkeeper's statue outside the ground there in 2015 – was filled in, another big screen was erected in the diagonally opposite corner of the ground, over the emergency entrance, behind which is also housed a TV studio.

Whether the time has been on display or not, stuff has always happened in Stoke games. This book relives the great goals at home and on the road, through European and cup adventures, scored by the likes of John Ritchie, Freddie Steele, Ricardo Fuller, Mark Stein, Mike Sheron, Peter Thorne and Jimmy Greenhoff. It harks back to the heady days at the end of the Second World War, but travels through every era since up to the modern day. It features over 600 goals against almost 100 different opponents scored by over 230 different Potters stars, past and present.

Many of the goals I have been able to select have been memorable for so many reasons other than timing, not least the drama of the moment, which is what I've tried to capture here in describing them. Often many need context, particularly the ones which predate most modern fans' memories. I hope you feel the entries are suitably evocative, particularly if you were there and remember the goal vividly. Because this book is all about moments, frozen in time, that live on in the memory for the better, for the most part, or occasionally, for the worse.

It isn't only goals scored which feature. Here you will find sendings off; penalties; fingertip saves; broken bones; fights; inspirational, or sometimes turbulent, crowds; mascot dust-ups; post-match shenanigans; and even the odd crucial or controversial penalty or goal conceded. Taken altogether, it is a different take on the history of the club, told minute by minute through the course of a game.

Dip in and relive your favourite moments, which have thrilled, frustrated, enraged and brought joy and tears to generations of Stokies. They are all here, recorded minute by minute, from Asmir Begović's incredible 92-metre goal after 13 seconds against Southampton in 2013 to Tim Coleman's 120th-minute winner in the longest FA Cup tie in history.

Enjoy!

Foreword

By Terry Conroy (1967–79)
Appearances: 335 Goals: 67

Wembley, 4 March 1972. Chelsea v Stoke City in the League Cup Final.

Looking back, I would have loved to have been with all the Stoke supporters, enjoying a day out, a dream come true for the many faithful followers. I can assure you, it's more fun watching than playing. Now, don't take that the wrong way; 90 minutes of running around very energy-sapping turf is no fun. We are trained for that, but it's still very hard work. The enjoyment of it all comes only at the end, when you are the victors.

My ambition, growing up, was to become a professional footballer, represent my country and score the winning goal in a cup final at Wembley. Isn't that every kid's dream?

I got that slightly wrong, though. I didn't get the winning goal, but I did score that March day in 1972, heading in the opening goal in the fifth minute in that never-to-be-forgotten game. After the ball flew in off my bonce, I became transfixed by the big *Radio Times*-sponsored Wembley scoreboard, showing: 'Conroy 5'.

My name was transfixed in time, and my eyes glued to it.

I promise you, I was in dreamland for the next ten minutes. Time at that point seemed to stand still for me. It can be like that sometimes as a footballer. You are almost always in the moment, but sometimes that moment overwhelms you. The enormity of

18

what I had just done froze me a bit and I was pretty useless for a while.

I was snapped out of it by Jackie Marsh, our right-back, giving me an earful. You can rely on him to do that!

For Stoke City to win a major cup at Wembley was a fairy tale and I am so delighted to have played a part in that. With the club's long and wonderful heritage, we deserved our place amongst the winners.

This was the day that we stood alongside the great teams that had graced Wembley before us. We were no longer 'little old Stoke'. The party was just beginning, around the pitch with our wonderful supporters, in the big Wembley bath with the trophy and some champagne afterwards and then on the open-top bus tour round the Potteries for a fabulous welcome home the next day.

Time has moved on since those wonderful days when I scored goals seemingly in every minute of the game. Now, through my position as matchday host at the Bet365 Stadium, I get to see the Potters' games, at least until Covid-19 intervened to keep them behind closed doors. But, as I write, the country is planning to reopen and we may even have fans back to watch Stoke's first home game of the 2021/22 season. That will be a wonderful time to be alive.

I am somewhat puzzled by the present-day game. Players don't play by the rules anymore, at least not as we knew them. Anything they can do to gain any advantage, they will do. The merest hint of a wind is enough to have the modern-day player diving. If I didn't own my TV set, I would put my foot through it. It seems as if cheating is everywhere.

Mind you, I blame the governing bodies for this. If they clamped down on pushing, shoving and, most importantly of all, constant backchat, then a lot of the problems would disappear. I understand passions run high during the game, but players take it too far. At every opportunity they seem to try to get an opposition player sent off. Discipline is non-existent. As soon as a foul is committed, straightaway the players are waving for a card to be shown. It's rife within the game.

I will guarantee that if the governing bodies laid down proper disciplinary behaviour, then in no time, the game would be all the better for it.

What current players don't realise is, their actions are copied by the youngest growing up, hoping to emulate their heroes.

Righting these wrongs won't happen overnight, but if the deterrent is severe enough, then it will become the game that we all grew up loving again. Have trust in the match officials.

And the players should manage themselves. I know during my time as a player the game was hard, but rarely did players dive. If you did, you'd get an earful from your own team-mates. Trying to get an opponent sent off or booked was a definite no-no.

Thankfully, at Stoke, we don't go in for that kind of thing and neither the players, the manager, nor, crucially, the fans will allow it. It doesn't stop some visiting players having a go time and time again.

But when they do I wince and think back to a better time, one that fills me with a warm glow, remembering some golden moments, like those with which Simon has filled this book. Moments in time, frozen and framed for you to remember them if you were there or visualise them in your mind's eye if you weren't that fortunate.

Enjoy.

Terry Conroy,
Alsager, March 2021

Stoke City Minute by Minute

The clock is ticking ...

Prematch

The bell goes in the changing rooms. In the stadium, the background current pop-chart ditty fades through into the ominous, brooding, glowering introduction of the guitar chords of Eminem's Oscar-winning 'Lose Yourself'. Fans around the ground get to their feet in anticipation, jigging gently from foot to foot in time with the music, and also from the cold, often bitter wind that swirls about even in summer months. A minute or so later the stadium announcer Steve Buxton screams in an ever-rising voice: 'Ladies and gentlemen, please welcome to the Bet365 Stadium the visitors [whoever they are] and your mighty, MIGHTY POTTERSSSSSSS!!!!!!!!!'

The opening chords to the Stoke City FC club anthem 'We'll Be With You', written by *Neighbours* theme-tune penners Tony Hatch and Jackie Trent, sung by the victorious 1972 League Cup squad, strike. Fans sing along: 'We'll be with you, be with you, be with you, every step along the way!', as the players emerge from the tunnel, mascots in hand, led by the match officials, who collect the ball off a little podium positioned by the corner flag (at least in the Premier League years ...).

As the players line up for photos in front of the main two-tier stand, the music segues into Tom Jones's 'Delilah', a song adopted and adapted by supporters, as legend has it, one day in Derby when the police asked them to stop singing lewd songs in a pub and the (in)famous fan known as 'TJ' (Anton Booth) broke into his favourite tune, which then was sung throughout the ensuing match and forever after.

The players shake hands along the lines and break to warm up, with the Potters taking the half of the pitch in front of the Boothen End, where fans are packed into the red and white seats, rising to greet their heroes with a tumult of noise, clapping and scarf or flag waving. The fever rises ...

Game on!

13 seconds

2 November 2013

As wind billows around the Britannia Stadium, Southampton kick off in the Premier League, but their early pass forward is intercepted by Erik Pieters, who knocks the ball back safely to goalkeeper Asmir Begović. The Bosnian international thwacks the ball downfield and a gust of wind propels it towards Artur Boruc's goal. It lands on the D of the Saints' penalty area, where it seems to take on supernatural powers and careers crazily over Boruc's head, bouncing once more before ending in the top corner of the Boothen End net. No one really knows how to celebrate. They are too busy being incredulous. It is a record-breaking goal in many senses: the first goal of Begović's career, the longest goal ever scored in recorded professional football at 92 metres (before being beaten by Newport's Tom King in January 2021 with a distance of 96 metres) and the quickest goal in Premier League history at just 13 seconds. Remarkably, it also makes Begović the season's joint leading scorer for Stoke, for a week at least.

19 seconds

6 December 2014

In yet another eventful edition of Potters fans' favourite Premier League grudge match against Arsenal, Stoke take the lead when a Steven Nzonzi cross is missed at the near post inexplicably, by Calum Chambers, who will later see red for two bookable offences to complete a miserable personal day. The ball ricochets off Héctor Bellerín and Mame Diouf, wrong-footing Gunners keeper Damián Martínez, and falls perfectly for Peter Crouch, right in front of goal, to just roll into the back of the Boothen End net with a gentle side-foot with his right peg. The chants of '1-0 to the rugby team' ring around the Britannia as Arsène Wenger pretends he didn't see that.

24 seconds

13 May 2000

Stoke get off to a tremendous start in the Second Division play-off semi-final first leg against Gillingham at the Britannia Stadium. Despite the Gills taking the kick-off and sticking an aimless long ball out of play in the Potters' left-back position, the throw is worked forward to Kyle Lightbourne, tight on the left touchline ten yards inside Gillingham's half. The beanpole striker hugs the line to beat one man then cuts inside to leave another grasping thin air. He then squares the ball to the on-loan Arnar Gunnlaugsson, just outside the penalty area, and the Icelandic international hammers a left-footed drive into the top-left corner from 18 yards to send the home support ballistic.

35 seconds

11 November 1989

In City's first game since the sacking of manager Mick Mills following the 0-6 thrashing at Swindon the previous weekend, caretaker manager Alan Ball restores attackers Vince Hilaire, Gary Hackett and Wayne Biggins to the starting line-up, as well as veteran centre-half George Berry, and is rewarded with an opening half hour of verve and ambition. Right from the off, City pile forward and midfielder Carl Beeston drives into the penalty area, exchanges passes with Dave Bamber and prods in past the onrushing John Keeley in the Brighton goal. The Ball era has started well.

52 seconds

1 January 1987

Stoke begin the new year perfectly, scoring within a minute of the kick-off of the Second Division game against Shrewsbury at the Victoria Ground. In front of the biggest home crowd of the season, 19,382, Carl Saunders starts and finishes a move, which also involves Phil Heath, Nicky Morgan and Brian Talbot. The 1-0 victory, on a rain-sodden pitch, is City's seventh in eight games in a golden patch around Christmas, with a goal aggregate of 24-6 over the run, which takes them from 20th position to fifth after this latest win.

1

26 December 1950

Having defeated Arsenal at Highbury the day before, Christmas Day, Stoke clinch a well-deserved double over the Gunners thanks to a goal by young striker Roy Brown. His right-foot shot proves too hot for new keeper Ted Platt, replacing the unfortunate George Swindin from the previous game, and the ball squirms into the net. Although that is the end of the scoring for the day, Brown's involvement switches to the other end of the pitch on 15 minutes, as Stoke keeper Dennis Herod picks up an injury which means he cannot continue in goal and Brown pulls on the jersey to tend nets instead. With no substitutes available, Herod plays 75 minutes on the right wing, smiting the bar with one tremendous shot. City survive a late Arsenal surge, even though wingers Malkin and Ormston also hobble around for the last few minutes of a tense encounter.

17 December 1960

Right-back Bill Asprey roams forward to pounce on a mishit clearance and fire in a right-footed shot from the edge of the penalty area, which struggling Plymouth's goalkeeper Geoff Barnsley saves. But the rebound goes straight back out to Asprey, who lashes home gleefully. The goal sets Stoke on their way to a club-record 9-0 win. Within two minutes, Plymouth's George Fincham has inadvertently bundled the ball into his own net in front of an unforgiving Boothen End to put Stoke two up. Neil Dougall's Argyle capitulate from that awful start.

15 April 1963

In a dramatic first minute of a vital game against promotion rivals Sunderland, Stoke are awarded a penalty by referee Mr J. Thacker, when Dennis Viollet is felled in the act of prodding home a loose ball. Viollet picks himself up to slot the penalty home in front of a jubilant Boothen End. More than 42,000 are jammed inside the

Victoria Ground just three days after City drew 0-0 at Roker Park in front of over 62,000. With a home 1-0 victory over Cardiff thanks to a Viollet goal on the Saturday in between also having over 30,000 inside the Vic, a total of 135,000 fans watch City in those four days, as the team pick up five points on their way to promotion.

2

15 February 1947

Stoke run riot on a snow-covered pitch as Johnny Sellars rushes in to tap home George Mountford's early shot, which has been parried by Chelsea keeper Harry Medhurst. Within another 25 minutes City will have racked up six goals as they hurtle up the First Division table towards a first challenge for the league title, all netted with Stan Matthews, John McCue and Frank Mountford watching from the stand injured.

30 November 1957

Right-winger Neville 'Tim' Coleman opens the scoring in the second minute at Craven Cottage with a brilliant individual goal, the first of a hat-trick. This opener comes as he jostles Fulham's former England international half-back Eddie Lowe and wins possession from him, racing forward to hit a low, bobbling shot into the far-right corner of the net. Coleman scores his second just after half-time when he fires Kelly's pullback into the roof of the net and Stoke are on their way to a superb 4-3 win away at their promotion rivals.

12 September 1962

Dennis Viollet, a January 1961 signing from Manchester United for £25,000, nets the first of a personal haul of four goals in a goal fest against Charlton Athletic at the Victoria Ground. This strike, a rising, right-footed, thumping drive at the Town End, flies into the top of the net past Addicks keeper Peter Wakeham. City go on to win 6-3 to record a first victory of what will turn out to be a promotion season and exceed the total of five goals scored in the six matches thus far within a vibrant 90 minutes.

21 March 1964

Stoke have won just three of their last 15 league games, but cut loose as a settled team, uninterrupted by injuries that have blighted their winter, find form. Dennis Viollet opens the scoring in what will become a 9-1 rout when Ipswich keeper Jim Thorburn saves Keith Bebbington's header, and the inside-right follows up a rebound to slot home. It is the first of a hat-trick for the 30-year-old. Ipswich, who have already lost 1-10 to Fulham and 0-9 to Manchester United this campaign, are on their way to another crushing defeat.

4 April 2009

Stoke City always beat West Brom, at least they did between Christmas 1988 and 2015, inspiring the famous terrace song. This crucial Premier League relegation battle at a sunlit Hawthorns starts brilliantly for the Potters when a long punt forward out of defence by Danny Higginbotham is misjudged by Albion's Shelton Martis, who lets it bounce over his head for the lurking Ricardo Fuller to latch on to.

The Jamaican races forward, cuts inside on to his right foot and hits a low shot towards Scott Carson's goal from 22 yards. Carson, who was almost signed by Stoke the previous summer, but opted for the Baggies instead, dives late and allows the ball to go through his flimsy right hand to nestle low into the back of the net for a fairly soft goal all round. City are on their way to their first-ever Premier League away win and their first in the top flight since Luton in May 1984.

24 January 2010

The Potters already have a hoodoo over Arsène Wenger's men, but the fear and dread felt by every Gunners fan, player and official is cemented by a superb start to this FA Cup fourth-round tie. Inevitably it arrives via a Rory Delap long throw after only 70 seconds. From a position level with the penalty area on the right-hand touchline, the ball flies at pace into the area on a low trajectory just above head height, watched by transfixed Arsenal defenders.

It seems only Ricardo Fuller is on his toes and aware of where the ball is heading. As the ball dips to waist height, he ghosts pasts three static defenders, distracted by the movement of Ryan Shawcross, to beat keeper Łukasz Fabiański to power a header into the top-right corner from six yards. Moments later Fuller should have a penalty when he is fouled by Mikaël Silvestre, but referee Martin Atkinson misses the foul. No matter, Stoke will win easily 3-1.

3

26 May 1947

In gorgeous sunshine on Whit Monday, City take the lead in their crucial penultimate match of the season at Aston Villa, when George Mountford flicks home Alec Ormston's right-wing corner to net what will prove to be the only goal. The 1-0 victory sets up a one-off game against Sheffield United at Bramall Lane. Win and City will lift the league championship for the very first time.

6 April 1992

In front of new broadcaster Sky TV's cameras, the Autoglass Trophy semi-final first leg gets off to a stunning start when first Wayne Biggins stretches to redirect a left-wing cross into the bottom-right corner from eight yards with a flick of his bull neck. Then, just two minutes later, Biggins, who will end the season as the club's top scorer with 28 goals in all competitions, slams a 22-yard short free kick right-footed straight at young debutant Peterborough keeper Ian Bennett, but the custodian mishandles the ball and it drops inside his right-hand post, sending the Boothen End into raptures.

At that moment, not only did Stoke lead 2-0 and seem on course for Wembley, but the Potters also sat atop the Third Division after Biggins's brace the previous Saturday saw them record a 3-0 win over Hartlepool.

Referee David Elleray adds a twist into the post-goal celebrations for Biggins's second when he notices the burly striker has not covered his wedding ring up and calls on the trainer to apply tape, confusing everyone into thinking he may have disallowed the goal. He hasn't. It stands. However, this pulsating semi-final has only just begun to unfold its drama and an hour later Stoke are somehow 2-3 behind to Chris Turner's Posh, who would join City in the play-offs after a late-season collapse in league form saw Stoke slump to finish fourth.

28 April 1993

Peter Fox's 15-year career at Stoke City is probably best remembered for two seconds right at its twilight. Approaching 36, and only playing due to an injury to Ronnie Sinclair and the return of loanee Bruce Grobbelaar to Liverpool, Fox pulls off not one but two of the great saves by a Potters keeper in quick succession to help City clinch a deserved promotion against Plymouth. Lou Macari's side had been at the top of the Second Division for months, but stuttered as the finishing line drew closer, so nerves were jangling as Peter Shilton's Pilgrims arrived at the Victoria Ground. Right at the start, City show the frailty which has led them to falter. Mickey Evans whips in a ball from the right and Steve Castle's six-yard near-post header is brilliantly tipped on to the right-hand post by Fox's left hand. Warren Joyce pounces on the rebound, but the veteran keeper hauls himself up and somehow raises his right hand instinctively to block the point-blank snapshot. It is a superb way for club servant Fox, who made 473 appearances in all for the Potters, to bow out. He had joined Stoke from Sheffield Wednesday in 1979 for £15,000 as cover for Roger Jones after becoming the Owls' youngest-ever player when he kept a clean sheet in a 2-0 win over Leyton Orient at the age of 15 in 1973. Established in the top flight, Fox was tipped for England honours in the early 1980s, but never quite broke into the squad. It was fitting, then, that he should pull off such a magnificent save with the former England great, former Stoke keeper and now Argyle manager in the goal at the other end. The save earnt him celebrity status, as Fox recognises: 'We went to Adrian Heath's wine bar in Newcastle afterwards and it's fair to say we were well looked after. I certainly don't remember having to buy a drink that night.'

28 July 2011

The Potters have not played European football since 1974, but get off to a great start in this Europa League third qualifying round at home to Croatian veterans of European competition Hajduk Split. Matty Etherington chests down a Rory Delap pass on the left wing and crosses perfectly for Jon Walters to outmanoeuvre his marker and head home from eight yards. Try as they might, Stoke cannot find a second goal, although Kenwyne Jones has an effort ruled out for offside, and the tie is in the balance as City travel to Croatia the following week.

12 May 2013

Stoke are celebrating turning 150 years old, making the club the second-oldest league club in the country and thus the world. Before the game, a parade of hundreds of former Potters greats are greeted by adoring crowds, who are all given a free commemorative T-shirt to mark the occasion by the club. The Premier League match against André Villas-Boas's Spurs gets off to a great start when Steven Nzonzi ghosts in at the near post to head home Charlie Adam's right-wing inswinging free kick off Hugo Lloris's post. City cannot sustain their lead and Clint Dempsey equalises before Adam is dismissed for a second yellow card in the 46th minute and Emmanuel Adebayor scores to secure victory for the visitors, in a contest which proves to be manager Tony Pulis's last home game in charge of the Potters after two spells covering ten seasons.

4

12 June 1947

In torrential rain, the biggest game in Stoke's history gets off to a pulsating start at Bramall Lane when first Dennis Herod misjudges Fred Pickering's third-minute shot, which bobbles in, then, a minute later, Alec Ormston runs in off the left wing to latch on to George Mountford's cutback to hammer home. At 1-1 the crucial game is finely balanced. Just one more goal will clinch the title for City, but Sheffield United are determined not to make it easy.

21 March 1964

City score their second goal inside the opening four minutes when Keith Bebbington crosses, John Ritchie dummies and Peter Dobing runs in from the left to fire home left-footed past visiting Ipswich keeper Jim Thorburn; 2-0 will become 9-1 and a record top-flight victory for Stoke before the end of the game.

10 April 1965

John Ritchie bags the first of his four goals to defeat fifth-placed Sheffield Wednesday. The burly 6ft 2in striker opens his account when he follows up visiting centre-half Vic Mobley's block on the line, from Jimmy McIlroy's shot, to net easily. It is his 19th league goal of the season, but by the end of the game he will have netted his 22nd.

31 March 1993

In a frantic opening few minutes to the season's fifth Potteries derby, tackles are flying in. John Butler marauds forward from right-back to beat a couple of lunging dives to hit the byline and pull the ball back towards the penalty spot. Vale have made the crucial mistake of giving Mark Stein half an inch and the 'Golden One' swivels to lash a perfectly struck right-foot shot low into the bottom left-hand corner, past keeper Paul Musselwhite, right in front of the gathered throng of Potters fans in the Hamil End.

Stoke are on their way to completing a league double and erasing some of the pain of two cup defeats to their neighbours during the campaign.

28 April 1993

Sixty seconds after Peter Fox's amazing double save, Graham Shaw bursts into the right-hand side of Plymouth's box. He squares the ball into the middle, where midfielder Nigel Gleghorn collects with his left foot, but stumbles slightly under a challenge. As he falls, he manages to slam the ball into the roof of the Boothen End net left-footed from six yards. It will turn out to be the winner and the most important of his eight goals since joining from Birmingham for £100,000 seven months earlier. City are on their way to promotion as Second Division champions, but they still have 86 minutes to hang on against player-manager Peter Shilton's Plymouth. Nerves are jangling.

29 November 2000

In front of a first-ever capacity crowd of 27,109 at the Britannia Stadium for this League Cup fourth-round tie, Stoke tantalisingly almost snatch the lead against Gérard Houllier's Liverpool when Pegguy Arphexad miscontrols a back pass and striker Peter Thorne pounces to rob him in a tackle outside the penalty area. The ball breaks slightly to the left, but Thorne races on to it and slams it goalwards. As the ground celebrates prematurely, the ball strikes a post and bounces back to the grateful keeper. City have wasted their chance to steal the lead and the visitors cut loose, setting themselves on course to lift a cup treble by the end of the season by scoring eight goals to inflict a record 8-0 home defeat in all competitions on the Potters, with Robbie Fowler bagging a hat-trick. Added to the previous week's FA Cup exit at the hands of non-league Nuneaton, this is one of the most miserable periods in Stoke City history.

17 August 2002

Having won promotion under Guðjón Thórdarson just three months earlier, Stoke get their First Division campaign up and running under new boss Steve Cotterill in the third game of the season. City striker Andy Cooke, a man who is a Stokie through and through, boasting tattoos to prove it, chases down a back pass from the left side of the penalty area directed towards Bradford keeper Gary Walsh. The former Manchester United custodian lingers too long instead of clearing quickly and Cooke slides in to hook the ball home from eight yards and bag the first goal of the season. Cotterill's reign, though, is to last only a further ten games and less than two months before he heads off to be number two to Howard Wilkinson at Sunderland, forever more to be known as 'Quitterill' by Stoke fans.

26 January 2015

After several cup upsets at the weekend, City put all thoughts of another one to bed this Monday night when diminutive Spanish genius Bojan latches on to a poor headed clearance by Olly Lancashire to lash a left-footed volley low into the bottom-left corner of Josh Lillis's net from 23 yards. The smile on Bojan's face as he celebrates in front of the cameras and with the Potters fans on the side of the Spotland pitch is a sign of the powers of the instigator of City's new attacking style, which has transformed them from Arsène Wenger's hated long-ball and throw merchants into a team which can destroy sides like Manchester United and City with flowing football. The little 'number ten' has dovetailed beautifully with skilful forwards like Marko Arnautović and Victor Moses, plus the more industrious Jon Walters and Glenn Whelan, prompted by midfielders such as Steven Nzonzi and Charlie Adam, to produce a wonderful blend of play under manager Mark Hughes. Arriving with fellow young stars Marc Muniesa and Moha El Ouriachi from Barcelona, Bojan was signed for just £1.8m in the summer of 2014. He had been the Catalan club's youngest-ever debutant, aged 17 years and 19 days, breaking Lionel Messi's record, and joined Stoke following loan spells at AC Milan and Ajax as his star waned at the Nou Camp. There was fevered anticipation as Hughes sought to change City's style and Bojan instantly became the supporters' darling. But just after the half-hour mark at Rochdale, he suffered a devastating knee injury which occurred as he chased a ball into the penalty area, merely caused by his motion over the uneven and muddy Spotland pitch. City win this game 4-1 to go through to the fifth round, but Bojan will not reappear in a City shirt until September. He manages to find his mojo again and notches seven goals in 31 appearances in the 2015/16 season, which sees him and Hughes's team at the height of their exciting potential. Injuries, loss of form and changes of managers eventually see Bojan farmed out on loan to Mainz, then Alavés, despite fan protests. He is then released in August 2019 to move to Montreal Impact in the MLS. His smile, verve and incisive attacking passing will always stand as a monument to that happy period from 2014 to 2016 in which Stoke turned from the Potters into 'Stokelona'.

5

16 November 1963

Following a thrilling 4-4 draw with Burnley in the previous home game a fortnight earlier, young striker John Ritchie starts the ball rolling for Stoke again, running in to slot home after Sheffield Wednesday keeper Ron Springett saves Tony Allen's left-footed piledriver. This is now the sixth consecutive league game in which Ritchie has scored and the ninth overall, setting a new club record to replace the previous one of six games set by Jack Peart in 1910. Ritchie's overall record still stands today, although Mike Sheron bettered the league-game run by one match in the 1995/96 season. Ritchie now has 13 goals in that spell, which began with a brace at home to Scunthorpe in a second-round League Cup replay. But his goalscoring is not over for the day just yet. He will end the game with four.

4 March 1972

It is early in the 1972 League Cup Final as Stoke attack Chelsea's goal at Wembley's tunnel end and win a throw in deep by the corner flag on the left wing. Skipper Peter Dobing's long throw loops to the near corner of the six-yard box, drawing keeper Peter Bonetti out to punch clear from Denis Smith's head. But it only falls to George Eastham on the left edge of the area, who clips it first time towards Jimmy Greenhoff, lurking centrally. The striker is beaten to the ball by John Dempsey, but his weak clearance only falls to Smith, whose first-time shot hits Dempsey, loops up in the air and is nodded into the bottom-right corner by the onrushing Terry Conroy from eight yards. Stoke lead 1-0. The glory of a first-ever major trophy is within touching distance.

28 August 1982

Mark Chamberlain, a winger signed from local rivals Fourth Division Port Vale, along with reserve goalkeeper Mark Harrison, in summer 1982, for a snip of a joint fee of £180,000, destroys

Arsenal's England left-back Kenny Sansom in a dazzling display. He provides the first of many goals for fellow debutant George Berry with a cross from the right byline, which sees the centre-half stoop to thunder home a header into the back of the Boothen End net. Five minutes into the second half Chamberlain beats Sansom yet again to cross for centre-forward Brendan O'Callaghan to head City's second. The 2-1 win sets up a superb season for the Potters, prompted by the incredible form of 21-year-old Chamberlain on the wing. By December he has impressed new England manager Bobby Robson so much that he makes his international debut as a substitute, heading home a Terry Butcher cross to net the sixth of nine goals against minnows Luxembourg in a European Championship qualifier. Chamberlain would go on to win eight caps, his other highlight: being man of the match in the Maracanã, a game which is now best remembered for John Barnes's mazy dribble and goal to put England on their way to a 2-0 victory. But the winger would begin to pick up injuries which curtailed his devastating pace and, by 1985, as Stoke were relegated ignominiously, he struggled, being sold to top-flight Sheffield Wednesday after City dropped down to the second tier for a tribunal-set fee of just £300,000. He would help the Owls finish fifth in the First Division and go on to play for Portsmouth, Brighton and Exeter, retiring in 1998 after a season at Fareham Town, where he also briefly managed. Always sunny and smiling, Chamberlain remains a firm favourite with City fans.

7 May 1984

Stoke are desperate for three points in the penultimate game of the season as they have come back from the dead of being next to bottom at Christmas to be on the cusp of an incredible survival. David Pleat's Luton are unusually subdued, especially after City striker Ian Painter, looking suspiciously offside from George Berry's flick-on, fires the ball right-footed high into the net from close range and turns to see the linesman keep his flag down. Despite Hatters protests, the goal stands and the Potters keep them at bay to secure that vital victory. This, though, will prove to be the club's last away win in the top flight until victory at West Brom in April 2009.

12 October 1997

In the first Potteries derby at Stoke's new Britannia Stadium, City start superbly when Kevin Keen crosses and Richard Forsyth heads home, unmarked, from close range.

22 December 2007

In a huge game between two promotion-chasing teams at the Britannia Stadium, John Eustace's neat pass is helped on by striker Mama Sidibé with a neat flick of his left foot, leaving the pacy Ricardo Fuller haring in on Dean Kiely's goal, having wriggled between West Bromwich Albion's central defenders. Fuller easily scores low to the keeper's right with the outside of his right foot and sets City on their way to a famous 3-1 win, in which the Jamaican nets a superb hat-trick.

26 December 2012

Stoke are on an eight-game unbeaten run under Tony Pulis in a fantastic start to the season which sees them in ninth place. The Boxing Day visitors are Brendan Rodgers's Liverpool, who take the lead in the second minute after Ryan Shawcross pulls over Luis Suárez to give away a penalty which Steven Gerrard nets. But City come roaring back and Walters fires home past Pepe Reina with a powerful right-footed drive after Martin Škrtel slips as he tries to deal with a long ball, leaving Walters to control and finish from 12 yards, low into the bottom-right corner. Stoke sense blood.

6

9 November 2014

City's new £1.8m signing from Barcelona, Bojan, announces himself with a superb individual goal. The little Spaniard picks the ball up in the middle of his own half on the left side, exchanges passes with Steven Nzonzi, then starts to motor towards the Tottenham goal. The home team's midfield and defence back off, seeming to part like the Red Sea, as Bojan advances with the ball glued to his right foot. Quick as a flash, he is 22 yards out and hits a low, right-footed shot through Danny Rose's legs to beat Hugo Lloris low to his right. It is Bojan's first goal for Stoke and the first time the fans get to see his wonderful smile.

19 December 2020

City swarm over visitors Blackburn from the kick-off and get their just reward when Morgan Fox picks up a quickly taken throw-in on the left wing and pings over an inch-perfect cross for Nick Powell, unmarked, to launch himself and nod home spectacularly from six yards with a throwback diving header. It's a different story after that as Rovers attack, but parsimonious Stoke have kept six clean sheets in the past seven games and manage to deliver another one to seal the narrow win over Tony Mowbray's men thanks to dogged defending, good goalkeeping by young Joe Bursik and the width of a post, struck by Barry Douglas.

7

23 February 1957

Neville 'Tim' Coleman starts a remarkable Second Division game against Lincoln with the first of his seven goals in an 8-0 victory, setting a world record for any winger in a professional game and a club record for an individual player, which still stands today. A rejigged Stoke forward line, missing the injured Frank Bowyer and with Johnny King at centre-forward in place of the dropped Andy Graver, alongside the recalled Joe Hutton at inside-left, sparks into riotous form. Despite the icy Victoria Ground pitch, which is speckled with the snow that fell an hour before kick-off and has been hastily marked with blue lines by the groundsmen, Coleman's first comes as Oscroft crosses from the left wing, then Hutton flicks the ball on to the far post, where the right-winger slides in unmarked to slot the ball home.

15 November 1980

Burly blond striker Lee Chapman, at just 20 years of age, is making a big impression in the First Division and will end the season with 17 goals. Ken Brown's Canaries feel the brunt. Chapman rises to head home skipper Ray Evans's free kick to give Stoke an early lead. It's the first of a hat-trick that starts to alert big clubs to his prowess.

14 October 2006

The second coming of Tony Pulis, following the purchasing of the club back in summer 2006 by Peter Coates from the Icelandic consortium who have been in charge since 1999, has begun with a whimper. Just one win in ten games sees City in 20th position in the Championship. But a visit to Elland Road sparks a new-look City into life, with recent arrivals Salif Diao and Rory Delap making their debuts as a new central midfield partnership which will eventually see the Potters into the Premier League, while loanee Lee Hendrie, from Aston Villa, pulls the strings. It bears fruit early on when Hendrie curls in a stunning free kick from 22 yards into the top-left corner of Neil Sullivan's net to give Stoke a fabulous start against managerless Leeds.

5 December 2015

Stoke tear Manuel Pellegrini's Manchester City to shreds as Mark Hughes opts to play Bojan as a false nine, flanked by Xherdan Shaqiri and Marko Arnautović as inverted wingers. The visitors cannot cope with the Potters' verve and flair. Early on, Shaqiri, known as the 'Alpine Messi', who up until now has not set the Premier League alight, sparks into life. There seems little danger when he picks up Glen Johnson's short pass on the right wing, but he shakes off the weak challenge of Fernando, bursts towards the penalty area, beats Aleksandar Kolarov with a stepover and sprint to the byline, then cuts the ball back right-footed for the onrushing Arnautović to prod home from four yards. Arnie's celebration, leaping two-footed at Shaqiri down by the tunnel, is one of the enduring images of the Austrian's eventful stay at the Bet365 Stadium.

1 February 2017

Thirty-six-year-old Peter Crouch nets his 100th Premier League goal, 15 years after his first, sliding in, six yards out, to prod home Marko Arnautović's square ball from the left side of the Everton penalty area. The big man celebrates in the most Crouch way possible, bringing out the robot for one last airing in front of the East Stand.

8

4 March 2000

Stoke are mourning club president and legend Stanley Matthews, who died aged 85 on 23 February and was buried after a funeral procession which began at the Britannia Stadium and travelled past his old haunt at the site of the Victoria Ground to St Peter's Church in Stoke, in front of thousands of fans. In City's first home game since Matthews's passing, marked by a minute's silence before kick-off, Peter Thorne cuts loose, netting four goals in a 5-1 thrashing of Chesterfield, on his way to bagging 20 goals between the start of March and the season's end. Thorne's first comes as he rises above keeper Mark Gayle and defender Ian Breckin to nod a deep left-wing cross into an unguarded net, while his second, ten minutes later, sees him head home debutant loanee Arnar Gunnlaugsson's far-post corner.

13 May 2000

Already 1-0 ahead, Stoke take a grip of the Second Division play-off semi-final first leg at the Britannia Stadium when Arnar Gunnlaugsson breaks away deep inside his own half. Carrying the ball at pace, he arrives at the edge of the Gillingham penalty area and puts fellow Icelandic international Brynjar Gunnarsson in on the left. His left-footed cross wrong-foots the entire Gills defence when it deflects back out towards the penalty spot, but not Kyle Lightbourne, who strokes home left-footed past keeper Vince Bartram.

10 November 2013

On his 100th consecutive Premier League appearance, striker Jon Walters skips through two weak Swansea tackles on the edge of the Liberty Stadium penalty area and slots a low, right-footed shot from the right corner of the six-yard box off the left post of Gerhard Tremmel's goal.

9 November 2019

Stoke begin new manager Michael O'Neill's first game in charge brilliantly, but thanks to Barnsley keeper Bradley Collins, who takes an innocuous-looking free kick out on his right touchline, 30 yards out of his goal, so badly it ends up at the feet of Stoke's Sam Clucas on the halfway line. Controlling instantly with his left foot, Clucas, knowing Collins is way out of his goal, simply chips a 60-yard, left-footed effort over the despairing keeper's head, which goes, one bounce, into the middle of the goal. The away fans, gathered at the other end of Oakwell, begin a Michael O'Neill party that lasts throughout the game, as the new man has already brought about a huge change in fortune, and an air of optimism, despite only being appointed the day before, after the club agreed terms with his former employers at Northern Ireland. City need the luck of the Irish; they are deep in a relegation mire at the foot of the Championship after the disastrous tenure of Nathan Jones.

9

20 August 1955

Two goals down to Doncaster Rovers inside the first five minutes on the opening day of the 1955/56 Second Division campaign, Stoke start one of the most remarkable first-day comebacks when diminutive centre-forward Johnny King scores one of the great individual Potters goals, picking the ball up halfway inside Rovers' half, weaving towards goal, beating three men, before cutting sharply on to his left foot on the edge of the D and lashing the ball in off the underside of the bar.

27 September 1969

Stoke deliver a superb footballing performance to defeat the previous season's FA Cup winners Manchester City at the Victoria Ground to sit in fifth place after 12 games. Jimmy Greenhoff, a £100,000 signing from Leeds during the summer of 1969, dovetails brilliantly with the returning John Ritchie, re-signed from Sheffield Wednesday for £28,000 by Tony Waddington, who has admitted he made a mistake in moving the striker on in the first place. The combination hits it off from the start and form one of the best partnerships in the Potters' history. Greenhoff gets the scoring started by nodding in Peter Dobing's cross past a youthful Joe Corrigan at the near post. It is his fourth goal since signing for Stoke and he goes on to score against his former club the following week, finishing the season as joint top league scorer, with Ritchie, with 14 goals.

13 February 2016

Manager Mark Hughes has splashed out a club-record and eye-watering £18.3m on out-of-favour Giannelli Imbula from Porto on transfer deadline day (1 February 2016) in an attempt to replace the departed Steven Nzonzi. The rangy midfielder starts to pay that back by scoring his first goal for Stoke in his second start. He wins the ball back midway inside the Bournemouth half and exchanges passes with Ibrahim Affelay, before laying the ball forward to Xherdan Shaqiri, on the left-hand corner of the penalty area. Imbula then runs on to take the return pass, but instead Shaqiri opts to cross. The ball is cleared back out to the edge of the area, where Imbula sets himself to hammer a left-footed volley into the far-right side of Artur Boruc's goal. It is a stunning strike and at this stage it looks like Imbula is a shrewd buy. He will, though, score just once more in a Stoke shirt and become something of a millstone around the club's neck with his five-and-a-half-year, costly contract.

20 January 2020

Stoke are in desperate straits at the wrong end of the Championship table, but new manager Michael O'Neill has already managed to win five of his first 12 games to begin to turn things around. At leaders West Brom, in a Monday night TV game, City start brilliantly when Bruno Martins Indi, filling in at left-back, cuts out an Albion through ball and plays it to Sam Clucas in the centre circle. The midfielder kills the ball and turns with one touch of his left foot, then plays in Tom Ince, racing down the right, with a lovely right-footed pass. Ince hares into the Albion penalty area and squares the ball left-footed to Tyrese Campbell, for the 20-year-old striker to score right-footed, hitting the ball first time so hard keeper Sam Johnstone cannot keep it out despite getting both hands to it. It is Campbell's fifth goal in nine games as he becomes one of the hottest young players in the Championship.

24 October 2020

City are scintillating in the first hour against highly rated Championship promotion hopefuls Brentford. James McClean drives forward from the halfway line, carrying the ball into the Bees' penalty area, and plays in Tyrese Campbell down the left-hand side. The striker jinks to his left and finds space to deliver a cross to the far post where centre-forward Steven Fletcher has lost his marker to rise and head home unmarked from two yards.

10

21 January 1950

Stoke get off to a great start against the First Division leaders when makeshift centre-forward George Mountford, usually a right-winger, latches on to a pass by his stand-in on the right wing, Johnny Malkin, to turn and slam home a rising shot from the edge of the penalty area. Matt Busby's Manchester United are never in the game after that. City will go on to record a famous 3-1 win.

29 April 1967

Gordon Banks makes his home debut (after losing 1-0 on his full debut at Chelsea the previous week) to help his new club defeat his previous one, Leicester. The England World Cup-winning keeper has arrived amidst a huge media storm after being nudged out at Filbert Street by the arrival on the scene of a precocious 17-year-old called Peter Shilton. But Banks still has plenty of football left in him and tells his new team-mates he has come to Tony Waddington's Stoke 'to win trophies'. He makes a great start by creating the first goal of a pulsating game. His gigantic punt downfield allows Peter Dobing to race through and side-foot past Banks's nemesis. Harry Burrows and youthful midfielder John Mahoney net the other two in a 3-1 victory. The match also marks Dennis Viollet's last game at the Victoria Ground before his retirement at the end of the season after a career in which he scored 251 goals in 535 games and the Boothen End rises to say 'farewell' to a real Potters hero.

25 September 1982

Richie Barker's Stoke City are an exciting proposition early in the 1982/83 season and sit fourth in the table after four wins in the opening six games. David Pleat's newly promoted Luton have already set their stall out to score more than the opposition do. It makes for a scintillating match, which has gone down in folklore as one of the best in Potters history. City take the lead

50

when Paul Maguire's left-wing inswinging corner is flicked up in the air by Brendan O'Callaghan at the near post. It falls for Mark Chamberlain, who loops a header against Alan Judge's bar, but George Berry rushes in to nod the rebound home from two yards. It's the first of eight goals in an end-to-end thriller.

1 April 2000

Peter Thorne is in the middle of the hottest spell of his career in the spring of 2000. At third-placed promotion rivals Bristol Rovers, he opens the scoring when Kyle Lightbourne's left-foot shot from the left edge of the penalty area is so mishit it ends up being a brilliant cross to the far post, where Thorne taps home right-footed from three yards. It is the first of 11 goals in seven games for Thorne, who misses out on scoring against Cardiff in the sixth game of his run, which would have equalled Mike Sheron's club-record spree of seven consecutive scoring matches, but netting more goals. No matter, Thorne's scoring for this game is only just beginning.

21 November 2015

City secure another Premier League victory, the fifth in seven games, when Erik Pieters marauds down the left wing and pings a cross to the near post, anticipating Bojan's run. The little Spanish imp continues his motion, running off the back of Jordy Clasie, but then improvises a beautiful, right-footed instep flick to perfection, catching the ball so sweetly it flies into the top-left corner past Saints keeper Maarten Stekelenburg before he can move. Sheer footballing genius. Meanwhile, at the other end, that is City's fourth successive away clean sheet and fifth in six games, while the 1-0 win secures their first-ever win at St Mary's and first at Southampton for 35 years.

4 July 2020

Stoke are in a slump since the resumption of Championship football following the three-month coronavirus break of spring 2020. They are yet to win in three matches and face a crucial clash with fellow relegation-zone inhabiters Barnsley. The pressure is on, but is greatly relieved when first Sam Vokes heads in Sam

Clucas's inswinging corner after eight minutes and then, two minutes later, Tyrese Campbell begins a one-man show, which sees him tuck home James McClean's cutback from the left byline with a clever back-heel at the near post from six yards. Impudent improvisation.

11

15 February 1947

Syd Peppitt, playing at inside-right, scores from a tight angle on the right side of the penalty area as Stoke make it 3-0 against Billy Birrell's Chelsea. Within a minute, Alec Ormston will have scored his second left-footed 15-yarder of the game to make it 4-0 with just 12 minutes gone. Stoke are on their way to their biggest win of the 1946/47 season, 6-1, and a rise up the First Division table to fourth position.

8 December 1979

Home-grown 22-year-old striker Garth Crooks bags the first goal of his second hat-trick of his career, and his first treble in the top flight, when he slides in to convert Paul Randall's right-wing cross from six yards. His second, three minutes later, sees Crooks show his predatory instincts when he intercepts Ally Robertson's back pass. City are on their way to a 3-2 win over West Brom in this mid-table clash.

22 November 2003

On the day England win the Rugby World Cup in dramatic fashion in the morning, Stoke are in a vital First Division relegation clash with managerless Bradford. The tense, tight game, littered with mistakes, is settled early on when John Eustace starts and ends a move which sees him nod home Lewis Neal's cross from three yards to score his first goal for the club since his move from Coventry. Eustace also hits a post late on. It secures a crucial 1-0 win, which is Stoke's only victory in a run of nine games, and only their third in a long run of 19 matches, before a December revival, inspired by the signing of Gerry Taggart.

17 October 2006

Having won 4-0 at Leeds just three days earlier to kick-start the return of Tony Pulis as manager, Stoke start brightly, with a raft of new signings combining well. But one of them, Rory Delap, on loan from tonight's opponents, Sunderland, goes into a tackle with former team-mate Robbie Elliott, just in front of the benches on the main stand side of the Britannia Stadium, and a horrifying crack is heard as Delap breaks his tibia and fibula. The incident upsets Stoke, and Sunderland take the lead through Dwight Yorke, but City will come back strongly in the second half to win 2-1, and when Delap is offered a permanent contract, despite his long-term injury, it feels as if the club as a whole has turned a corner in the way it treats its players. That mood is continued as Stoke march inexorably towards the Premier League, famously propelled by the fit-again Delap's long-throw missiles.

1 November 2008

This is the moment when Stoke, and Rory Delap in particular, begin to haunt Arsène Wenger's nightmares. Delap has a throw-in 35 yards from goal, way out on the right, and there should be no danger at all, in normal circumstances. But Delap is superhuman and his deep throw sees Ricardo Fuller outmuscle Kolo Touré to glance a far-post header past Manuel Almunia. Not for the last time by a long chalk, the Gunners, and their despairing fans, are rooted to the spot wide-eyed as a Delap Exocet comes flying in to blow their defences apart. It will soon become one of football's biggest clichés – and all the funnier for it, particularly as Touré puts his arm up to claim offside from this throw, which does little to reduce his embarrassment.

17 April 2011

It is the biggest game for Stoke since 1972 and once again Wembley proves to be a happy hunting ground as City overwhelm Owen Coyle's Bolton 5-0 in the FA Cup semi-final. The goal fest starts in balmy spring afternoon sunshine when Matty Etherington calmly rifles home a peach of a left-footed shot from 22 yards into Jussi Jääskeläinen's bottom-right corner after Bolton make a hash of a clearance and the ball falls perfectly to the left-winger to strike. It is all one-way traffic from hereon in. Ethers has proved an inspirational signing since arriving in January 2009 for £2m from West Ham, despite having a well-publicised gambling problem that the club helped him deal with, in return for which he delivered some wonderful performances. Along with right-winger Jermaine Pennant, he brought dynamic flank play to Stoke and helped make the team Premier League mainstays. Etherington bagged 16 goals in five seasons at the Britannia Stadium, finally succumbing to injuries, notably a back problem, which caused his premature retirement in December 2014, aged just 33. Bright and intelligent, Etherington loved to join in attacks at pace, and possessed an accurate left foot, never more seen than when scoring that first semi-final goal which opened the floodgates against Bolton.

7 March 2020

In a crucial bottom-of-the-table clash at the Bet365 Stadium, as Michael O'Neill's men battle to climb clear of relegation, City produce a superb team goal. The move starts at the back and works its way down the left wing, where Nick Powell produces a wonderful piece of skill to flick a back-heel pass through Leonardo Da Silva Lopes's legs to Sam Clucas. Stoke keep possession and go all the way back and across the back four before Tom Ince's threaded pass sees right-back Tommy Smith hit the right byline and chip a cross to the far post, where Powell steals in six yards out at the far post to head powerfully at goal. Hull keeper George Long should really save it, but the pace on the ball is too much for him and he parries it into the top-left corner of the Boothen End net. The tension around the stadium is relieved and City will let rip and score five goals against Grant McCann's sorry Tigers. Little do Stoke know at the time, but this is the last game with fans inside the ground before the coronavirus pandemic hits.

12

2 September 1981

After an opening-day win at Arsenal thanks to Lee Chapman's goal, Stoke rise to the top of the formative First Division table under new manager Richie Barker thanks to thrashing Dave Sexton's Coventry 4-0 at the Victoria Ground. The Potters are two goals up by the 12th minute, the first coming from Chapman again, a back-post header. City's second comes from Adrian 'Inchy' Heath, calmly finished into the bottom-left corner of Jim Blyth's net.

18 September 1982

Stoke win the fourth out of their first six First Division games thanks to a bright start at sunny Portman Road. The opener comes when Derek Parkin's long ball is flicked on by Brendan O'Callaghan on the edge of the box for Welsh midfield imp Mickey Thomas to race on to and slot home left-footed past Ipswich keeper Laurie Sivell's right hand.

22 November 1986

Keith Bertschin, signed from Norwich in November 1984 in a failed attempt to score the goals to stave off relegation from the First Division, finds his scoring touch. He bags the first of a hat-trick against Reading's third-choice central-defensive pairing when he nods in yet another George Berry near-post flick-on past a static defence.

26 December 1993

Toddy Örlygsson, a free-transfer signing from Nottingham Forest the previous summer, picks the ball up on the left side of the centre circle and embarks upon a mazy run. He nutmegs one Birmingham midfielder, dribbles round another and hits a 25-yard, right-footed shot from the right edge of the D, which flies past Kevin Miller in the Boothen End goal and goes into the bottom-left corner. Stoke win 2-1 to go into eighth place in their first season after promotion back to the second tier, under new manager Joe Jordan.

5 January 2010

A myth is born as, amidst arctic conditions, Stoke get their match on against Fulham at the Britannia Stadium this Tuesday night, whereas every other game in the country is called off. Not only can the Potters do it on a cold night in Stoke, they slaughter Roy Hodgson's visitors in a first half to savour. Turkish free spirit Tuncay bags City's first, nodding home from one yard on the far post after Robert Huth powers a right-wing Matty Etherington corner goalwards, with the Cottagers' defence literally and figuratively frozen.

13 March 2011

Stoke are all over Avram Grant's West Ham from the kick-off of this FA Cup quarter-final at the Britannia Stadium. Visiting keeper Rob Green has already made a stunning save from Etherington's header when Rory Delap slings in a throw from the left wing, near the corner flag, which sees Robert Huth rise to head powerfully home from six yards, right in the centre of the tunnel-end goal. City are on their way to Wembley.

26 December 2012

In a pulsating encounter, Stoke come from behind to lead Liverpool when Kenwyne Jones, unmarked at the near post, heads Glenn Whelan's corner into the bottom-left corner of Pepe Reina's goal and sets off to deliver his trademark somersault celebration, not once, but twice. City's verve and attacking *esprit de corps* is overwhelming Brendan Rodgers's men.

12 July 2020

Stoke face their day of reckoning. Just one point and one place above the Championship relegation zone, despite the Herculean task performed by new manager Michael O'Neill since taking the reins in November after Nathan Jones's sacking, City have four games in which to save themselves in this Covid-delayed season and they are on the ropes after a 5-0 hammering at Leeds just three days earlier. Managerless Birmingham, who sacked manager Pep Clotet in midweek as they are being dragged into the relegation soup, cannot live with Stoke's effervescent start. After Sam Vokes hits the bar with a header, the Potters take the lead at an empty Britannia Stadium when Danny Batth turns in Nick Powell's teasing left-footed cross from three yards at the far post. With a win, City will go above the visitors, but nerves remain jangling as long as the lead is narrow.

13

16 November 1963

John Ritchie rises like a salmon to powerfully head Gerry Bridgwood's right-wing cross into the right-hand side of the Boothen End net to put Stoke 2-0 up at home to Sheffield Wednesday. Ritchie now has 14 goals in his blistering spell of form over the past nine matches of his first full season in the team following his arrival from Kettering Town for £2,500 in 1962. Ritchie has only come into the side due to an injury to Dennis Viollet the previous month, but has grabbed his chance with both hands. The only question now is can he bag his first Stoke City hat-trick?

13 May 2012

City are hosting Owen Coyle's Bolton on the last day of the season, but the visitors need to win to have any chance of Premier League safety. Stoke are smarting after losing to Wigan in the same circumstances the previous season and watching them celebrate survival and make no mistake this time round. Wanderers keeper Ádám Bogdán has already made two good saves when Matty Etherington curls in a cross left-footed from the right wing. Jon Walters miscontrols the bouncing ball and it pops up for Bogdán to pouch, but he collects the charging Walters at the same time and the striker's head connects with the keeper's elbow. Bogdán spills the ball, which hits him in the face and bounces into the net, with the goalie following close behind. Bolton go ballistic as Walters has clearly fouled the keeper, but referee Chris Foy allows the goal. Controversial.

19 November 2012

Stoke haven't won away in 11 months in the Premier League, but start this Monday night game at Upton Park brightly and take a deserved lead through a well-worked corner routine. With their attention drawn by Crouch and Ryan Shawcross's runs in towards goal at the near post, the Hammers defenders fail to track Walters who runs from deep at the far post to appear in a pocket of space eight yards out at the near. He swipes home Glenn Whelan's precise corner right-footed. Post-match, Tony Pulis admits Walters has never managed to score from that routine in training: 'We have worked on it for the past three days, we tried it five or six times and Jonathan Walters has never scored from it, so I'm glad he saved it for today.'

14

8 December 1971

City take the lead in only the fourth semi-final of a major cup in their 108-year history, at a foggy Victoria Ground. George Eastham wins the ball back from West Ham in the centre of the opposition half and feeds Jackie Marsh. The right-back looks up and hits a long, deep ball towards John Ritchie, lurking about 15 yards out on the left side of the area, but the burly striker mistimes his jump and the ball bounces over him for strike partner Jimmy Greenhoff to hit a first-time shot. It flies against the far-right post, but rebounds directly to Peter Dobing, who slots into the Boothen End net from two yards. Stoke lead, but eventually lose this first leg League Cup tie 1-2 and have it all to do in the return match at Upton Park the following week.

7 December 1974

Jimmy Greenhoff scores one of the great Stoke City individual goals at Freddie Goodwin's Birmingham. Right-back Jackie Marsh chips the ball forward from halfway to the right flank where Jimmy Robertson heads it inside towards Greenhoff, who chests it down whilst facing away from goal on the corner of the penalty area. Quick as a flash, he swivels to lash a perfect, right-footed volley over the helpless Dave Latchford in the Blues goal from 25 yards. The ball forms a perfect arc as it flies into the top-left corner and the wonderful piece of individual skill is captured for posterity by the ITV cameras.

7 April 2007

City are hunting down a play-off place and visit Tony Mowbray's West Brom with supporters in jubilant mood as star striker Ricardo Fuller has signed a new long-term contract. The Jamaican celebrates by ripping the Baggies apart. For the opening goal of a 3-1 victory, Fuller latches on to Sam Sodje's bizarre, lofted pass back towards his own goal to flick the ball up, swivel and hit a right-foot volley into the far-left side of Dean Kiely's net, right in front of the adoring City fans, who, after the traditional post-goal chorus of 'Delilah', break into the introduction to Johnny Cash's 'Ring of Fire' which lasts most of the game.

19 April 2008

Stoke have just three games remaining in which to clinch promotion to the Premier League, with Hull City hot on their heels and visitors Bristol City not far behind. Enter Mama Sidibé for the greatest performance of his Potters career. The big Malian striker nets the first of a brace in a 2-1 victory when he rises at the far post to meet a Liam Lawrence free kick with the side of his head to power the ball high into Adriano Basso's net from four yards and set the packed stands alight.

15

9 March 1946

A quarter of an hour into City's FA Cup quarter-final second leg at Bolton's Burnden Park, fans begin to encroach upon the pitch from behind the Railway End goal at which Stoke's goalkeeper Dennis Herod is standing. Play continues as police usher the supporters back, but then two barriers give way under the tremendous pressure of people surging forwards to try and get a view of the game. In the ensuing melee and crush, 33 die with another 400 or so injured. Initially the game continues, with a policeman telling Herod that the people lying by the side of the pitch have fainted. Herod would later chillingly recount, 'I knew those people hadn't fainted, I knew they were dead.' The 'Burnden Park disaster', as it became known, was a shameful moment in football history, not least because referee Dutton insisted the remaining minutes be played while the bodies were taken away from where they lay. The game finished goalless, with Stoke going out, having lost the first leg 0-2.

25 August 1990

Cash-strapped Stoke begin the new season under Alan Ball with just one new signing, Mick Kennedy from Luton for £180,000, to tackle the Third Division. Noel Blake gets the optimism rocketing when he dives to head home a flicked-on corner from six yards and sets the Potters up for a 3-1 victory over Rotherham at the Victoria Ground.

9 August 2003

After masterminding a miraculous escape from relegation from the First Division, Tony Pulis puts together a team of free transfers which somehow gels delightfully to defeat Derby on opening day at Pride Park. Debutant striker Gifton Noel-Williams opens his account when fellow first-timer Keith Andrews crosses and the former Watford forward slides in to bundle over the line with a ricochet off his shins from three yards. After Chris Greenacre fires another debutant's, Carl Asaba, cross under Rams keeper Andy Oakes six minutes later, City go on to win 3-0 in glorious sunshine.

29 September 2011

Just a couple of minutes after Portuguese winger Roberto Hilbert has given Turkish visitors Beşiktaş the lead at the Bet365 Stadium in this Europa League group game, in a fevered atmosphere, Ryan Shawcross rises at the near post to try to flick on a Dean Whitehead left-wing, inswinging corner. It bounces off his right shoulder and falls for Peter Crouch to stretch one of his exceptionally long legs to prod the ball, at the top of its bounce, at his waist height, over the line from four yards.

4 December 2011

After the ground rises to pay tribute to the recently departed former Toffee Gary Speed before kick-off, Stoke win a tight game to secure a first victory at Goodison Park since 1981. Matty Etherington's corner to the far post is headed clear, but only to Dean Whitehead on the edge of the penalty area. Whitehead connects beautifully first time, right-footed on the volley, and the ball arrows through the crowded penalty area. As keeper Tim Howard dives to his right to save, Robert Huth dangles his left foot to divert the ball up and over the American and into the net.

5 December 2015

Mark Hughes's Stoke are playing superb football that even makes the national media sit up. Manuel Pellegrini's Manchester City are on the receiving end at the Britannia Stadium as the Potters hit a purple patch with Bojan playing as a false nine in peak 'Stokelona'. The Potters' second goal that kills off the subdued visitors arrives when Xherdan Shaqiri, head and shoulders above every other creative player on the pitch, fools Fernando with a beautiful piece of control on his unfavoured right foot, then turns swiftly to head towards goal 40 yards out, leaving the Brazilian in his wake. With his second touch, Shaq threads a through ball forward, which seems to be heading for Bojan, but ends up perfectly at the feet of Marko Arnautović, arcing into the area, 15 yards out. Arnie takes the ball first time to slide past the onrushing Joe Hart into the bottom-left corner. Stoke hold on comfortably to win 2-0 and should score more as they completely outplay the joint leaders. Potters fans have rarely seen football as sublime as this.

2 March 2019

Nathan Jones's Stoke team are in the middle of a run of keeping seven clean sheets in nine games, but are also often struggling to score. So when Tom Ince cuts in from the right wing to feed Peter Etebo in the centre of the field, 40 yards out from the Nottingham Forest goal, there seems little danger. But the Nigerian international, a £6.3m summer 2018 signing from Portuguese club Feirense, controls left-footed, then drives forward, taking three touches which shift the ball further on to his right foot, making space for a shot. When it comes, it arcs perfectly from 18 yards out into the bottom-right corner of Costel Pantilimon's net. It is his first goal for the club and the first in a 2-0 win. Etebo bags a second goal, also impressively netted from outside the area, at Blackburn a month later. But those two wins are the only ones in City's last 18 games of the Championship season.

16

24 August 1963

Stoke's first game back in the top flight after a decade's absence could not have got off to a worse start against Bill Nicholson's mighty Spurs, who won the first 20th-century double two years earlier and finished as FA Cup winners and First Division runners-up in the previous season. Tottenham and England centre-forward Bobby Smith nets after just two minutes when new Stoke goalkeeper Bobby Irvine, a £6,000 signing from Linfield and a Northern Irish international, parries a Jimmy Greaves shot, but Smith is there to mop up the rebound into an empty net. But City fight back to level when Jimmy McIlroy latches on to the electric Stan Matthews's pass to fire home past Bill Brown high into the top-left corner of the Boothen End net. The real surprise is that Matthews, now well into his 49th year, popped up on the left wing to exchange passes with Don Ratcliffe before finding McIlroy positioned just inside the penalty area. A magnificent upset is very much on.

24 March 1979

Having already grazed the bar at Ninian Park with a 25-yarder, Paul Randall latches on to Brendan O'Callaghan's flick-on of Roger Jones's goal kick, then takes the ball round keeper John Davies, before hammering it into the top-left corner to beat defender Phil Dwyer, who has retreated on the line. The Potters are on their way to a 3-1 win and a 14th game unbeaten as they push for promotion back into the top flight.

19 September 1993

Stoke are back in the second tier, now known as the First Division due to the creation of the Premier League, after three seasons away and announce their arrival in style with a cracking victory at Frank Clark's newly relegated Nottingham Forest. City get off to a superb start when first Nigel Gleghorn, then Mark Stein, flick on a long ball and Dave Regis races into the left side of Forest's area

66

at the Trent End. Regis slides a slightly scuffed left-foot shot past Mark Crossley into the far corner of the goal off the foot of the post to put City 1-0 up.

11 May 2002

City are on a roll after their remarkable late comeback victory over Cardiff in the Second Division play-off semi-final second leg. In the final, back in the capital city of Wales, but this time at the Millennium Stadium, even the curse which has apparently afflicted the south dressing room which Stoke have been allocated cannot stand in their way. The first 12 football matches after the stadium took over from Wembley, currently closed for refurbishment, have been won by the team in the north dressing room, and the stadium management have brought in a feng shui expert to carry out a blessing, then employed Welsh artist Andrew Vicari to paint a mural to try to defeat the 'bad spirits'. Early Potters pressure sees on-loan winger Arnar Gunnlaugsson sling an inswinging right-wing corner to the near post. 'Big Chris' Iwelumo flicks the ball on and it finds another loanee, striker Deon Burton, in oceans of space, whilst also being surrounded by seven Bees defenders. He controls and fires home right-footed from four yards to give Stoke the lead. Steve Coppell's Brentford are never in it from that moment.

28 December 2015

City open the scoring at Goodison Park in a classic encounter when Bojan races down the left and flicks inside right-footed to Marko Arnautović, who also flicks on first time right-footed to find Xherdan Shaqiri. The Alpine Messi slides the ball home from eight yards left-footed past Tim Howard into the bottom-right corner. It is his first goal in the Premier League since his club-record £12m move from Inter Milan in the summer, but Shaq's best is yet to come.

17

9 December 1972

Stoke have won just once since Gordon Banks's awful, career-ending car accident two months earlier and travel to Old Trafford for a relegation battle with 18th-placed Manchester United. The Potters take a deserved lead when left-back Mike Pejic starts and ends a neat move down the left, before breaking inside the penalty area and firing home left-footed from ten yards.

12 May 1984

Stoke have somehow produced a run of nine wins and 30 points in the 16 games since Alan Hudson's return to the club in January 1984 to put themselves on the brink of an unlikely First Division survival. On the last day of the season they face old rivals Wolves at the Victoria Ground, with the Wanderers already ignominiously relegated. A win will save Stoke and they get off to a great start when winger Paul Maguire, playing up front as usual striker Brendan O'Callaghan has converted to play at centre-half, nets a far-post header from Mark Chamberlain's pinpoint cross. It will be the first of four goals for Maguire. City will survive spectacularly.

17 April 2011

In bright Wembley sunshine, Stoke already lead 1-0 when a Rory Delap long throw is cleared by Bolton's defence. Andy Wilkinson pumps the ball back, high into the Wanderers area, where it is nodded away once again. But this time central defender and all-round man-mountain Robert Huth, on his way back into his own half having been up for the initial throw-in, turns to catch the ball perfectly on the volley with his right instep and swerve a 25-yard shot into the same bottom-right corner that Matty Etherington's opener found. I say 'perfectly'; he actually shinned it a bit, but I'm not going to be the one to tell him. Either way, Huth will never score a better goal and City are in dreamland.

23 February 2012

Tony Pulis has caused controversy by leaving nine first-team players at home after telling everyone in the Potteries to go out to Valencia and enjoy themselves. Over 5,000 follow the manager's advice and party like there's no tomorrow in the city square, painting it red and white. The players who do make the trip make a great fist of taking on the perennial Champions League qualifiers, who are currently third in La Liga only to Barcelona and Real Madrid, in the Mestalla, and Kenwyne Jones is twice denied by Valencia goalkeeper Vicente Guaita, when put clean through. His best chance comes with the score in this game at 0-0, put through by Wilson Palacios to scuff a left-footed shot that is palmed wide. Jonas scores shortly afterwards to make the tie safe for Valencia, 2-0 on aggregate, but Stoke's European adventure has been a wonderful one. Valencia end as beaten semi-finalists, only losing to eventual winner Atlético Madrid.

18

28 December 1953

Having drawn at Swansea Town two days earlier, Stoke celebrate Christmas with a thumping 5-0 victory over the Welshmen in the return game. Already 1-0 up thanks to a fifth-minute Johnny King goal, debutant Joe Hutton, a recent signing from Ayr United along with club captain Bobby Cairns, latches on to a return pass from King to fire a cross shot into the far corner of the visitors' net. Just 20 minutes into his fledgling Stoke career, Hutton has now scored one and made one, as it was his cross which King flicked elegantly home at the near post with his lethal left foot to open the scoring. Hutton will go on to score in his first three games for his new club as the supercharged Potters rack up 15 goals in the process.

18 April 1964

FA Cup holders Manchester United are defeated at the Victoria Ground almost before they take to the almost grassless pitch as Denis Law is injured. City's road to their 3-1 victory is set by wantaway midfield powerhouse Calvin Palmer, who slams a shot from 22 yards into Harry Gregg's top corner, collecting a John Ritchie pass before firing in a dipping drive that leaves Gregg watching motionless.

18 September 1982

Paul Maguire gets the first of a brace of goals which see City clinch a 3-2 victory at Portman Road. It couldn't be simpler after Mark Chamberlain bamboozles England captain Mick Mills, drawing two other defenders to him, and passes inside to release Sammy McIlroy, who simply moves the ball on for Maguire to slot home from eight yards unmarked. Maguire's second, and winning, goal is a penalty after Paul Bracewell is tripped. New Ipswich boss Bobby Ferguson hasn't seen his team win yet and they sink to the foot of the table, while Stoke rise to the heady heights of fourth in the First Division.

13 December 2003

Dutch left-winger Peter Hoekstra puts on a legendary one-man show against Steve Coppell's Reading. His first of a treble comes as Reading make a hash of an Ed de Goey goal kick and the ball runs through for Hoekstra to outpace and outmuscle Nicky Shorey, then trick his way round keeper Marcus Hahnemann to slot home right-footed from eight yards.

8 August 2006

Vincent Péricard, a free-transfer signing from Portsmouth, making his home debut, slides in to toe-poke Peter Sweeney's cross come shot home from three yards past Derby keeper Lee Grant. The big Frenchman has set the chance up with a lovely piece of control and back-heel to free Sweeney on the left edge of the box. It is the first goal of the second coming of Tony Pulis following his return from Plymouth after Peter Coates bought the club back from the Icelandic owners, and of City's 100th league season.

19 March 2016

Striker Jon Walters finishes a superb team goal as Stoke take a deserved lead at Vicarage Road against Quique Sánchez Flores's Watford. City play keep ball at the back for 19 touches, before the ball finds new club-record signing Giannelli Imbula, who drives forward 40 yards and feeds Ibrahim Affelay, just outside the Hornets box. The ball goes to the right wing, where right-back Phil Bardsley is overlapping and his low, driven cross is side-footed past Heurelho Gomes on the far post by Walters. The number 19 cups his hand to his ear in trademark celebration and City are on their way to another Premier League away win and a third consecutive ninth-placed finish under Mark Hughes.

7 March 2020

Tyrese Campbell causes havoc down Hull's right flank, outmuscling Sean McLoughlin to latch on to Tommy Smith's long ball, then cutting inside and leaving two men on the deck. His shot is blocked, but falls straight to Sam Clucas, who fires instinctively, high, left-footed into the far top-left corner of the Boothen End net from ten yards. Stoke lead Hull 3-0 early in the game and the fans are rejoicing as Michael O'Neill's men climb inexorably away from the Championship relegation zone.

19

21 September 1946

Stan Matthews, fit again after missing four matches, runs rings around Manchester United's left-back Billy McGlen. He sets up George Antonio to crash a shot in off the underside of keeper Crompton's bar as Stoke take the lead against Matt Busby's league leaders on the way to recording a third successive victory to climb to eighth place in the First Division.

19 April 1972

Having secured League Cup glory the month before, City are in FA Cup semi-final replay action against Arsenal yet again, seeking revenge for the previous season's heartache. Stoke begin this replay at Goodison Park brilliantly and are on top when Geoff Barnett hauls over Jimmy Greenhoff and the striker picks himself up to slot home the spot kick, awarded by referee Walker, low to the goalkeeper's left. Stoke lead 1-0. Wembley beckons again.

21 November 1992

Behind to Ashley Ward's 15th-minute opener, Graham Shaw goes on a one-man rampage through the Blackpool defence at a wet and windblown Bloomfield Road. He helps draw City level when he speeds through the puddles on the left wing to cut into the penalty area near the byline and fire the ball across at hip height for Kevin Russell to stoop and head home, or rather let the ball hit him and see it fly in, from three yards.

26 February 2003

Stoke are fighting a desperate battle against relegation in their first season since winning the play-off final and have already gone through three managers in five months. Tony Pulis finally has the team picking up points, despite the previous weekend's 0-6 thrashing at Nottingham Forest, and, in this vital relegation battle against Colin Lee's Walsall, City nick a crucial three points. It is former Port Vale striker Lee Mills who bags the only goal under the Britannia Stadium floodlights when he diverts Wayne Thomas's wayward shot past Jimmy Walker in the Saddlers goal. Only 10,409 see the win, City's lowest home crowd of the season, but the result picks Stoke off the foot of the First Division table and within a month they will be out of the relegation zone.

19 October 2008

In a superb, eventful, Sunday afternoon televised game, Stoke really lay out their credentials for Premier League survival in taking on Juande Ramos's Spurs at a frenzied Britannia Stadium. The day's events begin when Gareth Bale, oddly selected at left-back, hauls down City's Tom Soares, who has been put through into the Tottenham box. Bale sees red and Danny Higginbotham hammers the penalty home left-footed into the bottom-right corner of Heurelho Gomes's net, but only after the north Staffs breeze has twice blown the ball off the spot before Higgy can strike it.

18 August 2011

On FC Thun's astroturf pitch and against the sunlit backdrop of the Bernese Oberland mountainscape, Stoke win a second successive European away leg 1-0. This time it is thanks to midfielder Danny Pugh's left-foot strike from 20 yards which defeats the Swiss Super League leaders. The ball zips past home keeper David da Costa, right in front of Thun's resident drummer, who is leading the home chanting. He doesn't notice for a while and carries on his rhythmic beat while the Potters fans, at the other end of the ground, go ballistic. A conga breaks out, which lasts all the way through the half-time interval, accompanied by ongoing choruses of 'Doe, a Deer' from *The Sound of Music*. Da Costa is sent off in the last minute and, as Thun have used all their substitutes in a vain attempt to peg back Tony Pulis's men, midfielder Stephan Andrist ends up in nets, making a name for himself by tipping a Jon Walters strike round the post.

26 December 2015

Mark Hughes's team aren't just Stoke City anymore, they are 'Stokelona', due to the nature of their intricate passing and powerful running game. Having beaten the blue side of Manchester 2-0 earlier in the month, the Potters put the red half to the sword on Boxing Day. Bojan is the architect, but Manchester United help Stoke open the scoring when Memphis Depay tries to head the ball back to goalkeeper David de Gea on the right side of the penalty area, but it falls well short and Glen Johnson nips in to square the ball back to Bojan, who prods home gleefully from six yards to silence the visiting fans behind the goal.

20

5 May 1945

George Mountford, who has filled in manfully for Stanley Matthews while the England man has been serving with the RAF in Lancashire, starts a rout of neighbours Port Vale when he picks the ball up 40 yards from goal, races towards the penalty area and, having cut to the right, hits a powerful cross shot past Valiants keeper Prince. By the end of the game Mountford will have bagged four of City's six without reply in a War League North second-phase game, played three days before VE Day.

23 February 1957

Tim Coleman bags two in three minutes to net a first hat-trick of his Stoke City career. The right-winger first takes George Kelly's right-wing cross in his stride, sidesteps a challenge and strokes home. Then he swoops to prod home from a yard out amidst a melee of bodies, after Kelly's teasing cross has been headed up and against his own bar by Lincoln right-back Jackson.

28 August 1971

Stoke exact some sort of revenge on double-winning Arsenal for their tortuous FA Cup semi-final defeat the previous April. City take advantage of the unseasonal blustery conditions at Highbury and John Ritchie lashes a long through ball past Bob Wilson in the Gunners goal to win it 1-0.

23 November 1971

Stoke have already played six matches to reach this League Cup quarter-final at Eastville against a Bristol Rovers team sitting tenth in the Third Division. The Pirates are no match for the slick Potters. Jimmy Greenhoff has already given the visitors the lead with a cute finish from 15 yards, before Denis Smith flies in bravely to head City's second, breaking two fingers in the process. They are mere flesh wounds for the burly centre-half from Meir, who also clashes heads with a defender in the act of scoring and plays the rest of the game in a daze. Smith still does not remember anything of the last 70 minutes, which see Stoke win through easily 4-2, and the following day he is still staggering around semi-consciously whilst taking his daughter in a pram to the local shops, when two ladies accuse him of being drunk in charge of a young child! Smith would end his career a club legend, having broken his leg five times, his nose four times, and his ankle, collarbone and cheekbone once each, amongst many other more minor injuries, causing *The Guinness Book of Records* to list him as 'the most injured man in football'.

31 March 1975

Stoke are vying for the league title for the first time in almost 30 years, propelled by the resurgent Terry Conroy, who has scored five goals in two games since his return from a long-term knee injury. The Irishman is playing up front, rather than on the wing, due to the career-ending injury for John Ritchie earlier in the season and he delivers a superb performance against Bob Paisley's Liverpool. League leaders at kick-off, the visitors cannot live with Stoke, who produce a brilliant display of flowing football in front of 45,954, their biggest crowd of the season, on Easter Monday. Conroy nets both goals in a 2-0 victory, his first coming from the spot after Phil Thompson fouls Welsh midfield powerhouse John Mahoney.

22 November 1975

Geoff Salmons revels in downing his former club, scoring both goals in a 2-1 win at the Victoria Ground. His first is a corking drive with his magical left foot from the edge of the penalty area. Eight minutes later, Salmons secures the points with a penalty in off the post, given after his own shot is handled off the line. Sheffield United end the day plumb bottom of the First Division.

7 November 1978

Stoke are flying at the top of the Second Division under new manager Alan Durban, but are also making progress in the League Cup. Drawn at fellow Second Division side Charlton in the fourth round, Stoke go 2-0 up at the Valley, having taken the lead through a Sammy Irvine shot from 20 yards after 36 seconds, when striker Viv Busby finishes an Irvine cross at the near post, with Charlton defenders appealing for handball. City win 3-2 and move on to the fifth round where they are drawn against Third Division leaders Watford.

3 December 2016

Stoke score an exquisite goal against Sean Dyche's Burnley when Mame Diouf roams down the right wing and clips the ball into the near post to Jon Walters. Eight yards out, the Republic of Ireland striker hits the ball on the volley first time and loops a delicate right-footed shot perfectly into the far-left corner of former England keeper Paul Robinson's net, in off the post.

21

16 March 1963

After the big freeze of the winter of 1963, which has meant Stoke have not played between Boxing Day and 2 March, City are on the ropes with their promotion challenge faltering. Having begun the restart of the season after the thaw with a 3-0 victory over lowly Walsall, thanks to a Jackie Mudie hat-trick, Stoke are thrashed 0-6 at Norwich and look demoralised 20 minutes into their next home game a week later, when struggling Grimsby take the lead against the run of play through ex-Port Vale player Portwood's fine cross shot. City are in need of inspiration and find it in the form of Dennis Viollet within a minute of going behind. Straight from the kick-off, the Potters work the ball to Stan Matthews on the right, who finds a pass through the mud to Viollet. The former Manchester United star swivels and fires a right-foot shot right into the corner, past Town keeper Wright. The momentum swings to Stoke and by half-time they lead 2-1 thanks to Mudie's smart header from a Don Ratcliffe cross.

14 April 1984

Against Bob Paisley's all-conquering Liverpool, Mark Chamberlain is in rampant mood on the wing, taking the visitors' left-back Alan Kennedy to the cleaners. Chambo cuts in from the right and hits a powerful shot, which Bruce Grobbelaar palms out, only for Ian Painter to follow up and prod home from eight yards at the Town End. City lead 1-0 and Liverpool barely create a chance all game. Stoke's incredible escape from relegation is very much in full swing.

21 December 1986

A year on from being thrashed 6-2 at Stoke, Leeds keeper Mervyn Day gives an interview before their trip to the Victoria Ground in which he determinedly states he won't concede six again. Day was right; he didn't concede six times – it was seven! Right-back Lee

Dixon scores the best of those when he latches on to a loose ball, headed clear at a corner at the Town End, and performs a balletic overhead kick, catching the ball perfectly with his right foot to plant it in the left side of the goal. It puts City 3-0 up and it will be five by half-time, with the 7-2 win beginning a run of 14 goals in just three games.

10 September 2011

Stoke's new talismanic, club-record signing Peter Crouch, £10m from Tottenham, makes his debut against one of his many former clubs, Liverpool. But it is the big man's strike partner who nets the decisive goal of the game against Kenny Dalglish's Reds. The winning penalty comes after Jamie Carragher hauls over Jon Walters, who dusts himself off to blast the spot kick home right-footed, right down the middle, while Pepe Reina dives to his left. City hang on despite an incredible series of misses by Jordan Henderson, who sees Asmir Begović pull off three saves in a row, two from him when clean through and one on the follow-up from Charlie Adam, while Ryan Shawcross throws himself to block another effort in an amazing sequence. Later, Luis Suárez also misses an open goal after Begović's fumble. Charmed.

31 January 2015

Jon Walters has a perfect day, notching the first goal of his 'perfect' hat-trick against Queens Park Rangers at the Britannia Stadium when Stephen Ireland tackles Mauricio Isla, and the midfielder's cheeky back-heel finds Walters, 22 yards out on the left edge of the penalty area. The striker takes the ball in his stride and plants it right-footed into the far bottom-right corner under keeper Rob Green's somewhat flimsy left hand.

22

9 February 1946

Stoke are flying in the first major competition to restart after the Second World War, the FA Cup. In this fifth-round tie, in front of 40,452 at the Victoria Ground, centre-forward Freddie Steele bags both goals in a 2-0 win, two of 43 he will score overall this season. The goals are carbon copies of each other, towering headers from Stan Matthews corners from eight yards. The second, in the 72nd minute, seals the tie as Stoke keep a clean sheet in the second leg at Hillsborough to progress through to the quarter-final. One fan is so excited about impending cup glory he gifts two eggs to each player to 'help them get their strength up in this time of rations' to take on Bolton in the quarter-final.

28 October 1961

After over 14 years away (the length of most players' careers), 46-year-old Stanley Matthews makes his second debut for Stoke, 29 years after the first, in front of a baying 35,974 (up over 27,000 on the previous home gate), thus repaying his £3,000 fee instantly. He makes Huddersfield and England left-back Ray Wilson's life hell, drawing in sometimes two or three other Town players to mark him as he torments and dazzles them with a display of artistic footwork to thrill the watching throng. Matthews plays an unusual part in the first goal of a famous 3-0 victory, though. As Town take a defensive throw-in, Stan jostles the receiving player, who miskicks directly to the waiting Jackie Mudie, who instantly arcs a cross into the penalty area where Jimmy Adam, a £5,000 signing from Aston Villa just two months before, outmuscles his marker and heads home. Matthews was reuniting with both Mudie, with whom he starred for many years at Blackpool, and who had joined City seven months earlier for £8,500, and inside-right Tommy Thompson, who he had last played with in 1957 for England in a 2-1 victory over Scotland at Wembley.

18 April 1964

Dennis Viollet races in to adroitly flick home a low, driven corner past Harry Gregg to put his new club 2-0 ahead of his old one, Manchester United. His side-footed finish comes as he times his run perfectly to meet the ball into the box from Jimmy McIlroy; a perfect 'old crocks' combination goal, the signature of Tony Waddington's first team.

27 March 1971

Stoke's search for a first-ever Wembley cup final begins in astonishing fashion when a lucky break gives City the lead in the FA Cup semi-final. At the Leppings Lane end at Hillsborough, a right-wing corner is curled in by Harry Burrows to the near post, where it falls to Peter Storey, Arsenal's defensive midfielder. Inexplicably, he tries to control and dribble out, giving City's centre-half Denis Smith the chance to close him down, and when Storey finally realises he needs to whack it clear, Smith is on him, blocking with his left foot. The ball is hit so hard that it cannons off Smith and flies directly above keeper Bob Wilson's head and into the Gunners' net off the underside of the bar, right in front of the Potters fans. Advantage Stoke.

25 September 1982

Luton's Paul Walsh has already equalised George Berry's opening goal, but the big central defender with the huge Afro, which Berry himself once described as a 'tactic to fool opposing players', puts City ahead again in this pulsating encounter between two free-scoring teams. Mark Chamberlain is the provider with the most legendary cross in Potters history, coming as he is pinned on the right-hand goal line with his back to the penalty area, being nudged towards the corner flag. Somehow Chambo defies the laws of biomechanics to swivel and hit the ball right-footed, ending with his legs crossed, chipping it into the middle 180 degrees from where he was facing just a split second ago. No one anticipates he can deliver from there except Berry, who rises to head home from six yards. A stupendous goal in a bonkers game.

7 April 2007

Ricardo Fuller has ripped holes at will in West Brom's defence in a devastating eight-minute period. Having scored the first and then forced Jonathan Greening to put through his own net for the second, a minute later Fuller sets up Jon Parkin for an eight-yard tap-in from another driving run down the left flank. City are 3-0 up in this vital play-off clash, and go on to win 3-1 at the Hawthorns.

23 March 2014

Mark Hughes's Stoke side are made of stern stuff and, when Christian Benteke gives Aston Villa an early lead at Villa Park, they come back impressively to score two goals in four minutes, the first from sparkling winger Peter Odemwingie, a January transfer-window arrival from Cardiff. The Nigerian forward chips the ball up to Peter Crouch, on the edge of the Villa penalty area, then races forward to take the return and hold off Ryan Bertrand to poke the ball between keeper Brad Guzan's legs. Crouch then gets in on the act against his former club by tucking in Erik Pieters's cross side-footed, after the Dutch defender latches on to Marko Arnautović's back-heel.

23

15 January 1962

Stan Matthews latches on to a long through pass to beat centre-half Ian King, then weave his way around Leicester and England goalkeeper Gordon Banks, to slot the ball neatly, right-footed, inside the far post. Under the lights at a bewitched Victoria Ground, it is Stan's second goal since his return from Blackpool two months earlier and the first of five, as Stoke hammer Leicester 5-2 in an FA Cup third-round replay at the Victoria Ground. The *Daily Mirror* nicknames Stan 'the miracle in football boots' for tantalising left-back Richie Norman for the full 90 minutes, aged 46.

18 November 2000

Stoke's FA Cup first-round tie with non-league Nuneaton at the Britannia Stadium is so dull that Pottermus, the cheeky Stoke mascot, decides to liven things up. Approaching his opposite number, Brewno the Bear, cavorting in front of the away end, and appearing to be joining in the laughs, the rotund Hippo raises by far the biggest cheer of the afternoon when he steals Brewno's head and races off, Hippo-fashion, towards the Boothen End, with the now beheaded Bear in hot pursuit. Pottermus makes the most of the speed expected of a two-time Mascot Grand National champion to hare the full length of the Sentinel Stand to huge cheers, before graciously returning Brewno's bonce. The game ends goalless, but the moment lives on in legend.

7 November 2020

Michael O'Neill's Stoke produce a classic away performance at Reading's Madejski Stadium to soak up the Championship leaders' huge pressure and strike three times on the break. The first goal sees tyro striker Tyrese Campbell pounce on a loose clearing header from Tomás Esteves and fire into the bottom left-hand corner, with his supposedly weak right foot, from 18 yards with Royals keeper Rafael Cabral unsighted.

24

10 December 1966

Left-winger Harry Burrows hits a thumping drive from 25 yards, which takes a deflection on its way into the corner of Aston Villa's net. The goal is the first of a hat-trick for the former Villan against his old team-mates on a mudbath of a Victoria Ground pitch in a 6-1 win. He has made a habit of netting against his previous team-mates, having scored three in two games, without reply, to secure a double over them in the previous campaign.

24 November 1992

In a pulsating encounter, played in atrocious conditions at Vale Park, part three of the five-game Potteries derby classic of 1992/93 is underway as City take the lead in their FA Cup first-round replay. Eight days after the original goalless draw at the Victoria Ground, Lee Sandford pops up to prod home Vince Overson's header from a deep free kick, sending the away fans in the Hamil Road end into raptures and City into an early lead.

14 May 2011

Stoke are up against it in the first half of their first-ever FA Cup Final, with wave after wave of Manchester City attacks getting ever closer. As Yaya Touré drives forward yet again, he feeds Mario Balotelli on the left corner of Stoke's penalty area. The Italian shifts the ball onto his right foot then curls a shot past the lunging Andy Wilkinson and Robert Huth, which appears to be arrowing right into the top corner of Thomas Sørenson's net. But the Great Dane launches himself to reach the ball with his outstretched right fingertips and divert it millimetres past his left post. A superb save, which keeps Stoke in the final.

25 August 2011

City are just 90 minutes away from reaching the Europa League group stage and begin a rout of their Swiss visitors FC Thun when a left-wing, inswinging Jermaine Pennant corner is headed in at the far post from six yards by new signing Matthew Upson for his first goal for Stoke.

20 October 2011

Stoke take a giant stride towards the knockout phase of the Europa League, on a Britannia Stadium pitch which has had to be widened to meet UEFA specifications and so has its Premier League pitch markings clearly visible three yards inside the new ones, with a comfortable 3-0 victory over Maccabi Tel Aviv. Already 1-0 up thanks to a towering Kenwyne Jones header, striker Cameron Jerome notches a second when he takes advantage of a feeble attempt by the visitors to play offside to nod Matty Etherington's inswinging free kick past flailing keeper Guy Haimov from six yards. Seven minutes later Jerome breaks the offside trap again, but is forced wide in going round the keeper and sets up Ryan Shotton to make it 3-0.

25

20 May 1982

On a tense night at the Victoria Ground, in a game played after the end of the regular season due to postponements, City just need to beat already-safe West Brom to survive and send Leeds down. Hundreds of Leeds fans have travelled down from Yorkshire and are cheering on Albion, who couldn't care less and it shows. Plus, they beat Leeds two days earlier and are exhausted. Stoke are on top throughout and finally make their dominance pay when veteran centre-half Dave Watson steals forward at a corner and bundles in the opener from close range. The result is never in doubt after that and City go on to win 3-0.

15 September 2001

Stoke have just sold striker Peter Thorne to Second Division rivals Cardiff for £1.7m and the fans are not happy, venting their spleen as City take on Alan Pardew's Reading. The Royals cannot cope with Peter Hoekstra, given a free, roving role by Guðjón Thórdarsson. Hoekstra hits a post, then turns provider to set up Bjarni Guðjónsson to score from five yards.

26

23 October 1996

New Arsenal manager Arsène Wenger brings his Premier League second-placed Gunners to the rather less glamorous environs of the Victoria Ground, ST4. The swanky Londoners are at full strength, but still have a tough night against Lou Macari's mid-table First Division Potters, who take the lead when Kevin Keen's dink into the penalty area catches Arsenal and England captain Tony Adams flat-footed. As it falls near the left corner of the six-yard box, Mike Sheron nips in behind Adams to flick the ball home right-footed, almost over his shoulder with his back to goal, on the run. The Boothen End goes nuts behind David Seaman's goal as the ball nestles into the bottom-right corner. Arsenal despise being behind and have five booked as things turn tasty. City are only denied, late on, by an Ian Wright goal which has more than a hint of handball about it when the striker controls and finishes. Stoke lose the replay 2-5, but only after taking the lead, again through Sheron, much to the delight of the travelling hordes.

21 January 2007

After Danny Higginbotham has given Stoke the lead at Derby from the penalty spot in the 15th minute, after Dean Leacock's needless handball at a corner, Dominic Matteo grabs a second, clinching goal against Billy Davies's Championship leaders to secure a great away victory on a freezing night. It is Matteo's first Stoke goal, a belting near-post header from six yards from Lee Hendrie's inswinging left-wing corner, which bounces under Steven Bywater's despairing dive.

24 May 2015

It is Steven Gerrard's last game before retiring and Stoke are hosting Liverpool in a carnival atmosphere. City overwhelm the visitors with a devastating display of finishing in which everything they hit seems to fly in. The ball is set rolling when Mame Diouf scores a quick-fire brace of goals, the first after Reds keeper Simon Mignolet parries Adam's powerful drive into the striker's path for a tap-in. His second sees him lash home from the edge of the penalty area, right-footed, high into the top-left corner. City are on a roll.

26 December 2015

Just seven minutes after Bojan has opened the scoring, Marko Arnautović ensures Stoke inflict a fourth successive defeat on Louis van Gaal's Manchester United, increasing calls for the Dutch manager's head. The Austrian winger picks the ball up 30 yards out after Bojan's free kick on the left side of the penalty area hits the wall and rebounds. He controls with one touch of his right boot, then, with little backlift, unleashes a fearsome drive which swerves into the left side of David de Gea's goal from 25 yards. City should score more than the two goals which clinch the three points and move them to within four points of a European spot.

1 October 2020

Stoke are at Premier League Aston Villa for a League Cup fourth-round match and get off to a wonderful start when Sam Vokes rises highest at the near post to flick a header in at the far post from Jordan Thompson's corner. Stoke hold on despite Villa's pressure and the Potters have now lost just once in seven games in all competitions, winning four of their past five, keeping four clean sheets, as the Michael O'Neill revolution really takes hold. This was the last game, though, for Bruno Martins Indi, on his way to a season-long loan at AZ Alkmaar in his native Holland, who was made skipper to mark the occasion. Three days later Aston Villa would thrash Liverpool 7-2.

27

15 February 1946

Racing clear on to George Mountford's tidy pass to beat Harry Medhurst in goal easily, Syd Peppitt bags his second, and City's sixth, of a whirlwind first half hour to go 6-1 up against Chelsea. Stoke end the game in fourth position in the First Division, set fair for a climactic end-of-season title challenge.

23 February 1974

Behind 0-2 to Don Revie's 29-game unbeaten Leeds, who are chasing Burnley's all-time record of 30, Stoke begin a stirring fightback when John Mahoney surges towards the visitors' box only to be fouled by Norman Hunter. As David Harvey aligns the Leeds defensive wall, Alan Hudson flicks the free kick inside to Mike Pejic, 22 yards out, who unleashes an unstoppable, left-footed banana shot into the Town End net. *The Sentinel* call it Pej's 'Rivelino special'. The unthinkable is on.

6 January 1996

Lou Macari's Stoke are making good progress in the First Division, but Premier League Nottingham Forest are pushing for the European places. Frank Clark's visitors are clear favourites to progress in this FA Cup third-round tie, but Stoke are much the better side. Graham Potter hits a post and Nigel Gleghorn has a header cleared off the line. City score just once, when Kevin Keen strides forward and probes a pass into the edge of the penalty area, finding Simon Sturridge, who hits it first time with his right foot, low past Mark Crossley into the bottom-left corner of the Town End net. Sadly, Stoke can't hang on and Stuart Pearce's fierce drive takes City back for a replay at the City Ground, which Forest win 2-0.

24 August 1996

Stoke's first home game of the last season at the Victoria Ground sees former boss Alan Ball return as manager of visitors Manchester

City, relegated from the Premier League in crazy circumstances the previous season. Stoke love humbling Ball, and take the lead when Richard Forsyth follows up when Eike Immel parries Simon Sturridge's shot back out to fire home from ten yards at the Town End. Ball is on the brink and being taunted from the stands.

14 November 1998

Kyle Lightbourne hammers a fierce drive past Scott Howie to secure a first win over Reading in five years, a first at the new Madejski Stadium and a first away FA Cup win against league opposition for 26 years.

11 August 2007

Nineteen-year-old Ryan Shawcross, signed on a season-long loan from Manchester United just a few days before this opening game of the season, scores the only goal against Cardiff when Liam Lawrence curls in a corner from the right wing into the near post and everyone misses it. The ball lands at Shawcross's feet at the far post, eight yards out. He hits it first time, right-footed, sweeping it into the back of Ross Turnbull's net to set City on to the path of glory and Shawcross on the road to a legendary Potters career. He will captain the side from the age of 22 and be a mainstay of both Tony Pulis's and Mark Hughes's teams, which deliver mid-table finishes over a decade in the Premier League, an FA Cup Final, a League Cup semi-final and a European campaign. Shawcross also scored 14 Premier League goals, as well as seven Championship goals in this promotion season.

28

26 September 1970

Stoke have won only two of the first nine games, but explode into life against Bertie Mee's Arsenal. The avalanche of goals starts when Peter Dobing sends a probing pass in to Jimmy Greenhoff inside the Gunners' penalty area. Greenhoff finds Terry Conroy on the right wing and the Irishman's first-time cross finds John Ritchie, six yards out, at the back post. The big striker leaps to head perfectly in an arc over the diving Bob Wilson and the ball nestles in the far bottom-right corner of the Boothen End net. Stoke will end the day 5-0 winners.

5 April 1975

City rise to third place, level on points with the top two, Everton and Liverpool, and fourth-placed Derby, and one point ahead of fifth-placed club Ipswich with three games remaining in the tightest championship race in years, with a comfortable 3-0 victory over relegation-threatened Chelsea. Terry Conroy, playing up front in the absence of John Ritchie, who suffered a leg break earlier in the season, starts things off by finishing a lovely pass by Geoff Salmons low past keeper John Phillips. Conroy has now scored eight goals in four and a half games and will bag another one later in this match.

14 February 1981

Stoke are 0-1 behind at Elland Road, but enter Lee Chapman. The young striker latches on to Paul Bracewell's through ball to hammer left-footed past John Lukic. He will go on to bag a hat-trick in City's first away win at Leeds in 21 years.

25 September 1982

All hell breaks loose at the Vic as Peter Fox tries to shepherd a long ball back into his box, but Luton forward Paul Walsh attempts to steal it off him. Fox falls on the ball, handling it in the D as he does so. But it squirms from his grasp and Walsh goes on to beat George Berry to score. But the goal doesn't count as referee Gilbert Napthine has called the play back for Fox's handball and dismisses the Stoke keeper, who is distraught, but slopes off to spend the rest of the game watching through the tiny window in the home-team dressing room. Luton and Walsh are livid the goal doesn't stand and this tumultuous game has taken yet another twist.

25 September 1991

Stoke are behind to Ian Rush's early header when Ian Cranson rises seven yards out to meet Ian Scott's inswinging corner from the left wing. Cranson, who has a bandage on a cut over his left eye, powers his header past Bruce Grobbelaar into the top-right corner of the Kop end net to put City level against Graeme Souness's Reds in this League Cup second-round first-leg tie.

12 February 1992

Kick-off is delayed by 15 minutes as 23,645 cram into the Victoria Ground on a Wednesday night to watch Lou Macari's second-placed City take on Bobby Gould's top of the Third Division West Brom. Mark Stein taunts the Baggies' defence for the whole game, hitting the side netting and then rising unmarked on the edge of the six-yard box to nod home Vince Overson's near-post flick-on from a left-wing corner. Stoke's 1-0 victory sees the pair change places in the table.

21 November 1992

Level at 1-1 at rainswept Bloomfield Road, and with City's unbeaten run of 13 league games under threat, Graham Shaw exchanges passes with Mark Stein and sends a perfectly weighted through ball across the rain-sodden turf for his strike partner to run on to. Stein takes aim 18 yards out and beats Lee Martin in the Tangerines goal easily, low to the bottom-right corner, much to the delight of the sodden supporters on the terraces.

8 May 2011

Arsène Wenger's Arsenal still maintain faint hopes of winning the league title, while Stoke are warming up for next week's FA Cup

Final. City get the scoring underway when Jermaine Pennant whips a right-wing free kick into the near post and Kenwyne Jones evades the attention of Johan Djourou to bundle home the simplest of finishes beyond the wrong-footed Wojciech Szczęsny. He simply lets the ball come off his midriff and it bounces in at the near post. 'One-nil to the rugby team' resounds around the Britannia Stadium in response to Wenger's comments about the Potters using oval-ball tactics. It won't be his day.

29

6 November 1982

Stoke are already ahead when Peter Hampton roves forward and, as the West Ham defence parts before him, the left-back lashes a fierce left-foot drive into the far-bottom corner of Phil Parkes's net. That pearler puts Stoke on their way to a 5-2 victory over John Lyall's men, who were equal top at start of play, to move into seventh spot in the First Division.

17 April 1996

Striker Mike Sheron has scored in the previous six First Division matches and nets in a club-record seventh game in a row when Simon Sturridge's flick finds him on the edge of the penalty area. Sheron chests it down to the right side, lets it bounce, then smashes the ball home from 16 yards into the far bottom-left corner. It sends the Boothen End, behind that goal, into ecstasy. A moment of Potters history.

13 December 2003

Dutch winger Peter Hoekstra is on fire. He already has the first of his treble, but his second is utterly sublime. Picking the ball up from Lewis Neal's accurate cross-field pass, wide out on the left wing, Hoekstra takes the ball down on his left instep, speeds towards the penalty area and looks up. Not liking his options for crossing, the wily winger deceives Reading keeper Marcus Hahnemann by lashing the ball left-footed inside the near post from out on the left edge of the box. It is a stunning strike.

14 December 2011

Kenwyne Jones wins the ball back from the Beşiktaş backline and flicks it to Ricardo Fuller, who drives at the Turks and then lets loose from 25 yards. The ball takes a nick off Egemen Korkmaz's thigh and flies past Rüştü Reçber, leaving the veteran keeper flat-footed, into the top-right corner. City lead 1-0 in Istanbul in this dead rubber at the end of their Europa League group stage, but will lose 1-3.

18 December 2013

It's goalless with David Moyes's Manchester United in the League Cup quarter-final when the heavens open. But, instead of rain, they deposit an unbelievable number of hailstones, at great speed, on to the Britannia Stadium. Referee Mark Clattenburg, unable to see the players, quickly takes them off the pitch, with the teams re-emerging ten minutes later when the elements are somewhat calmer. United go on to win 2-0.

Manager Bob McGrory (right) congratulates, from the left, Stanley Matthews, Freddie Steele and Joe Johnson on winning their England caps in the same team to take on Scotland in 1937.

Baby-faced Frank Bowyer, a wonderful volleyer of the ball, who, if wartime goals are taken into account, is the only player to have scored more than 200 goals for Stoke.

Flying keeper Jimmy O'Neill makes a save at Preston's Deepdale in the 1962/63 season during the run of only two defeats in 32 games which saw Stoke contend for promotion. This game ended 1-1.

You can't see his face, but in that ruck of delighted Stoke players is one Stanley Matthews (third Stoke player from the right). Forty-eight years young, Matthews has just scored the clinching second goal against Luton Town at the Victoria Ground in May 1963 in the 47th minute. The 2-0 victory sends City back to the First Division for the first time in a decade.

Sir Stanley Matthews is chaired from the Victoria Ground pitch by Lev Yashin (left) and Ferenc Puskás after the end of his farewell game in April 1965 to the strains of 'Auld Lang Syne', which echo around the ground.

On a sticky Victoria Ground pitch, Harry Burrows challenges a former Villa team-mate for the ball. Stoke will win this game 6-1, with Burrows bagging three goals against his old employers, competing his hat-trick in the 54th minute.

In the 45th minute, Terry Conroy rounds Hull keeper Ian McKechnie to score the first goal of Stoke's incredible comeback from 0-2 down to a 3-2 victory in the FA Cup quarter-final in March 1971 at Boothferry Park.

John Ritchie turns to celebrate putting Stoke 3-2 ahead against Hull in the 81st minute of the 1971 FA Cup quarter-final, with Terry Conroy leaping in delight.

Stoke striker 'Big' John Ritchie celebrates putting City 2-0 ahead at Hillsborough in the 31st minute of the 1971 FA Cup semi-final. Ritchie, the club's record goalscorer with 176 goals in 351 games, is immortalised in a bust behind the Boothen End of the Bet365 stadium.

Mike Bernard follows up to prod home, after Bobby Moore, in goal due to Bobby Ferguson's concussion, saves his spot-kick in the 32nd minute at Old Trafford in the fourth game of the tie. The goal puts Stoke 1-0 ahead and on course for Wembley.

A tale of two penalties in the 1972 League Cup semi-final epic against West Ham. Above, Gordon Banks flings his arms up to deflect Geoff Hurst's 117th-minute penalty up and over the bar to keep City in the tie at Upton Park. Perhaps the most famous save in Stoke City history.

Gordon Banks celebrates with the Potters fans behind his goal after the final whistle at Old Trafford proclaims that Stoke have reached their first ever major final, the 1972 League Cup Final at Wembley.

The most famous goal in Stoke City history flies into the back of the net in the 73rd minute as George Eastham, slightly obscured behind the post, prods home left-footed from four yards following Chelsea keeper Peter Bonetti's save to clinch the 1972 League Cup Final at Wembley 2-1.

The 1972 League Cup-winning team celebrate with the trophy at Wembley, with winning goalscorer George Eastham (third from left) leading the way.

Jimmy Greenhoff, scorer of both goals in the final victory over Hull City, in the 16th and 67th minutes, accepts the Watney Cup from Bobby Charlton at the Victoria Ground in August 1973. Stoke were the last ever winners of the short-lived competition.

Alan Hudson, Stoke's mercurial midfielder (left of picture), is bossing things once again, this time at QPR.

Cometh the hour, cometh 'Big Bren'. Just 11 seconds into his Stoke debut, Brendan O'Callaghan, a £40,000 signing from Doncaster, rises at the near post to flick a 78th-minute header into the Boothen End net to defeat Hull.

Young striker Ian Moores in action against Manchester City at the Victoria Ground in February 1975. Moores scored two goals in a magnificent 4-0 victory, in the 44th and 84th minutes.

Paul Richardson dives to head into Notts County's net in the 87th minute to secure a famous 1-0 win at Meadow Lane, which guarantees promotion back to the First Division for Alan Durban's team.

Lee Chapman celebrates scoring the opening goal of a 2-1 home win in the tenth minute against newly-promoted West Ham in February 1982, closely pursued by Alan Dodd.

Stoke celebrate a late equaliser in the 80th minute by Mick Doyle (hidden by substitute Paul Bracewell) at St Andrew's against Birmingham City.

Brendan O'Callaghan dives to head home Mickey Thomas's cross in the 75th minute to clinch a famous 1-0 win over Manchester United in March 1983, then, right, celebrates with the fans on the Boothen End.

One of the greatest games in Potters history sees George Berry (extreme left) put City 2-1 ahead against Luton in the 22nd minute. The game eventually ends 4-4, with a red card and missed penalty thrown in for good measure. Berry's telepathic understanding with right-winger Mark Chamberlain led to many goals like this one being scored.

30

15 January 1947

England winger Stanley Matthews sweeps home right-footed past Spurs' Ted Ditchburn to settle an FA Cup third-round replay in front of 38,639 fans, with the gates closed an hour before kick-off. Matthews races in to finish a lovely piece of interplay by Frank Baker and Alec Ormston on the left wing after the ball is cut back by the latter, who also has a shot cleared off the line by Spurs' Willis, while Baker also hits a post.

23 April 1968

Peter Dobing, who has been subject to an unfair amount of Boothen End booing during a disappointing season for the Potters, has the bit between his teeth as Stoke take on a Leeds team gunning for the title. There are just five games left in the season, and with a point Don Revie's men will go top. But Dobing has other ideas. He is a whirlwind up front all night, producing one of the great individual performances from a Stoke striker. He scores his first goal of three when he races onto George Eastham's through ball. But he still has 35 yards to goal, with England centre-half Jack Charlton almost literally hanging off his back. Dobing shrugs the 'Giraffe' off and ploughs on to the byline. Looking up and cutting inside he realises that none of his team-mates have kept pace with him. All alone, he gives Leeds keeper Gary Sprake the eyes and shoots inside the near post, leaving the Welsh goalie bemused. There is a moment's delay as the crowd work out that the ball has somehow ended up in the back of the net. City lead in their fight against relegation.

29 April 1974

On the final day of the league season Tony Waddington's team clinch fifth spot, the club's second-highest finish ever, thanks to John Ritchie, who takes Sean Haslegrave's pass and buries it past Alex Stepney. Tommy Docherty's United are already relegated and their fans riot, burning banners and causing mayhem on the terraces. City qualify for the UEFA Cup for only the second time in their history.

1 October 1983

John Lyall's table-topping Hammers cannot cope with Stoke's physicality. From a Robbie James near-post corner, Sammy McIlroy flicks on and Dave McAughtrie, City's young Scottish centre-back, hits the ball back over his own right shoulder with his right foot, into the bottom-left corner of the Boothen End net to give the Potters the lead from seven yards. It's a cracking, instinctive finish in the pouring Potteries rain.

11 November 1989

City lead 2-1 against Brighton as they attempt to win just their second game of a dreadful season with caretaker manager Alan Ball in charge. Combative midfielder Chris Kamara flicks home his first goal of the season at the near post after Carl Beeston's driving run to the byline and sharp pullback. Stoke should have a fourth, but George Berry puts a 60th-minute penalty wide and instead City have to hang on after Kevin Bremner's late goal has nerves jangling. But they do and the Ball era has begun with a much-needed victory.

23 August 2008

It is Stoke's first-ever Premier League home game and Paddy Power have written the team off after a 1-3 defeat at Bolton on opening day. But they reckoned without this redoubtable City team, who take the lead against Martin O'Neill's classy Aston Villa when Ricardo Fuller beats Martin Laursen out on the right wing and cuts into the penalty area. He appears to be fouled by Laursen and goes to ground, but Rory Delap picks up the loose ball and then tumbles under another Laursen challenge, and referee Mark Halsey points to the spot. Liam Lawrence slots low to the bottom left. City are up and running and 27,500 crammed in to the Britannia Stadium are loving it.

17 April 2011

With Bolton already capitulating in the FA Cup semi-final as Stoke run riot, Jermaine Pennant steals the ball off Wanderers' Martin Petrov inside the Stoke half on the right wing. Pennant scampers forward to the edge of the penalty area and scythes the retreating Trotters defence in two with a pass which sends Kenwyne Jones clean through with only Jussi Jääskeläinen to beat. Jones controls with his left and scores with his right foot, low to the keeper's left. Double somersaults ensue from the Trinidadian international, as Potters fans can barely believe what they are witnessing.

24 May 2015

City's third against Brendan Rodgers's Liverpool comes as a result of a comedy of defensive errors. Stoke make easy progress down the right wing and Mame Diouf's deep cross is headed back towards his keeper by Emre Can. Before Simon Mignolet can get there, Jon Walters nips in to shoot left-footed. Mignolet blocks, but the ball pops up and Walters reacts first, with the defence flat-footed, to nod home from three yards, then celebrates in front of the Liverpool fans behind that goal, like the boyhood Everton fan he was.

1 December 2015

Mark Hughes's Stoke have been drawn at home against Championship Sheffield Wednesday in the League Cup quarter-final, and get things moving when Glen Johnson takes a short throw-in down by the right corner flag and Joselu turns to lob a deep cross to the far post. It is going over Jon Walters's head, but Ibrahim Affelay is running from deep and connects perfectly on the volley from 16 yards to drive, left-footed, low into the bottom-right corner for his first Potters goal. City are on their way to a semi-final.

31

27 March 1971

Stoke are in dreamland in the FA Cup semi-final at Hillsborough when Arsenal midfielder Charlie George hits a tame back pass towards his keeper Bob Wilson without looking and it is easily intercepted by Stoke striker John Ritchie. The big man collects it right-footed, then hurdles the floundering Wilson, before knocking it unchallenged, left-footed, into the net at the Leppings Lane end. He celebrates by whirling back towards the halfway line with both arms raised in delight, taking the acclaim in a moment now frozen in time for posterity as part of the Ritchie bust, behind the Boothen End at Stoke's Bet365 Stadium.

At 2-0 up by half-time, what can possibly go wrong for the Potters?

17 August 1996

Mike Sheron's opening goal is overshadowed when Mark Prudhoe is injured by a tough challenge by Oldham's Stuart Barlow and has to go off. As all the substitutes on the bench are outfield players, centre-half Ian Cranson dons the gloves and performs heroics at Boundary Park, conceding only once, near the end, when Steve Redmond buries a free kick. Sheron's second comes after John Gayle flicks on a long Cranson punt, and Cranson's heroics see Stoke start the season in sweltering heat with a 2-1 away win.

4 January 2003

'Big Chris' Iwelumo scores one of the most memorable volleys in Potters history when he feeds Peter Hoekstra on the left and then runs 50 yards into the penalty area to lash the Dutchman's cross home with a waist-high, right-footed volley past Wigan keeper John Filan. City down Paul Jewell's Second Division table toppers to avoid an FA Cup upset in the third round.

26 December 2007

Just four days after Ricardo Fuller has bagged a hat-trick against West Brom, Liam Lawrence gets in on the act with a treble of his own. It starts when Fuller is hauled over by Dennis Souza during a mazy jink down the right byline and the Irish international side-foots home into the bottom-right corner, sending Barnsley keeper Heinz Müller the wrong way, then celebrates with the Potters fans in the corner behind the Oakwell goal.

13 May 2018

Swansea lead thanks to Andy King's tap-in at the Liberty Stadium in this game between the already relegated Potters and the all-but-down Swans, when the impressive Badou Ndiaye equalises with a right-foot lob from 25 yards past Łukasz Fabiański, who will later save a penalty. Both clubs end the day in the Championship, despite Stoke's comeback win.

32

5 May 1945

George Mountford bags his second goal of the game, intercepting a weak back pass by Griffiths to bear down on Prince in the Valiants goal to stroke home. Stoke end up putting neighbours Port Vale to the sword in a War League North match 6-0.

26 January 1972

In an absolute mudbath at neutral Old Trafford, West Ham keeper Bobby Ferguson has already had to go off and Bobby Moore is in goal, when John McDowell miscontrols a throw-in and John Ritchie pounces to drive towards goal. In his desperation to repair his mistake, McDowell hauls Ritchie over on the left side of the penalty area and a spot kick is awarded by referee Pat Partridge. After some discussion, Mike Bernard steps up to take the penalty, which is awful and straight at the England captain. Moore saves easily, but cannot hang on to the ball amidst the slime and Bernard follows up to tap home left-footed. City lead 1-0 in this fourth game of the epic League Cup semi-final.

8 February 1975

Stoke have never won at White Hart Lane, but already lead through Jimmy Greenhoff's 23rd-minute tap-in. The stage is set for Alan Hudson to deliver a truly magnificent goal when he picks the ball up centrally, 30 yards out, exchanges passes with Ian Moores on the edge of the area, and then fires home right-footed from 15 yards past Barry Daines. Denis Smith and Eric Skeels are imperious in repelling Spurs' weakened attack and 75 years of failing to beat Tottenham away comes to an end against Terry Neill's men.

22 September 1993

City win the ball in defence from a wayward Manchester United pass and it falls to Toddy Örylgsson, who sets off towards the Town End with the ball glued to his right foot. Halfway inside the

United half, he finds Mark Stein, lurking out on the right wing. The striker drives in, facing up Gary Pallister, then suddenly dips his right shoulder, darts to the right and hits the ball hard, right-footed, into the far corner of the net from 18 yards, from wide on the right edge of the penalty area. The whole move has taken just nine seconds. Sumptuous.

11 November 1995

Simon Sturridge has broken his duck for the season with a brace against Luton in the 15th game just the week before this visit to Roots Hall, but after Southend take the lead it becomes the 'Studger' show. He scores the first of his hat-trick when his movement loses his marker and he side-foots home Kevin Keen's indirect free kick from the byline, after Graham Potter is fouled, but referee Mr Pierce awards a free kick, not a penalty.

24 August 1996

Former Stoke manager Alan Ball is on the ropes as returning Manchester City boss and the Potters take a two-goal lead when Mike Sheron pounces on sloppy passing at the back to outpace Kit Symons and crunch into a challenge with German keeper Eike Immel, which sees the ball rebound off Sheron to fly into the Town End net against his former club. Sheron now has three goals in the first game and a half of the new season. Despite Uwe Rösler picking up a loose pass and pulling a goal back, Stoke hold on to record a second successive victory. After the game, Ball resigns.

16 April 2000

Wembley is ablaze with red and white as Stoke take on Bristol City in the Auto Windscreens Shield Final. The Potters' opening goal is a peach. Graham Kavanagh picks up a loose ball 30 yards out, then slaloms through the Robins defence, beating three players before hammering a left-foot shot inside the near post past Billy Mercer, who has anticipated a cross shot.

9 May 2015

Matty Etherington looks up and hits a long, left-footed ball from deep on the left wing into the Spurs penalty area. The visiting keeper Hugo Lloris and defender Eric Dier both go for the ball and make a complete hash of the clearance. It falls to Steven Nzonzi, who calmly slots past Lloris with a precise finish, then celebrates by laughing uproariously at the comedy which preceded his goal. The game is done when Spurs' Vlad Chiricheș becomes the seventh player to be sent off in seven league games between Stoke and Tottenham at the Britannia Stadium for hauling down Mame Diouf in the 52nd minute to earn a second yellow.

33

23 February 1957

Tim Coleman bags his fourth goal of the half, on his way to recording a world-record seven in a game for a winger, when he cuts inside to latch on to a through ball, speeds over the icy, rutted Victoria Ground quagmire and fires home, taking advantage of Lincoln's Tony Emery, who fails to cut out the pass when he really should. A 4-0 lead at half-time is wonderful, but there are more goals in this game for Stoke and Coleman.

18 May 1963

Pint-sized striker Jackie Mudie settles nerves amongst the 33,644 Victoria Ground crowd willing City to promotion by giving Stoke a half-time lead. It comes as resilient Luton are undone after keeper Ron Baynham parries away a McIlroy shot, which falls to Mudie, who flicks it up and over the prone keeper and covering defenders. One, Brendan McNally, tries to keep the ball out by scissor-kicking it off the line, but the Victoria Ground mud means he cannot get off the ground and he only succeeds in helping it on its way into the net.

4 September 1982

Stoke are already 1-0 up at St Andrew's, thanks to Phil Hawker's own goal, when new right-winger Mark Chamberlain goes on the rampage again. It was his cross that Hawker volleyed home inadvertently, but this time there is no luck about the goal. Chamberlain picks the ball up on the right, just inside his own half. As he advances towards Jim Blyth's goal, the dazzling winger beats four men in a mazy dribble, including the hapless Hawker again, before lashing a right-foot shot into the far corner. It is one of the great solo goals scored by a Stoke player and an unbelievable way to notch Chamberlain's first in a Potters shirt. His second will arrive just three minutes later when he lashes home from close range. Peter Griffiths adds a fourth goal five minutes before half-time to complete one of Stoke's most famous top-flight away wins – the day Mark Chamberlain destroyed Birmingham City.

5 May 1997

It's one big party at the Victoria Ground as Stoke say farewell to their home of 119 years. City notch the first in a 2-1 win against perennial bunnies West Brom, when Graham Kavanagh latches on to a ball down towards the right byline, flicks it up and over Richard Sneekes's head, and then crosses hard at waist height for Gerry McMahon to dive to head home at the near post from five yards.

9 December 2003

Tony Pulis's Stoke are languishing just above the First Division relegation zone and are conceding goals far too regularly for the manager's liking, so he brings in experienced loanee centre-half Gerry Taggart from Leicester. The big Irishman makes his debut at West Ham and marshals the defence superbly. At the other end, fellow loanee debutant Frazer Richardson, from Leeds, side-foots home the rebound after David James parries Ade Akinbiyi's shot to secure a 1-0 victory, City's first at Upton Park for 30 years.

9 November 2014

Stoke already lead 1-0 at White Hart Lane thanks to Bojan's first Potters goal, but suddenly it is two when Danny Rose misjudges a Ryan Shawcross header. It allows Mame Diouf to break away down the right wing unmarked and cross for Jon Walters, also unmarked, to finish from a central position, eight yards out, with his left foot. City hold on for a second Premier League victory at Mauricio Pochettino's Spurs, aided by Kyle Naughton's late red card.

34

25 December 1950

Stoke have only ever won once at Arsenal's Highbury stadium, but centre-forward Roy Brown finds the net to end all thoughts that Stoke would be hammered 6-0 as they had been on the previous season's visit to North London. Latching on to the ball inside his own half, Brown races through past the Gunners' last line of defence, the ageing Leslie Compton, who struggles to turn and keep up with the young striker, to fire past keeper George Swindin. No matter that Arsenal are down to ten men with leading scorer Doug Lishman off the field injured at the time, City, already 1-0 up, have also hit the underside of the bar through Alec Ormston and are on their way to a comfortable 3-0 victory.

20 August 1955

Having equalised in the 29th minute with a tap-in, following keeper Ken Hardwick's fumble of Harry Oscroft's shot, after his stupendous opening goal, Johnny King bags his third Stoke City hat-trick, diving full length a foot off the turf to head home from six yards. City have turned around a two-goal deficit after five minutes to lead 3-2 by half-time at Doncaster's Belle Vue and go on to complete a 4-2 away victory to set off their promotion bid perfectly.

18 August 1979

Viv Busby nets City's first goal back in the top flight after winning promotion under Alan Durban. He heads past Jim Blyth to set Stoke on the way to a 3-2 victory over visitors Coventry, whose fans are housed in the new 4,250-seater Stoke End stand.

30 August 1997

After Sir Stanley Matthews has cut the tape on the new Britannia Stadium, in beautiful sunshine, Stoke's new home is given the perfect start when Graham Kavanagh carries the ball forward on the right-hand side, looks up and chips to the far post, where

Richard Forsyth steals in to prod the ball home with the outside of his right foot past Swindon keeper Fraser Digby. It is Stoke's first league goal at the new ground, but the day doesn't end well as Steve McMahon's Robins score twice late on to take the points.

12 October 1997

City seal a 2-1 victory in the first Potteries derby at the Britannia Stadium when Graham Kavanagh breaks forward, drawing in the Vale defence, and releases the ball at the perfect moment for Kevin Keen to shoot into the net. Despite having equalised only 13 minutes earlier through Tony Naylor's floated header, Vale cannot maintain that momentum and Stoke should have a third, but Forsyth's header, which seems to have gone over the line, is clawed away by Paul Musselwhite and the referee plays on despite City's pleas. That win, though, is currently City's last against Vale. In six subsequent games City have lost two and drawn four.

22 February 2005

From 23 October 2004 to 22 February 2005 the only scorelines in matches involving Stoke City were those of 0-0, 1-0, 0-1 and 1-1. It is already 1-1 at the Britannia Stadium against Craig Levein's Leicester when Gifton Noel-Williams heads in Kevin Harper's inch-perfect cross from six yards to add to Dave Brammer's thunderbolt from 20 yards ten minutes earlier. Stoke's eventual 3-2 victory in a Britannia Stadium snowstorm breaks the binary sequence of 18 league games under Tony Pulis.

31 January 2015

Jon Walters bags the second of what will prove to be a 'perfect' hat-trick against Harry Redknapp's QPR, who have lost every away game so far this season. This goal arrives courtesy of midfielder Stephen Ireland, who plays in Walters, racing through 30 yards out. The striker controls with one touch of his right foot, then wallops the ball into the bottom-right corner from the edge of the penalty area past Rob Green with his left.

24 January 2017

Stoke put struggling Sunderland to the sword. Marko Arnautović has already hammered one shot past Vito Mannone, when he picks the ball up 15 yards outside the penalty area on the left-hand side. He plays a one-two with Xherdan Shaqiri, then repeats the move with Peter Crouch just inside the area, to receive the ball back on his left foot. The Austrian hammers past Mannone again for a team goal that is pure Potters poetry. City go on to win 3-1.

35

12 October 1946

Stoke are in majestic form at Stamford Bridge. Freddie Steele opens the scoring, nodding home after George Mountford's piledriver shot cannons down off the underside of the bar and bounces out for Stoke's centre-forward to finish. It is the first of five goals City thrash past Billy Birrell's Chelsea to announce their title credentials loud and clear.

23 February 1974

Don Revie's Leeds are 29 games unbeaten and chasing down Burnley's all-time top-flight record of 30. The visitors lead 2-1, but City draw level when a long ball finds John Ritchie and he nods it down for Alan Hudson, who has only been at the club for a month since his £200,000 transfer from Chelsea, but has already made such a difference. Huddy turns, holds off the attentions of Terry Yorath, and fires past David Harvey in the visitors' goal from eight yards.

1 September 1984

There are very few high points in Stoke's 1984/85 season, but little did Potters fans know how badly it would unfold, with the team setting a then-record low-points total in the top flight of just 17, when Sammy McIlroy opens the scoring against Howard Wilkinson's Sheffield Wednesday. The goal comes after Mark Chamberlain shows sparkling form down the right wing, bamboozling Nigel Worthington before cutting the ball back for McIlroy to sweep home from six yards to open the scoring. City will win 2-1, but it will prove to be one of only three victories in this woeful season.

9 December 1995

Lou Macari's Stoke are upwardly mobile after five wins in six, while West Brom have lost the last seven. City steal the points when

Ian Clarkson slips while crossing from the right wing and the ball spoons up into the penalty area. Simon Sturridge challenges for it, but it's headed away by Paul Raven. It falls for Paul Peschisolido, lurking 12 yards out on the far post. Pesch swivels to hit a hip-high volley with his right foot, low past Albion keeper Naylor, who really should keep it out, but allows the ball to squirm under his left hand into the corner, much to the delight of the Stokies behind the goal.

30 October 2004

It is Tony Pulis's 100th game in charge, but it is remembered for only one thing, and that's not even Chris Greenacre's late winning goal. Instead, it is for the incident when Gerry Taggart almost throttles Millwall's very annoying Dennis Wise to death and escapes with only a yellow card from referee Uriah Rennie. The incident follows the two players falling out as team-mates whilst at Leicester and then, when Wise leaves his studs in on Taggart earlier in this game at the Britannia Stadium, the big Northern Irishman waits to exact his revenge. It arrives when he flattens Wise, then grabs him with a chokehold that leads to a 12-man melee and, remarkably, just the two cautions from the man in black. Not that Gerry was overly hard, but his own recollection of the incident is: 'He [Wise] was on the floor and I grabbed him. He'd done me earlier and he was having it. I got on top and was strangling him – and as I'm strangling him, he's grabbing my ****s, squeezing – and I've just gone, "It doesn't hurt Wisey." The melee is going off and the referee drags me into no man's land, then starts winking at me as if to say, "Don't worry, I'm not going to send you off." Then he says to me, "I've got to give you a card ... but it's only a yellow." I've thought, "Cheers Uriah, next time I see you at the dogs [the two used to meet at Owlerton dog track occasionally], the first drink's on me!" It was probably two red cards! Top man, Uriah.'

6 December 2014

Stoke extend their lead against Arsène Wenger's Gunners as Mark Hughes's men deliver one of the best first-half performances of his managerial tenure. The goal arrives as Jon Walters, tight on the right touchline, makes space to swing a cross low to the near post, where Bojan loses his barely existent marker to nip in and slot past Emiliano Martinez delightfully with a neat, left-foot finish from eight yards.

3 December 2016

City secure another three Premier League points against Sean Dyche's Burnley at the Britannia Stadium, when Marc Muniesa scores his first Premier League goal. The Spaniard starts and finishes a wonderful, flowing move, picking up the ball just outside his own penalty area and beating three men, before first Imbula and then Shaqiri move the ball quickly out to Marko Arnautović, haring down the left wing. The Austrian beats Jon Flanagan with a stepover and hits the byline, before cutting the ball back to Muniesa, 12 yards out, who lashes a first-time volley low into the bottom-left corner with his left foot, past a bewildered Paul Robinson. Muniesa has the widest smile the Brit has ever seen, not least because it is the first time he has scored in front of his young son.

24 October 2020

As City pile on the pressure against Thomas Frank's visiting Brentford, James McClean runs on to a cute Tyrese Campbell pass on the left edge of the penalty area at a tight angle to fire a left-footed drive low into the bottom-left corner, beating keeper David Raya with the aid of a slight deflection off Charlie Goode. His goal makes it 2-0 in this Championship encounter, which sees Stoke playing some of their best football of the season.

7 November 2020

City grab a second goal to unsettle the Championship leaders Reading at home in this lunchtime televised kick-off. It comes as Veljko Paunović's Royals try to play out and a chipped pass from keeper Rafael Cabral is intercepted out on the right wing by Tommy Smith, one of six Stoke players pressing in the opposition half. His header bounces forward towards Tyrese Campbell, who tries to flick it on, but misses, and it just carries on through to veteran Scottish centre-forward Steven Fletcher, who slots home, unmarked from 12 yards, right-footed for his fourth goal for Stoke after his summer free-transfer signing from Sheffield Wednesday.

36

11 May 1963

A huge crowd of 66,199 are packed into Stamford Bridge for a crucial match between Stoke and Chelsea at the top of the Second Division. After a wobble which has seen the Potters lose three matches in a row, with just four games remaining in the season, both need the points, but it is City who take them in a tense and tetchy encounter thanks to a superb strike from 20 yards on an angle by Jimmy McIlroy which flies in off Peter Bonetti's far post. The goal is made by Matthews and Mudie and is hailed by *The Sentinel*'s headline as the '3-M goal'. Scribe N.G. wrote, 'It was a triumph for skill and delicate touches against weight and bombast.' City ride their luck, with Barry Bridges hitting the bar and Jimmy O'Neill making two fine saves at the death. After the game, Stanley Matthews, aged 48, is announced as the Footballer of the Year, 15 years after winning his first award, the very first in the prize's history, in 1948. He had had to survive a brutalising by Eddie McCreadie and Ron 'Chopper' Harris as Chelsea tried to kick the winger out of the game that resulted in Eddie Clamp's famous intervention as Stan's minder, telling Harris, 'If you do that again you'll end up in hospital' after one particular nasty challenge.

7 December 1974

Jimmy Greenhoff has already scored a sublime volley at St Andrew's and Stoke lead 2-0 when the striker rises at the near post to glance home Jimmy Robertson's cross past Birmingham keeper Dave Latchford. Jimmy's day doesn't end so well, though, as Joe Gallagher breaks his nose in a challenge later in the game.

23 October 1982

Impish Welsh midfielder Mickey Thomas has joined from Brighton in the summer to complete Richie Barker's classic midfield alongside Sammy McIlroy, Paul Bracewell and Mark Chamberlain. The cheeky scamp scores an absolute belter of an individual goal, trapping a Mark Lawrenson headed clearance on his thigh and in one movement lashing a left-foot half-volley from 32 yards, which, as Thomas cuts across the ball when he hits it, curls beautifully into the left side of Bruce Grobbelaar's goal. Stunning.

19 April 2008

Mama Sidibé is the hero of the hour, responding to Pottermouth's poetic 'Battle Cry', which has been doing the rounds on local radio, inspiring City for the last three games of the 2007/08 promotion season. Having already scored once, Sidibé beats Brian Carey to a bouncing clearance on the halfway line, then races on to Ricardo Fuller's flicked pass to dribble 30 yards and beat Adriano Basso in the Bristol City goal with a low right-foot, side-foot finish into the bottom-right corner. Stoke win 2-1 and Sidibé has doubled his personal goal tally for the season in one game, writing himself into Potters folklore in the process.

37

31 October 1992

Graham Shaw adds a second goal to seal a 2-0 victory at Turf Moor to inflict Jimmy Mullen's Clarets' first home defeat of the season. His first came as he tapped in after two close-range shots were saved by Marlon Beresford, but his second is a long-range effort, taking a bouncing ball on the run and firing a right-footed cruise missile of a shot into the far top-left corner. City are up to second place in the Second Division table to the delight of the 4,500 travelling fans.

15 December 2007

Ricardo Fuller, City's talismanic striker, hasn't scored for ten games, but he makes up for this at a wet and windy Bloomfield Road. A goal down to an early Mike Flynn strike, Fuller equalises when he picks up a loose ball at the far post, after Paul Rachubka palms out Liam Lawrence's free kick weakly, controls and lashes high into the far top-right corner of the goal on an angle. It is the first of a purple patch of five goals in two games.

5 January 2010

Stoke are 3-0 up by the interval as visitors Fulham are blown away by City's whirlwind first-half performance and the snowy, ice blast of the Potteries weather conditions. Abdoulaye Faye has just converted Matty Etherington's free kick, sliding in, left-footed, from two yards to make it 2-0 and then, three minutes later, a flowing move sees Tuncay and Etherington combine to swing a cross into the Boothen End penalty area, where Rory Delap flicks on at the near post. His header finds Mama Sidibé at the far post and the Malian hammers it left-footed from 12 yards into the ground, then, one bounce, past the helpless Mark Schwarzer into the top-right corner.

25 August 2011

On a balmy summer's evening, Stoke seal their progress through to the Europa League group stages when they take a 3-0 half-time lead against visitors FC Thun. The third goal arrives when Jermaine Pennant's corner causes havoc in the penalty area and is squeezed clear to the edge of the box by the Swiss defence, where Glenn Whelan steams in to lash a right-footed drive into the top-right corner of Dragan Djukić's net. No coming back for Bernard Challandes's men after that.

38

22 February 1975

Stoke hit the top of the First Division last weekend and seem to have taken the lead at lowly Luton when Alan Hudson slots into an empty net, but John Ryan races back to clear. Hudson claims (to this day) that the ball was clearly two yards over the line, but referee Reynolds disagrees and waves play on. When Geoff Salmons puts a penalty wide early in the second half, the goalless draw becomes inevitable. Despite the dropped point, Stoke remain at the head of the table of the top tier of English football, but this will be the last day on which that is the case, not only in this nearly-but-not-quite season, but ever.

29 November 2008

Amidst all the furore about Rory Delap's long throw and the carnage it is wreaking amongst Premier League defences, Phil Brown's Hull think they have come up with strategies to negate it. The fun starts when substitute Dean Windass is sent out from the dugout to warm up in front of Delap, who is about to take a throw in front of the main stand towards the tunnel-end goal. Windass times his jog down the line to perfection, interrupting Delap's run-up not once but twice. At that point, referee Keith Stroud loses his patience and books the Tigers striker, despite him never getting on to the pitch. But the comedy isn't over. A few moments later Hull keeper Boaz Myhill comes outside his area to clear a through ball. But he dithers, clearly in two minds as to whether it's a bright idea to put it out for a throw with Delap already warming his hands up. Instead, after teetering around on his tiptoes for a moment, Myhill turns the ball out for a corner, rather than a throw, amidst much hilarity in the stands.

31 January 2009

It all kicks off at the Britannia Stadium when Mark Hughes's Manchester City, featuring the world's most expensive signing,

£32.5m Brazilian Robinho, purchased by the newfound wealth of their new owners from Abu Dhabi at the start of the season, get physical with Stoke. Surprisingly, it is diminutive winger Shaun Wright-Phillips who goes in with all studs showing in a tackle with Matty Etherington. Rory Delap takes exception and the already white-hot atmosphere combusts when he fouls Wright-Phillips, then whacks the stationary ball into his midriff as he lies prone on the floor. Delap sees red, but referee Martin Atkinson misses Wright-Phillips's retaliatory kick on the midfielder, for which he is later suspended on review. Stoke now have ten men and at least 50 minutes to negotiate against the billionaires, but the crowd are completely behind their gladiators and rouse them to a stupendous 1-0 victory.

1 February 2014

Stoke start the game in the relegation zone in Mark Hughes's first season in charge thanks to wins for Sunderland and West Ham in the lunchtime kick-offs, but the Potters are in inspired form against David Moyes's Manchester United. Charlie Adam is the star. It is his left-foot free kick from 35 yards which is heading for David de Gea's goal, when United midfielder Michael Carrick sticks out his right leg at an awkward angle to deflect it past his flat-footed keeper from eight yards. Stoke's revival is on.

4 July 2020

Tyrese Campbell bags his second of this vital relegation clash against Barnsley, which proves to be City's first victory following the resumption of football after the coronavirus hiatus of spring 2020. This goal is as a result of a training-ground corner routine. Sam Clucas pulls the ball back to the edge of the area from a left-wing corner. All of City's players race towards goal aside from Campbell, who runs out from his starting position on the six-yard line to find oceans of space in which to strike a crisp, left-footed drive first time into the bottom-right corner. Stoke have now scored two goals from corners because Barnsley choose not to put men on their posts. Championship safety looks likely, but there are more twists to come in the final five games.

18 July 2020

Covid-19 has meant that the season is continuing throughout the summer. Somehow Michael O'Neill has forged a team from Stoke's fractured, legacy squad and they lie five points from the relegation zone before this, their penultimate game. A point should be enough, but Lee Gregory makes all three safe, pouncing after Bees goalkeeper David Raya palms out Sam Clucas's long-range, left-foot shot low to his left. The 1-0 win allows City to celebrate an unlikely survival, albeit in front of empty stands.

39

15 January 1962

Left-back Tony Allen roars on to the magnificent Don Ratcliffe's cutback to slam home from the left edge of the area past Gordon Banks, bulging the net gloriously, to put Stoke 2-0 ahead in an FA Cup third-round replay against the previous season's beaten finalists Leicester. Stoke go on to lead 3-0 at half-time and eventually win 5-2 to advance and face top-flight Blackburn in the fourth round, which ends in a controversial defeat with one fan threatening to sue the referee!

28 November 2012

As Tony Pulis's Stoke defeat Alan Pardew's Newcastle 2-1 at the Britannia Stadium, one incident stands out, when beanpole striker Peter Crouch loses his teeth in a clash with the Magpies defender Fabricio Coloccini in front of the main stand, not far from the technical areas. Crouch later recalled, 'Coloccini gave me an elbow and it was one of those that was intentional. I went to jump and he had one eye on me, elbow in the chops. I lost all four of my front teeth. They all fell out at the same time, but I caught two of them. The other two were on the floor and the physio came on and my mouth was gushing with blood. So now my front four teeth are all false and at times I get called the fourth Bee Gee.'

26 September 2020

After Preston's Tom Barkhuizen is sent off for a sliding challenge on Morgan Fox as the pair compete for a loose ball, City score their first goal of the season to secure a first win at Deepdale since September 2005. The goal comes 18 minutes after the red card as Jon Obi Mikel interchanges passes with Tashan Oakley-Boothe and Steven Fletcher down the right side of the area and squares for Lee Gregory to convert left-footed from three yards at the far post. It proves to be Gregory's last goal for Stoke due to injury, lack of opportunities and an eventual loan move to Derby on deadline day in February 2021.

40

8 May 2011

Former Gunner Jermaine Pennant is on fire against his old club and races forward, with the ball on his right foot. From 25 yards out, he unleashes a right-footed drive which deflects off Johan Djourou, up and over Wojciech Szczęsny in the Arsenal goal and goes in just under the bar in the top-right corner. Arsène Wenger's afternoon just got a whole lot worse. City lead 2-0.

41

15 January 1962

Young star Peter Bullock, not yet 21 and having become Stoke's youngest-ever player aged 16 years and 163 days five years earlier (a record he still holds), nets his 16th and final goal for Stoke as the Potters go 3-0 up by half-time against the previous season's beaten FA Cup finalists Leicester in a third-round replay. Bullock latches on to Don Ratcliffe's inside pass to hit the ball first time on the half-turn and score past Gordon Banks in the Foxes goal. Bullock would play just once more for Stoke before being sold to Birmingham City for £10,000. This victory marks the last time Stoke knocked a top-flight team out of the FA Cup when the club was in a lower division.

12 May 1984

Paul Maguire nets the second of his four goals which keep Stoke in the First Division after a remarkable second half of the 1983/84 season secures a great escape. This goal is his best of the lot, a superb overhead kick, spectacularly flying past Wolves keeper John Burridge at the Town End.

14 October 1995

Lou Macari's Stoke put Graham Taylor's Wolves to the sword. Graham Potter stabs in his first for the club to give Stoke a 2-0 half-time lead. Shortly after the break Mike Stowell is clattered by his own defender Eric Young and Dean Richards has to go in goal. He concedes two more as City win 4-1 at Molineux, the first victory since 1967.

23 March 1996

Mike Sheron bravely flies in to head Ian Clarkson's chip past Mike Ammann from seven yards at the near post. It is Stoke's first goal of 1996 away from home and proves to be the first of a run of Sheron scoring in seven consecutive games to set a new club record, which ends when he nets against the same opponents in the return fixture at the Victoria Ground. At this time Sheron was the hottest goalscoring property outside the Premier League, following his arrival from Norwich after being swapped for misfit Potters striker Keith Scott by manager Lou Macari in November 1995. His partnership with Simon Sturridge propelled Stoke to the play-offs by the end of that season and, a year later, after scoring 39 goals in 76 appearances, he was sold to QPR for £2.75m in order to finance the club's move to the new Britannia Stadium.

4 March 2000

Peter Thorne, recalled to the starting line-up because of an injury to Paul Connor and Kyle Lightbourne's international call-up for Bermuda, already has two goals. He completes his hat-trick, his first for Stoke, when he half-volleys a loose clearing header, left-footed, curling past Chesterfield keeper Mark Gayle into the bottom-left corner from 20 yards. It is the first-ever hat-trick scored at the Britannia Stadium. City lead 3-0 at half-time for the first time since Leicester away in August 1995.

9 May 2009

Stoke just need one more win to secure Premier League status and travel to fellow strugglers Hull in balmy sunshine, getting off to a great start when Ricardo Fuller swivels to fire the Potters ahead after a Liam Lawrence near-post corner ricochets into his path. Within touching distance now.

9 April 2011

Stoke are 1-3 down at White Hart Lane, but Kenwyne Jones nets an absolute cracker of a strike to pull it back to 2-3. It comes after Gareth Bale dwells on the ball, allowing Andy Wilkinson to prod through to Jones. The striker turns, cuts inside and fires an unstoppable left-foot shot into the top-right corner of the net from 30 yards, leaving Heurelho Gomes grasping thin air.

24 May 2015

Stoke score five goals before half-time for the first time since 1986 when midfielder Charlie Adam, a former Liverpool player himself, latches on to yet more poor defending from the visitors. This time Lucas Leiva loses control, allowing Adam to pounce to lash a left-foot shot low to Simon Mignolet's left from 18 yards. City now have a positive goal difference at the end of a Premier League season for the first time.

13 May 2018

Peter Crouch heads the 1,000th Premier League goal of the season and Stoke's final one in a ten-year stay in the top flight as City are already relegated, but come back to win 2-1 in their final match of the season at Swansea's Liberty Stadium. In brilliant sunshine, Stoke youngster Lasse Sørenson, who became the youngest player to start for Stoke in the Premier League (18 years, 204 days), provides Crouch with the cross to nod home from eight yards, extending his own Premier League record for headed goals to 53. Manager Paul Lambert is sacked after failing to keep Stoke up in his 15 games in charge, of which this was just his second victory. The fans sing one last Premier League 'Delilah' to say goodbye.

42

11 January 1947

In Stoke's first FA Cup tie since the Burnden Park disaster the previous March, Stoke score twice in three minutes against Joe Hulme's Second Division Spurs at White Hart Lane. First Tottenham's George Ludford puts through his own goal in trying to clear Alec Ormston's shot, which seems to be going wide, then City's Frank Mountford smashes home a spectacular 30-yard screamer past Ted Ditchburn. Fittingly, given that the night beforehand the two sets of players met up for a drink near Ludgate Circus, the game ends in a draw, with Ludford righting his own-goal wrong by forcing in from close range with three minutes to go to send the tie to a replay at the Victoria Ground. The fever with which that game is anticipated sees an estimated 20,000 queue up for just 7,000 presale tickets on Monday morning. Absenteeism on the day of the replay is said to be over 40 per cent in both the Coalfields and Potteries.

9 December 1972

In a crucial relegation battle at the foot of the First Division table, Stoke secure a vital win when John Ritchie stabs home Geoff Hurst's far-post knockback of Terry Conroy's corner kick. Frank O'Farrell's United are, unbelievably, on their way down to the Second Division for the first time since the mid-1930s. Old Trafford's floodlights come out in sympathy, failing during the half-time interval, but thankfully coming back on so Stoke's 2-0 victory stands.

23 August 1975

Brian Kidd dawdles on the ball on the left side of Arsenal's defence and, instead of clearing, chips it back to keeper Jimmy Rimmer. Although the laws then allowed Rimmer to pluck it from the air without being penalised, Jimmy Greenhoff steals in and challenges the keeper. Rimmer flaps at the ball, which rebounds to the edge of the area, where Alan Hudson pounces to control and fire home right-footed, low to the left corner. Rimmer recovers to get a hand to it, but can't prevent it bouncing in off the post and into the North Bank net for the only goal on a balmy day at Highbury.

16 January 1998

Over 2,000 fans register their disgust at the state of the club by turning up for the game 15 minutes late in front of Sky TV's cameras for this Friday-night encounter with Bradford. Managerless Stoke turn around an early deficit with a Richard Forsyth penalty and then a winner from Peter Thorne. Kevin Keen sets up the striker for his tenth goal of a stuttering season with a cute flick pass that Thorne slots past Gary Walsh on the run, right-footed from 23 yards, low into the bottom-left corner. Thorne will not score again until the final day of the season, as relegation is confirmed by a 2-5 home defeat by Manchester City.

23 February 2008

Top of the Championship table, Stoke maintain their lead thanks to a superb Liam Lawrence right-footed shot from 25 yards, wide on the right-hand side, outside the penalty area, which takes Ipswich keeper Steven Bywater completely by surprise and sails into the top-left corner.

20 October 2011

Cameron Jerome has had an eventful first half against Maccabi Tel Aviv. He has scored himself, created a goal for Ryan Shotton, hit the bar, had a header cleared off the line, been booked for dissent and now he gets a second yellow card for raising an elbow which catches Yoav Ziv, who goes down like the proverbial sack of spuds, writhing in agony, or putting it on according to the livid Stoke players and fans. Ziv's card has been marked by Stoke's supporters as Jerome wanders down the tunnel prematurely to a standing ovation.

20 April 2013

Cameron Jerome beats his man, hits the byline and cuts the ball back left-footed to the near post for Peter Crouch to side-foot home, right-footed, under the despairing dive of QPR's Rob Green to give City the lead at Loftus Road in a crunch relegation battle. Jon Walters seals a vital three points with a late penalty and Tony Pulis's men are all but safe, while Harry Redknapp's Rangers are all but down.

7 December 2013

André Schürrle has given José Mourinho's Chelsea the lead at the Britannia Stadium, but Mark Hughes's Stoke equalise when an inswinging corner comes in from the left and is missed by everyone at the near post, allowing it to bounce to Peter Crouch, eight yards out, in the middle of the goal. He controls on his stomach, swivels and fires in left-footed, beating the lunging Gary Cahill and keeper Petr Čech, and then going through Ramires's legs on the line.

12 April 2014

Dutch left-back Erik Pieters floats a cross over towards the far post from wide out on the left wing, but he slightly miscues it and, with the aid of the swirling Britannia Stadium wind, the ball flies over Newcastle keeper Tim Krul's head into the far top-right corner of the tunnel-end goal, off the inside of the top of the post, to give Stoke a 1-0 victory over Alan Pardew's Newcastle.

43

5 May 1945

George Mountford completes his first-half hat-trick against Port Vale, latching on to Tommy Sale's through ball to race clear and score past Vale keeper Prince from 15 yards on the right-hand side of the area.

26 September 1970

John Ritchie scores his second goal of the game against visitors Arsenal to set Stoke on their way to a 5-0 rout. As the Gunners flounce around with the ball at the back, Frank McLintock miscontrols and, quick as a flash, Ritchie pounces to snaffle the ball off the Arsenal captain, then bear down on the penalty area. He leaves John Roberts on the deck, then veers to the left side of the area, beating Pat Rice, before firing a low, left-foot shot into the bottom-left corner of the Boothen End net, past the onrushing Bob Wilson. A wonderful solo goal.

24 March 1979

Stoke are all over hosts Cardiff, lead 1-0 and have already hit the post as well, when Sammy Irvine hits a speculative high ball to the edge of the Ninian Park penalty area. It comes down with snow on it, but perfectly on to Brendan O'Callaghan's left boot, which strikes it sweetly into the bottom-right corner of John Davies's net. It's a cracking volley on the run to put Stoke on their way to a crucial 3-1 victory that keeps them in second position in the Second Division with just nine games remaining.

18 January 1997

A minute after scoring the opening goal, a deft near-post flick from five yards from Mark Stein's pullback, striker Mike Sheron seizes on Graham Kavanagh's slide-rule pass on the left side of the penalty area to roll a right-foot, side-foot finish into the far bottom-right corner of Andy Petterson's net from 16 yards to give

Stoke a 2-0 lead at the Valley. City hold on for a 2-1 victory over Alan Curbishley's Charlton to rise to fifth spot in the First Division.

17 May 2000

The Second Division play-off semi-final is finely balanced after Stoke's 3-2 win at home over Gillingham, but Priestfield becomes a hotbed when referee Rob Styles steps in to show two controversial red cards to Potters players in swift succession, for little apparent reason. First, Clive Clarke picks up a second yellow card in a minute for apparently throwing the ball away after a disputed throw-in call went against him. Then, at a corner, jostling takes place and before you know it Mr Styles shows another red, to City's inspirational Graham Kavanagh, allegedly for an elbow. No one in the crowd or on TV actually seems to see anything. Stoke succumb to three Gills goals, the first from the corner before which Kav was sent off, to bow out, mostly thanks to the referee, whose name is still never uttered without cursing in the Potteries.

11 December 2011

Matty Etherington is the hero as Stoke defeat Harry Redknapp's Tottenham at the Britannia Stadium. First, he nips in, after Peter Crouch controls, and then reverse passes a right-wing cross back across goal, to slot home, right-footed, from five yards. Then, he taps home a Jon Walters flick-on from a right-wing Rory Delap throw at the far post. Superb anticipation and positioning from the left-winger, a former Spurs player, who joined Stoke from West Ham in January 2009 for £2m. Ethers scored 16 goals in 177 games and became a firm fans' favourite, winning Player of the Season in 2009/10. He was unlucky not to win an England cap and also to be injured in the run-up to the 2011 FA Cup Final and not be fully fit for the big game. Etherington was a key component of Stoke's feared wing play, with his right-wing compatriot Jermaine Pennant also producing a purple patch in his career under Tony Pulis.

9 September 2017

Stoke produce a flowing move which starts with new signing Darren Fletcher spraying the ball out to the right-hand edge of the penalty area to an unmarked Mame Diouf. The Senegalese striker controls and crosses low, right-footed, to find Eric Maxim Choupo-Moting, a close-season signing from Schalke 04 on a free transfer, to slot his first Stoke goal from six yards, lunging in right-footed to beat David de Gea all ends up at the Boothen End to put City 1-0 up against José Mourinho's Manchester United.

44

3 May 1952

Despite Stoke's fate being in the balance as they battle against relegation from the top flight for the first time since 1923, there are only around 11,000 fans in the Victoria Ground for the visit of Middlesbrough. City have to win and Roy Brown scores twice, on 12 minutes and then again just before half-time. His first comes from Frank Bowyer's toe-poked pass which dissects Boro's defence. His second arrives when Bowyer's fierce shot ricochets back to Brown, who fires in a low shot that visiting keeper Hodgson touches on to a post, but the ball flies in. It saves the blushes of Frank Mountford, who has missed a penalty in between Brown's goals. But instead of putting City on the brink of salvation, Brown's brace only sees Stoke level as they conceded two goals to a header from Boro's Geoff Walker and a swerving left-foot shot from Lindy Delapenha in between. Stoke have just 45 minutes to save themselves from the drop.

24 August 1963

City are level against Bill Nicholson's Tottenham Hotspur all-stars in their first game back in the First Division since 1953, when Jimmy McIlroy pounces to net his second of the game to nudge City in front again. Bill Asprey's long ball forward is misjudged by Spurs defensive hard nut Dave Mackay. Pouncing on the loose ball, new arrival Peter Dobing, a club-record signing at £37,500 from Blackburn in the summer, makes a lovely swerve to his right before cutting the ball back to McIlroy, arriving at speed on the edge of the box to shoot on the run. The ball strikes a defender to deflect just past keeper Bill Brown's outstretched hand and nestle in the corner of the Boothen End net to the delight of the 40,017 crowd rammed into the Victoria Ground. City hold on in the second half, with midfielders Eddie Clamp and Eric Skeels prominent in keeping the likes of Cliff Jones and Jimmy Greaves quiet to secure a famous win. McIlroy was a key member of Tony Waddington's promotion-winning team the previous season, signing from Burnley, where he had won the league title, for a cut-price £25,000. He would go on to score 19 goals in 116 games for the Potters, but create many more, thanks to his trademark slide-rule passing and tactical brain.

21 March 1964

Dennis Viollet grabs his second of the game to make it 4-1 at half-time against the champions of 1961/62, who, now under rookie manager Jackie Milburn, are struggling at the foot of the First Division table. By the end of this match, Ipswich will have conceded 100 league goals in the season by their 34th game. Viollet makes it 95 when Ritchie flicks on George Kinnell's free kick to the far post and the striker is on hand to thump a powerful volley home.

23 April 1968

Already 1-0 ahead in a vital end-of-season match against title challengers Leeds, Peter Dobing nets his second of the game with a superlative strike. Collecting the ball 30 yards out, Dobing works the ball on to his deadly left foot and rifles it into the top corner past a disbelieving Gary Sprake. Stoke are now odds-on to avoid relegation.

1 February 1975

Stoke are playing champagne football on a quagmire of a Victoria Ground pitch against Tony Book's Manchester City. Thankfully, the TV cameras are there to capture Alan Hudson almost literally walking on water as he orchestrates midfield. He begins the move for the opening goal in a 4-0 victory deep in his own half, firing a right-foot pass up to Jimmy Greenhoff, just inside the visitors' half. The striker controls right-footed, then turns to spray a pass out to the right wing, which finds John Mahoney perfectly. The Welsh midfielder looks for a forward pass, but instead cuts it back inside to Hudson, who has sprinted 50 yards to join the attack he started. Huddy stutters, then dips his shoulder, sprints past Asa Hartford down the right side of the penalty area and chips a perfect right-foot cross, on the run, on to Ian Moores's head. The young, lanky striker accepts the gift gratefully, heading low into the bottom-right corner of Keith MacRae's net from six yards at the Town End. It is imperious and exciting: a tremendous move and goal, in awful conditions.

21 December 1986

Stoke make it 5-0 just before half-time when Tony 'Zico' Kelly chips a cheeky free kick, right-footed, over the wall and past visiting keeper Mervyn Day, who has promised his supporters in a prematch interview he won't concede six again like he did on Leeds' last visit to the Victoria Ground. They don't. They end up letting in a magnificent seven for Stoke.

20 April 1997

It is the last Potteries derby at the Victoria Ground and City are smothering Vale, with 18-year-old left-back Andy Griffin blanking the dangerous Port Vale winger Jon McCarthy from the game. Stoke's talismanic striker Mike Sheron opens the scoring, collecting a pass from Carl Beeston with his back to goal, then turning sharply, leaving two Vale players on the deck, nutmegging Neil Aspin with an adroit flick and beating the covering defenders to the ball to hammer goalwards from 22 yards. The ball takes a wicked deflection off Lee Glover to spin past Paul Musselwhite into the bottom-left corner of the Town End net.

23 November 1999

Amidst the excitement of the Icelandic consortium's takeover of the club, and installation of Guðjón Thórðarson as manager, City travel to Wycombe. There is huge optimism on the terraces, which proves to be justified for once as Graham Kavanagh fires in the first goal under the new regime, right-footed from 22 yards, low into the bottom-right corner of Martin Taylor's net. Kav celebrates with his team-mates, then double high fives his new manager on the way back to the halfway line.

11 May 2002

Stoke kill off any hopes Steve Coppell's Brentford may have of a comeback and secure a return to the second tier of English football when Bjarni Guðjónsson curls in a right-footed free kick from the left-hand side, just outside the penalty area, which takes two deflections on its way past Paul Smith in the Brentford goal, the last off striker Ben Burgess's left foot. Stoke hold on to their 2-0 lead comfortably at the Millennium Stadium and are back in the First Division four years after relegation, killing off the hoodoo of the south dressing room to boot.

9 January 2005

Over 6,000 Stokies are at Highbury for an FA Cup third-round tie against Arsène Wenger's Gunners. In a tight first half, Stoke are defending well, but right-back Wayne Thomas manages to free the defensive shackles to steal into Jens Lehmann's penalty area and prod home a loose ball from three yards high into the North Bank net, after the keeper has saved Ade Akinbiyi's header from eight yards. It sends the Potters fans at the Clock End at the other end of the ground ballistic, and Thomas runs the entire length of the pitch, pursued by his team-mates, to celebrate taking the lead with them. Euphoric.

24 October 2010

The bias of Premier League referees towards the big boys is never more apparent than when Andre Marriner somehow fails to send off Manchester United's Gary Neville, who just cannot cope with Stoke's flying left-winger Matty Etherington. Already on a yellow card for a clumsy challenge on City's mercurial winger, Neville, playing his 600th United game, scythes down Etherington once again out on the left flank. But Marriner declines to show him the obvious second yellow and deserved red to reduce United to ten men. Alex Ferguson makes the most of his good fortune and substitutes the former England captain at half-time, humiliatingly letting him take the pitch after the break before getting his number held up and making him jog off the pitch to be replaced by Wes Brown. Neville retires almost immediately, openly admitting he should have been sent off.

4 April 2015

Steven Ireland wins the ball off Chelsea's Eden Hazard on the right corner of Stoke's penalty area and plays it up to Jon Walters, 20 yards inside the Potters half. Walters controls, then lays the ball off to Charlie Adam. The Scottish midfielder takes two touches on his left foot, looks up, spies goalkeeper Thibaut Courtois off his line and larrups a left-foot shot from 62 yards. Surely it can't go in, but Adam has slightly cut across the ball and it sails goalwards, arcing left, to be plumb on course. Courtois struggles to move his feet to get back and only gets his fingertips of his left hand on to the ball as it then nestles in the back of the net. Adam celebrates with the world's worst robot in front of the benched Peter Crouch, whilst sporting a huge gap-toothed smile. Walters still claims the assist to this day.

45

6 March 1971

Terry Neill's Hull are 2-0 up against Stoke in this FA Cup quarter-final at Boothferry Park. The Potters need inspiration to mount the necessary comeback and find it when Sean Haslegrave sends a probing left-footed ball forward from the halfway line on the left side and Irish winger Terry Conroy races on to it, outpacing Billy Wilkinson. Conroy dances round keeper Ian McKechnie on the edge of the area, then slots low, right-footed from six yards, wide to the left, to begin a famous comeback.

26 January 1972

West Ham have somehow come back from conceding the opening goal only 13 minutes ago to lead 2-1 thanks to two cracking finishes past Gordon Banks. But straight from the kick-off, Stoke attack down the right. Terry Conroy passes inside for George Eastham to square to Peter Dobing. The skipper shifts the ball on to his right foot, then shoots from 20 yards. It takes a slight deflection on its way past the diving Bobby Moore, who is in the Hammers goal due to an injury to Bobby Ferguson, and nestles in the bottom-right corner of the Stretford End net. It's 2-2 at half-time in this pulsating League Cup semi-final second replay. Wembley is within touching distance.

19 September 1992

After Tony Parkes's gaffe has gifted Bob Taylor an opening goal for Ossie Ardiles's Baggies, Steve Foley drives forward from midfield, takes advantage of a lucky ricochet to race into the penalty area at the Town End of the Victoria Ground and, from 15 yards, chips left-footed over advancing visiting keeper Stuart Naylor as he goes to ground. An epic clash is unfolding which will spark both Stoke's record unbeaten run of 23 games under Lou Macari and 20 years' worth of singing 'We always beat West Brom'.

26 April 2008

In the penultimate game of the season, Stoke are tantalisingly close to promotion to the Premier League, but must weather the emotion of Colchester United's last-ever game at Layer Road. The only goal of a dour match comes when a Rory Delap throw is headed goalwards by Richard Cresswell from six yards, but Dean Gerken saves well, low to his left. Liam Lawrence pulls back the loose ball and Cresswell instinctively touches it in with the toe of his left boot at the near post from one yard out. It sends the few Stokies in the ground and the 10,000 watching at the Britannia Stadium on a big screen absolutely crazy. Promotion is close enough to touch now.

31 January 2009

Seven minutes after Rory Delap has been controversially sent off for kicking the ball at a prone Shaun Wright-Phillips because of an awful tackle by the diminutive Manchester City winger on Stoke's new winger Matty Etherington, Ethers, making his home debut, gets revenge by running on to Glenn Whelan's cute chip down the left wing to float a cross to the far post where City's other January signing, James Beattie, awaits. Beattie runs his marker Wayne Bridge under the ball, then backs off to leap and power a header perfectly into the bottom-right corner of Joe Hart's net. Stoke lead 1-0 with ten men. Can the unthinkable happen?

6 December 2014

Stoke round off the perfect half of football with a third goal against Arsène Wenger's woeful Arsenal. This goal comes from Bojan's deep corner from the left wing, which is headed down and towards goal by Peter Crouch. A slight deflection sees it bounce perfectly for Jon Walters four yards out and he lashes the ball into the roof of the net from an angle to send the Boothen End into hysteria.

24 May 2015

Steven Nzonzi drives forward from midfield unchallenged, his long legs carrying him towards Liverpool's penalty area, he shifts the ball on to his right foot and lashes a 25-yard shot, curling into the far top-right corner of Simon Mignolet's net. Stoke lead Liverpool 5-0 at half-time and the ground is alight with joy.

28 December 2015

At Goodison Park against Roberto Martinez's Toffees, City score a second to secure a half-time lead when Bojan's precise ball forward finds Xherdan Shaqiri all on his own on the right edge of the Everton penalty area. The ball bounces once before Shaq reaches it on the half-volley, whilst at full tilt, and clips a perfect, arcing shot over the advanced Tim Howard into the far top-left corner. A wonderful goal is celebrated with folded-arms cheek from the Swiss winger. Did he mean that? You bet.

12 July 2020

Stoke kill off any thoughts managerless Birmingham have of mounting a comeback and secure a vital three points on the way to averting relegation from the Championship when Sam Clucas scores a wonderful individual goal. The midfielder takes a flick from James McClean and speeds into the left corner of the penalty area, then moves the ball across himself on the run and fires a right-footed, curling shot into the far side of Lee Camp's goal. Adam Davies, given his debut in the Potters goal, has little to do as nerves settle and safety edges that little bit closer.

45+1

23 November 1999

All the optimism about the takeover of the club by an Icelandic consortium is becoming reality, especially when new signing, Icelandic international Einar Daníelsson, on loan from KR Reykjavík, dances through the Wycombe defence on the left side of the penalty area, leaving two defenders and keeper Martin Taylor on the ground, to slot home left-footed from five yards. It's a wonderful solo goal that symbolises the turning of a new page in Potters history.

26 January 2016

City travel to Anfield for the second leg of the League Cup semi-final a goal down to Jürgen Klopp's Liverpool after the home leg. But Mark Hughes's team are brilliant and take the lead when Jon Walters wins the ball back on the edge of his own centre circle, exchanges first-time passes with Bojan, then plays in the little Spaniard out on the right with a deft flick of his right boot. Bojan's cross is low, finding Marko Arnautović, looking suspiciously offside, in acres of space, seven yards out. The Austrian calmly side-foots, left-footed under keeper Simon Mignolet. City are level on aggregate and have the momentum. Could Wembley await?

Half-time

24 May 2015

Stoke leave the Britannia Stadium pitch 5-0 ahead at half-time for the only time in the stadium's history. As the players arrive in the home dressing room celebrating a stunning half of football against Liverpool, they look at each other and simply burst into laughter at the absurdity of it all!

13 September 2010

As Stoke kick off the second half of their Premier League home game against Aston Villa, manager Tony Pulis emerges from the Britannia Stadium tunnel. The ground rises as one to applaud the capped manager as it had been widely advertised before the game that he would not be in attendance because his mother had died earlier that day. It's an emotional moment and one which exemplifies the manager's dedication and professionalism at a time of great personal torment. Inspired, Stoke fight back to win 2-1.

46

19 September 1992

City were 0-1 down just before half-time in this classic clash with West Brom, but now Kevin Russell lunges to slam a loose ball into the roof of the Boothen End net, left-footed from three yards, after Stuart Naylor saves Steve Foley's header from Mark Stein's right-wing cross. This topsy-turvy game swings Stoke's way as they now lead 2-1.

21 November 1992

Kevin Russell ghosts across the lumpy, bumpy, mud-strewn puddles that pass for a pitch at Bloomfield Road to score a wondrous solo goal to secure a vital win and a 14th league game unbeaten, as Stoke hit the top of the Second Division table for the first time in 1992/93. Russell picks the ball up ten yards inside the Blackpool half, he beats one man in midfield with a dip of the shoulder and a swerve to the left, races between two more defenders with a burst of pace, darts into the penalty area with the ball on his left foot, but holds off a challenge to switch the ball, on the run, to his weaker right foot and plants a low shot into the bottom-left corner.

47

12 June 1947

In appalling conditions, despite it being summertime, Stoke's left-back John McCue slips in the Bramall Lane mud in trying to clear and Walter Rickett dashes in to shoot home past Dennis Herod. It puts City 1-2 down in the biggest game in the club's history, in which a victory would see the Potters lift the league title. Can they come back?

18 May 1963

With promotion tantalisingly close as City lead relegation-threatened Luton 1-0 at half-time, but with nerves jangling as only a win will seal the deal, the butterflies are blown away as evergreen 48-year-old Stan Matthews latches on to a glorious Jimmy McIlroy through ball that splits the Luton defence to hare goalwards across the Victoria Ground mud, bereft of even a tuft of grass after one of the most punishing winters on record. With hearts in mouths as Matthews bears down on goal in front of them from fully 50 yards out, leaving the defence running in treacle behind him, the Boothen End watches as the veteran waltzes around keeper Ron Baynham, selling him a dummy to go right, then switching back left and slotting home left-footed, sparking scenes of jubilation. When his team-mates catch up with him as he trots back to the halfway line, Matthews is engulfed by congratulations. What a time to score your first goal of the season.

15 May 1968

After a terrible second half to the season, which has seen Stoke record just six wins in the final 23 games, City have secured their First Division status thanks to a goalless draw at Leicester in their penultimate game. To celebrate, Stoke win their final match of the season, against Liverpool, 2-1. Cultured midfielder Willie Stevenson is the star, four months after signing from the Reds, as he spreads the ball around, revellng in being captain for the night, also breaking up inert Liverpool attacks, he then sends mercurial winger Terry Conroy away down the left-hand side of the penalty area. Conroy gets to the byline then pulls the ball back for Peter Dobing to nod home. City lead 1-0 and 27,693 fans celebrate.

19 August 2017

Jesé Rodriguez enjoys a dream start to his Stoke City career by scoring the winner against Arsenal. A sloppy pass from Granit Xhaka towards a flat-footed Mesut Özil gives the ball back to Stoke on the halfway line. Geoff Cameron feeds Jesé, who breaks forward and exchanges passes with Saido Berahino before rifling a left-foot shot low into the far-right corner at the Boothen End from eight yards out on the left side of the penalty area. Gunners manager Arsène Wenger keeps up his side of the bargain by complaining bitterly that his side were denied a goal (Nacho Monreal was offside) and a penalty by referee Andre Marriner. But far from this being the kick-start Jesé's career needs, the former Real Madrid Champions League winner, on a season-long loan from Paris Saint-Germain, spends most of his time not playing for the club, posting on social media about his DJ activities and becoming public enemy number one, in a hotly contested head-to-head with Saido, as the club sink towards an ignominious relegation.

48

22 April 1964

Dennis Viollet grabs an equaliser for Stoke to make it 1-1 on the night and 2-2 on aggregate in their first-ever major cup final, the 1964 League Cup Final against Leicester. The Foxes, at home in the second leg, have taken the lead thanks to Ian Stringfellow's burst past George Kinnell and Bill Asprey to score in the sixth minute. At the other end, Gordon Banks has already pulled off stunning saves from Calvin Palmer and John Ritchie, with the big centre-forward also heading on to the bar, before Viollet latches on to Jimmy McIlroy's incisive through ball to slot home. Game on!

49

26 January 1972

Right-back Jackie Marsh launches a deep cross into the West Ham box. John Ritchie and his marker John McDowell both rise out of the Old Trafford mud. McDowell climbs higher, but his headed clearance only reaches Terry Conroy on the edge of the penalty area. The Irish winger hits the ball first time, right-footed on the volley with perfect technique and it scoots low across the slick mud to beat Bobby Ferguson, restored to the West Ham goal after being knocked out by a Conroy challenge in the first half, low to his right-hand side. Conroy's celebration sees him stand still in his white change shirt in the gleaming lights, waving his arms in the air in exultation. City hold on and win through to their first-ever Wembley final 3-2, ending this exhausting and epic semi-final tussle.

14 February 1981

Lee Chapman bags a superb left-footed shot from 25 yards to put City ahead at Elland Road. The ball flies past John Lukic in a blur and Chapman is on his way to his second hat-trick of the season and a £500,000 move to Arsenal.

25 August 1990

On the opening day of the season, Alan Ball's Stoke clinch a 3-1 victory over Rotherham at the Victoria Ground to begin their Third Division campaign when veteran Welsh midfielder Mickey Thomas slams the ball into the far bottom corner, left-footed from the edge of the penalty area. All the optimism soon dissipates, though, and, by February and an awful 0-4 defeat at Wigan, Ball is sacked with the club in its lowest league position in its history, 16th in the third tier.

19 September 1993

Having already bagged a penalty to put Stoke 2-0 ahead at a sunny City Ground, Mark Stein nets one of his special strikes to seal the win for City. The little striker, wearing a classic purple away shirt, still beloved to this day, latches on to a flick from midfielder Micky Gynn to curl a first-time, left-footed volley into the left corner of Mark Crossley's goal from 18 yards. Stoke win 3-2 and end comfortably in mid-table in their first season back in the second tier. But only after talismanic manager Lou Macari and hero striker Stein both move on.

10 November 2001

When Darren Powell miscues a clearance from a long ball, Peter Hoekstra steals in on the left wing to nick the ball and square it across into the penalty area. Chris Iwelumo controls and then very deliberately side-foots left-footed past Brentford's Ólafur Gottskálksson to put City 2-1 ahead in the battle of third v second in the Second Division.

22 March 2003

Peter Hoekstra has already bagged from the spot against Ray Lewington's Watford at Vicarage Road. Stoke are desperate for points in a torrid relegation battle, but have Mark Crossley to thank for two great saves. The keeper's long free kick downfield sets up the vital winning goal and it is a special one. Andy Cooke chests the ball down and it falls just behind Hoekstra, who swivels to smack it superbly, left-footed, into the top-right corner, giving Watford goalkeeper Alec Chamberlain no chance. It is a wonderful goal that proves to be the winner as Stoke survive under Tony Pulis.

4 April 2009

With four points from a possible 45 thus far, Stoke have the worst away record in the top four divisions. Striker James Beattie has been one of the inspirations behind City's resurgent form since signing, alongside Matty Etherington, in January 2009, to help City pull away from the relegation zone. He clinches a crucial three points and a first away win in the Premier League at the 16th attempt, when a long ball by Danny Higginbotham is flicked on by Ricardo Fuller into Etherington's path. The winger loses the ball as he drives into the penalty area under challenges from Albion's Jonas Olsson and Gianni Zuiverloon, but it falls neatly to Beattie to lash home left-footed into the top-left corner, right in front of the visiting fans. Scott Carson's rather flimsy wrist merely helps the shot on its way into the back of his net for his second contribution to a Stoke goal of the game. City are almost safe now thanks to Beattie's sixth goal in ten games.

19 March 2011

Alan Pardew's Newcastle are self-destructing at the Britannia Stadium and give away a free kick on the edge of the D, 25 yards from goal. Danny Higginbotham takes a huge run-up and leathers the ball left-footed right at the spot where Robert Huth and Ryan Shawcross were standing, at the left-hand side of the visitors' wall. But both have peeled off, and the ball rockets into the roof of the Boothen End net with Magpies keeper Steve Harper rooted to the spot. Stoke lead 3-0 and by the end of this Premier League game it will be four.

26 December 2012

Stoke have already come from behind against Brendan Rodgers's Liverpool in a pulsating first half when Jon Walters grabs a clinching third. He shows great technique to control Kenwyne Jones's flick from Andy Wilkinson's long throw, chest the ball down on to his right foot 16 yards out and volley high past Pepe Reina's right hand into the top corner at the Boothen End. Stoke kill the game easily as the visitors are forlorn. City are now eighth, above Liverpool, and are unbeaten in 16 games at fortress Britannia.

19 January 2019

Moritz Bauer crosses from the right wing, down by the corner flag, into the Leeds penalty area. Liam Cooper heads the ball weakly away and Mateusz Klich makes a hash of a further clearing header on the edge of the box. The ball drops perfectly, 14 yards out, for Sam Clucas to steam in and hit a first-time half-volley with his left foot which thunders into the bottom-right corner of the Boothen End goal, sparking wild celebrations. New manager Nathan Jones's first home game has sparked into life as City lead the Championship's top side 1-0.

50

16 February 1952

One of the most remarkable goals in Stoke's long history is scored at Villa Park when injured City goalkeeper Dennis Herod, stuck out on the right wing as a 'nuisance', with Sammy Smyth replacing him between the sticks, races on to a long punt out of defence to hare clear to go one on one with Aston Villa's Con Martin. Martin saves Herod's initial shot, but the Stoke keeper follows up to fire into the roof of the net to score the winning goal in a 3-2 triumph. Rather bizarrely, not only was Herod a goalkeeper playing out of position, but Martin was actually a former centre-half who had found a talent as a goalkeeper late in his career, mainly thanks to his youth spent playing Gaelic football in his native Ireland.

23 February 1957

After Johnny King bags a goal three minutes after the break, Tim Coleman nets his fifth of the game, on his way to setting a club and world record for a winger of seven goals, against Lincoln City. His fifth arrives when a neat King pass finds him 15 yards out and, unmarked yet again, he scores right-footed, with Lincoln keeper Downie well beaten again.

27 April 1974

Alan Hudson, a £200,000 signing from Chelsea, returns to Stamford Bridge for the first time and scores the only goal of the game. In swirling wind, Denis Smith knocks down a free kick for Huddy to slam home from 12 yards. City will end a remarkable season in fifth position, qualifying for the UEFA Cup, when they languished in 17th the day Hudson made his debut just three months earlier.

17 August 1974

Brian Clough's Leeds are marmalised on the opening day of the season. Stoke, prompted by Alan Hudson, purr forward. John

Ritchie feeds John Mahoney and the Welsh international breaks through a Billy Bremner tackle and, 27 yards out, lashes a left-foot shot past David Harvey into the left side of the Boothen End goal. City lead 1-0, but will end the day comfortable 3-0 winners.

31 March 1975

City are in imperious form as the First Division title race hots up on Easter Monday. Already 1-0 up thanks to Terry Conroy, the impish Irishman nets a second to kill off Bob Paisley's Liverpool when he scampers clear and nets after Ray Clemence saves his initial effort, but he follows up to fire home. Stoke end the game in third position on 45 points, level with their visitors and one point off Everton at the top, but having played one game more. With four matches remaining, the title could be coming to the Potteries!

25 September 1982

Stoke take the lead against David Pleat's Luton for the third time when Paul Bracewell forces the ball over the line from eight yards. His downward header, after Alan Judge has dropped Mark Chamberlain's teasing cross, bounces twice, somehow beating two despairing Luton defenders on the line. It ends up being jammed into the net just over the line by the left post by Town right-back Kirk Stephens. The goal puts City 3-2 up in this wonderful First Division game, even though they have been without the sent-off Peter Fox for 22 minutes already and have right-back Derek Parkin in goal, replacing the first-half replacement keeper, Bracewell.

16 October 1982

Mickey Thomas and Mark Chamberlain have already put Stoke 2-0 up with emphatic finishes after terrible Brighton defending, when the classic early-80s corner routine bags City a third goal. Paul Maguire floats a right-footed chip from the left wing to the near post, where centre-forward Brendan O'Callaghan flicks it on. Sammy McIlroy, fresh from leading Northern Ireland to glory in the World Cup finals in Spain during the summer, races in to head home from four yards in front of the adoring Boothen End. Richie Barker's Potters are up to seventh.

14 April 1984

Stoke have hauled themselves out of the relegation zone, but face mighty Liverpool, who will go on to win the treble of league, European Cup and League Cup this season, at the Victoria Ground. The second and clinching goal in a classic 2-0 win comes when Sammy McIlroy curls in a free kick right-footed from the left wing and Colin Russell, on loan from Huddersfield and a former Liverpool player, flicks the deftest of headers past Bruce Grobbelaar into the right corner of the Boothen End net.

30 October 1993

City have lost manager Lou Macari to Celtic and talismanic striker Mark Stein, sold to Chelsea for £1.5m after scoring 68 goals in 123 games. But in a topsy-turvy game against Viv Anderson's Barnsley at the Victoria Ground, City draw level at 3-3 when Toddy Örlygsson taps a short free kick on the right side of the D to Nigel Gleghorn, who curls home left-footed into the far-left corner of the Town End goal.

7 December 2013

Jon Walters speeds down the right wing and, on the run, passes accurately inside to Steven Ireland, who has made space for himself with a cute run off the back of Chelsea captain John Terry. Ireland controls the ball with his right foot, at full pace switches it to his left, then curls a perfect shot into the far bottom-left corner of Petr Čech's net from 18 yards at the Boothen End. City lead 2-1, but the drama in this Premier League game is only just beginning.

28 November 2018

The visiting Derby supporters are wearing snakes in 'honour' of their former manager Gary Rowett, now in charge of Stoke. Rowett's new team are level with Frank Lampard's Rams, but in a tetchy game City are down to ten men after Peter Etebo's 33rd-minute dismissal, which led to a fracas that saw Derby's Bradley Johnson bite Joe Allen on the shoulder. But City defend manfully and Saido Berahino sets up Sam Clucas to run down the left wing and cross low into the middle of the penalty area. Tom Ince races in and slots home left-footed, low to Scott Carson's left at the Boothen End, the keeper getting a glove on it, but nothing more. The goal secures a gutsy 2-1 victory, but Rowett, who spent over £50m on talent in an attempt to get Stoke promoted back to the top flight at the first time of asking, only lasts until early January before being dismissed.

51

21 March 1964

Dennis Viollet bags a hat-trick as he follows up Ipswich keeper Thorburn's save from Peter Dobing and it falls for him to slot home. A minute later John Ritchie bags the first of a brace, his first goals in 11 games, firing a left-footed shot home before heading McIlroy's cross in off the bar on 65 minutes. After that mini-blitz Stoke lead Town 7-1, with more to come.

13 September 1972

Terry Conroy scores Stoke's first-ever European goal, finally beating West German keeper Josef Elting, who has already made seven saves to keep the Potters at bay, with a low shot from eight yards, setting City up for a 3-1 home win over Kaiserslautern.

28 April 1990

It's fancy-dress time at Brighton's Goldstone Ground as Alan Ball's City say farewell to the Second Division, after finishing plumb bottom, with a final away-day trip in a carnival atmosphere. Striker Tony Ellis gets the party started, chipping Perry Digweed from 20 yards to bag a superb goal to send the 3,000 travelling, inflatable banana-toting fans wild. It makes the score 1-1 and by the end of the game the fans, many of whom are sporting official 'relegation party' T-shirts bought for £3.99 from the club shop, are on the pitch to celebrate a 4-1 win thanks to further goals by Ellis, Wayne Biggins and Ian Scott in a ten-minute spell late on.

15 April 1992

In a tense second leg of the Autoglass Trophy at London Road, Stoke win a free kick 25 yards out, slightly to the right of centre. Up steps midfielder Paul Ware, a local lad made good. He takes a good run-up and larrups the free kick right-footed past the wall and into the bottom-left corner of the Peterborough net to send Stoke through to Wembley and the travelling hordes behind the goal into ecstasy. The story goes that, on the way to the game, manager Lou Macari saw Ware winning so many hands at cards on the coach that he told him that with luck like that he'd be taking all free kicks and any penalties. Prophetic.

28 December 2008

Stoke lead thanks to Abdoulaye Faye's early header at Upton Park, but the match takes a turn for the worse when first Carlton Cole scores from 12 yards, then Ricardo Fuller gets into an argument with captain Andy Griffin, who was carrying an injury which impaired him from clearing from Cole when he had the chance. Fuller ends up slapping the full-back as the ball is on the centre spot for the restart and is sent off by referee Mike Jones. City lose 1-2, leaving them in the relegation zone and without their star striker for three games.

3 November 2011

Maccabi Tel Aviv have not lost at home in 12 European games, but Stoke are in dominant mood at the Bloomfield Stadium. After missing a range of chances, Salif Diao and Andy Wilkinson play foot tennis, which ends up with the ball landing with Jon Walters, who uses his body to shield it from Savo Pavićević, allowing midfielder Dean Whitehead to run on to the ball on the edge of the area. Whitehead barrels through, then finishes low, left-footed past keeper Barak Levi from six yards on the left side of the six-yard box, in off the far post. Peter Crouch's tap-in completes the victory, which is celebrated by the visiting fans amidst a downpour of biblical proportions that sees many visit a local laundrette after the game to do their best Nick Kamen impressions to get dry.

52

24 April 1963

Stoke celebrate the club's centenary with a glittering occasion under the Victoria Ground lights against Miguel Muñoz's perennial European champions Real Madrid, clad in their famous all-white strip. The game is preceded by music from Foden's brass band and the teams emerge from the new main-stand tunnel side by side. Stan Matthews, now aged 48, is captain for the evening and the game is level at 1-1, thanks to Jackie Mudie's goal, when Don Ratcliffe skips down the left wing and crosses for Jimmy McIlroy to shoot past substitute goalkeeper Araquistáin, with the ball taking a deflection off a defender on its way into the net.

28 December 2003

John Eustace releases Ade Akinbiyi to race through and win a dour game at Turf Moor, breaking clear of Graham Branch before stabbing, left-footed, past Brian Jensen from ten yards. Moments later John Halls is sent off for picking up a second yellow card and ten-man City deliver a backs-to-the-wall defensive display to be proud of to secure Stoke's fourth victory in what will be a run of seven wins in eight games as they climb up the Championship table.

1 February 2014

Robin van Persie has just equalised for David Moyes's Manchester United at a windswept Britannia Stadium, but Charlie Adam isn't finished yet. When a deep cross into the penalty area is headed back by Jon Walters towards Marko Arnautović, it looks like the Austrian will strike it. But Arnie manages to miss the ball completely with a huge swipe of his left foot. Instead, it falls for Adam to rifle a left-footed pearler into the top-right corner of David de Gea's net from 25 yards, with the keeper nowhere. Stoke hold on for their first Premier League win against Manchester United after 11 previous attempts.

27 October 2015

Charlie Adam drives at the visiting Chelsea defence, slides a pass through to Jon Walters on the edge of the penalty area and watches as the striker takes one touch to control the ball, swivels adroitly and hits a right-footed shot high and in off the bar of former Stoke keeper Asmir Begović's net at the Boothen End to give City the lead in this League Cup fourth-round tie. Stoke hang on until the 93rd minute when Loïc Rémy bags the equaliser and Phil Bardsley is sent off for two yellow cards. But City win a pulsating tie in a penalty shoot-out after clinging on through extra time, when Jack Butland saves Eden Hazard's penalty, high to his right, with an extended left hand at the Boothen End, who respond by telling José Mourinho he will be 'sacked in the morning'.

53

19 October 2008

A frantic game is level at 1-1, but visitors Spurs are down to ten men after Gareth Bale's early red card. Stoke begin the second half in the ascendancy and Mama Sidibé crosses from the right wing for Rory Delap to side-foot home unmarked on the far post from three yards. Delap's goal celebration, screaming at the Boothen End whilst holding on to the goal net, is one of the great modern Stoke City photographs. Stoke will hold on to win their second game of the season 2-1 and send Tottenham to the foot of the Premier League table with just two points. Within days, Spurs manager Juande Ramos is sacked and Harry Redknapp installed as manager.

7 November 2015

Ten days after knocking José Mourinho's Chelsea out of the League Cup on penalties, City are at it again, this time in the Premier League, although the visiting manager is serving a stadium ban, so is watching on TV in his hotel room. City nick a tight match when Glen Johnson races on to Xherdan Shaqiri's through ball on the right side of the penalty area to cross for Jon Walters. The striker miscontrols and flicks the ball across to Marko Arnautović, who leaps acrobatically to hit a right-footed, hip-high volley into the Boothen End net. It is Arnie's first league goal at the Britannia Stadium since May 2014 against Fulham.

28 August 2018

Saido Berahino finally ends his two-and-a-half-year goal drought with the scruffiest goal, not that he or any of the 7,290 fans who bothered to turn up to see Stoke defeat Premier League Huddersfield in this League Cup second-round tie care. The East Stand is left empty due to general indifference following relegation from the Premier League, but Gary Rowett's City are by far the better team. They finally make their dominance tell when the £12m striker, signed from West Brom in January 2017, seizes on the rebound after a James McClean shot on the turn hits the bar and bounces out six yards. Berahino throws his head at the ball, slightly miscues it and it floats towards goal, with Jon Stanković trying to clear, only succeeding in thwacking the ball high into the Boothen End net. It is a real 'I was there' moment. Berahino's previous goal was scored against Crystal Palace for the Baggies on 27 February 2016.

54

10 December 1966

Harry Burrows combines beautifully with Welsh international inside-left Roy Vernon to prove that Stoke can exist without striker John Ritchie, controversially sold to Sheffield Wednesday at the peak of his powers just a month earlier. Burrows already has two against his former club Aston Villa, but completes his hat-trick when he speeds on to a Vernon through ball to ghost over the sticky mud of the Victoria Ground's surface, leaving his marker in his wake, to fire past visiting keeper Colin Withers.

12 April 1993

Lou Macari's Stoke are coasting towards promotion from the Second Division and secure victory at Millmoor to move just two wins away from securing a return to the second tier of English football.

The win comes courtesy of a Mark Stein brace, his first being a sharp turn in the penalty area to wrong-foot the defence and clinically finish past keeper Billy Mercer. But his second is a goal that is amongst the best scored by a Stoke player in living memory. The little striker receives the ball about 25 yards out on the right side of the pitch, but with his back to goal and a Rotherham marker within a yard or so.

Stein's strike partner Dave Regis makes a run to take another defender away, creating space for the 'Golden One' to control the ball with his right foot, turn adroitly to his left, shift the ball once on to his right foot and shoot instantly into the far top-left corner. The ball arrows over Mercer's despairing dive and, satisfyingly, hits the underside of the bar, then the top of the inside of the post, before cannoning into the net to the delight of the travelling hordes gathered behind that goal. Around 4,500 Stokies have travelled to Rotherham on this sunny Easter Monday, approximately half of the overall 9,021 gate.

158

20 October 2011

Pantomime villain Yoav Ziv has made himself public enemy number one by rolling around to get Cameron Jerome sent off and is being mercilessly booed by the Britannia Stadium faithful. With his side 0-3 down and out of this Europa League game, the Israeli international left-back is challenged by Ryan Shotton by the touchline in front of the East Stand. In doing so, Shotton treads on Ziv's left boot and it comes off. It must be getting to him because, instead of just putting it on and doing it up, Ziv chooses to thwack the loose boot directly at the nearby assistant referee, who it hits in the chest. Ziv sees red and the whole stadium waves him off with peals of laughter bellowing down from the stands. Couldn't have happened to a nicer fellow.

55

13 January 1958

With Molineux packed to its rafters with visiting Stoke and Villa fans for an FA Cup third-round second replay, City win a penalty against their top-flight opponents and reigning FA Cup holders, when half-back Vic Crowe inexplicably handles a Don Ratcliffe cross from the left wing under no pressure, flicking the ball away from an imaginary Stoke forward behind him. City's diminutive Scottish playmaker, right-half Bobby Cairns, slams the ball right-footed to Nigel Sims's left to give Stoke the lead as a rare cup upset looms.

16 November 1963

Centre-forward John Ritchie completes his first Stoke City hat-trick aged just 22. It is his shot which Sheffield Wednesday keeper Ron Springett dives to keep out, but Peter Dobing rushes in to force the ball home. It is stopped on the line and Ritchie slides in to score in the Town End net. Stoke lead 4-1, having led 3-0 earlier in the game after Dobing's goal in the 39th minute, but somehow Wednesday fight back. Despite the game ending in glory for Ritchie, as he has bagged a treble and made it 15 goals in nine games since being given his chance in the team by manager Tony Waddington, the Potters can only leave the pitch with a point after a second consecutive 4-4 home league draw. They are still looking for an elusive second home league victory of the season after ten matches.

22 April 1964

In the 1964 League Cup Final second leg, midfield powerhouse and Stoke captain Calvin Palmer picks up an injury in a tackle, which is exacerbated moments later when he dribbles through to shoot, but kicks a Leicester defender in doing so. Palmer has to leave the pitch for 15 minutes to receive treatment and in those days of no substitutes the Potters are down to ten men. In the time he is off, the Foxes grab a crucial second goal through David Gibson, who heads a cross into the roof of the net. Stoke's chance of a first-ever trophy is ebbing away.

19 April 1972

City lead 1-0 in the FA Cup semi-final replay at Goodison Park thanks to Jimmy Greenhoff's early penalty, but referee Keith Walker evens things up when he spots something no one else does, including Arsenal's players, when Peter Dobing challenges George Armstrong just inside the Potters' penalty area. It is barely a push, but Charlie George gratefully slots the spot kick high into the top-right corner, sending Gordon Banks the wrong way. Controversial, but there is worse to follow.

24 September 1974

In a tight game at Portman Road, John Ritchie is posing Ipswich's defence plenty of problems. But the veteran striker's season is ended by a dreadful Kevin Beattie challenge that referee Brian Daniels doesn't even think is a foul. It results in the first of four broken legs to Stoke players in the season that derail City's title challenge and they will finish fifth for the second successive season under Tony Waddington, but this time just four points off top spot. As physio Mike Allen reaches the prone striker, Ritchie shouts at him, 'It's broken.' He is right; his leg has a double fracture and it proves to be a career-ending injury for the 33-year-old. And what a stellar career. Across two spells at the club, Ritchie bagged 176 goals in 351 games, making him the club's leading all-time scorer.

30 October 1993

Long throws did exist before Rory Delap signed for Stoke. John Butler rains one into the Barnsley penalty area from the left wing and Vince Overson rises, unmarked, eight yards out to head into the bottom-right corner of Lee Butler's net at the Town End of the Victoria Ground. Stoke lead 4-3, but the scoring isn't over yet.

4 May 2003

In front of a packed house, Stoke need to match Grimsby's result to avert relegation, which seemed very unlikely when Tony

Pulis took charge the previous October. Opponents Reading are saving themselves for the play-offs, so City are the better team and secure the vital three points when Lewis Neal crosses from the left wing and finds Ade Akinbiyi, on the run at the near post. The dreadlocked striker's flick header beats keeper Marcus Hahnemann and Ade celebrates by taking off his shirt, laying it out in front of the baying Boothen End and allowing his team-mates, led by Chris Greenacre, to bow to his feet and shirt, whilst showing off his muscular physique, in a vest. Iconic.

12 April 2008

Stoke are still in second position in the Championship, but have won one in eight games and are 0-1 behind at Coventry. Up steps Ricardo Fuller who dribbles down the right edge of the penalty area only to be felled by Scott Dann, and then slots the resultant penalty calmly into the very bottom-right corner of Kasper Schmeichel's goal, right in front of the jubilant, and relieved, visiting fans.

15 September 2011

Stoke secure a famous draw in the Europa League group stage at Dynamo Kiev's ancient Valeriy Lobanovskyi Stadium, in the park by the river Dnieper, when Kenwyne Jones releases Ryan Shotton down the right wing and the young winger pulls the ball back from the byline for debutant Cameron Jerome, lurking at the far post, surrounded by five defenders, to control and stab, right-footed, high into the net. Jerome then runs over to the 1,000 travelling fans, massed on the wooden benches in the corner, to celebrate wildly.

15 May 2016

Stoke's record signing, £18.3m Giannelli Imbula, repays a small portion of his astronomical fee with a smart left-foot drive from 22 yards, low to West Ham keeper Darren Randolph's left-hand corner. Imbula's first goal in 11 games brings City level against Slaven Bilić's visitors on the final day of the season to lift the Potters to a third successive ninth-placed finish in the Premier League under Mark Hughes.

56

1 June 1971

At Roma's Stadio Olimpico, in an Anglo-Italian Cup group match, the Potters pull off a remarkable 1-0 win. In front of 37,360 increasingly angry home supporters, John Ritchie grabs the goal in a tetchy game, rifling home a superb left-footed volley. The screaming locals let off rockets and firecrackers during the game, and tear gas employed by police inflames things further as the fans riot and invade the pitch, tearing down the goal nets and dugouts after the final whistle. Stoke's travelling party shelter inside their changing room for two hours for their own safety, while the army, toting machine guns as deterrents, battle with supporters. The following morning, manager Tony Waddington and chairman Albert Henshall become the first English football officials to be granted an audience with Pope Paul VI and hand him a Stoke City pennant to mark the occasion. Safely back in Blighty, Waddo observes tersely, 'English football is just not compatible with the Italians.'

31 January 2004

Stoke have won seven of the last eight as Tony Pulis finds a formula which delivers points. In a topsy-turvy game against Colin Lee's Walsall at the Britannia Stadium in the pouring rain, Carl Asaba has already levelled at 2-2 with his 100th career goal, after a 15-game drought. Then, he anticipates a slightly mishit shot by Gifton Noel-Williams to dart in and divert the ball into Andy Petterson's bottom-right corner from eight yards at the Boothen End. City win 3-2 to rise to 12th in the table, when they had been in relegation trouble just two months earlier.

13 November 2010

Stoke haven't beaten Liverpool in 26 years, but Ricardo Fuller sets them on their way to victory when he latches on to Matty Etherington's cross come shot in a goalmouth scramble following a left-wing Rory Delap throw. Fuller's first shot is blocked by Martin Škrtel, but the Jamaican international follows up to poke home left-footed from five yards at the Boothen End.

57

20 March 1959

City are superb in the second half at Anfield, in a game played on a Friday night due to the following afternoon's Grand National, and equalise to make a pulsating game 3-3 when Bobby Howitt pulls the ball back to the edge of the penalty area and right-back Bill Asprey fires in one of his renowned thunderbolt shots. As keeper Younger dives to cover the ball, defender White flicks his head at it, but only succeeds to deflect it past the committed keeper and into the net.

21 April 2003

Tony Pulis's Stoke are desperate for points in the battle against the drop. There are just three games left and things are looking up after Saturday's win over Wimbledon, but on Easter Monday City visit Highfield Road to take on a Coventry team just one place above them, albeit several points. It's a crucial game, which is won with just one goal when Stoke receive some wonderful luck. Icelandic international Brynjar Gunnarsson is fouled and the Potters are awarded a penalty. Chris Iwelumo steps up and slams the spot kick against the right-hand post, but the Scottish international sees it rebound against the prone Sky Blues keeper Gary Montgomery's legs and into the net for an own goal to warm your heart.

13 February 2010

Half-time substitute Rory Delap slings one of his trademark throws into Manchester City's penalty area for Ricardo Fuller to leap on to and head powerfully, low past Shay Given into the bottom-right corner to secure a draw in this FA Cup fifth-round tie at Eastlands.

58

18 March 1972

After taking three games to see off Frank O'Farrell's Manchester United in the League Cup earlier in the season, Stoke take on the Red Devils again in the FA Cup quarter-final. After George Eastham is found by Willie Morgan out by the left corner flag, Jimmy Greenhoff puts City ahead when he heads Eastham's cross against keeper Alex Stepney from four yards, then follows up to prod home the rebound from a yard at the Stretford End.

15 November 1980

Lee Chapman has already scored twice against Ken Brown's struggling Canaries; a header from a free kick and a low shot from a Paul Richardson cross. He completes his hat-trick when visiting keeper Roger Hansbury drops Adrian Heath's shot and Chapman pounces to net from close range. It is Chapman's first career hat-trick, but his second, at Leeds, is only three months away.

14 October 2006

Stoke, prompted by three new arrivals, Salif Diao, Rory Delap and Lee Hendrie, are showing signs of producing some devastating attacking, but it is left-back Andy Griffin who nets the crucial second goal, picking up Hendrie's cute inside pass on the left corner of the Leeds penalty area, turning to shift it to his right a couple of yards and then slamming a right-footed drive inside the left-hand post of Neil Sullivan's goal.

1 March 2008

Another goal arrives from a Rory Delap long throw, this time from the right-hand side, flicked home from six yards by Mama Sidibé to secure a crucial 1-0 win at Carrow Road in the midst of a horrible eight-game, otherwise winless run as City search for promotion.

24 March 2012

One of the iconic goals in Stoke City history arrives when Asmir Begović launches a long downfield kick, which is aimed at 6ft 7in Peter Crouch, who had signed on deadline day the previous August from Spurs for a club-record £10m. Crouch's flick-on is returned by Jermaine Pennant's cushioned header back to the lanky striker, who then turns into a combination of Pelé and Johan Cruyff by deftly controlling the ball at waist height with his right foot, then pivoting on his standing left to volley a rocket of a shot, with the same right foot, which accurately dips into the far, top-left corner of the Boothen End net from 30 yards, way out on the right side of the Britannia Stadium. It whistles over a despairing Joe Hart to put Stoke 1-0 ahead against Roberto Mancini's Manchester City and sends the stadium ballistic, taking the Mickey out of the visiting fans by doing the 'Poznan'. Even Tony Pulis runs down the front of the main stand fist clenched, while Crouch puts his hand over his mouth in disbelief, which was what Potters fans felt when the strike was not voted as goal of the season, missing out to a Papiss Cissé goal for Newcastle against Chelsea.

30 August 2014

Mame Diouf picks up a clearance from a corner at Eastlands, chests it down 30 yards from his own goal and sets off on one of the great solo runs. The Senegalese striker outpaces Aleksandar Kolarov, who gives up the chase on the halfway line, and is quickly faced down by Vincent Kompany, 15 yards inside his own half. But Kompany is static, whilst Diouf is at full pelt and brushes his weak challenge aside, nutmegging him in the process, and bears down on the penalty area. He veers to the right, then hits a right-foot shot low under Joe Hart from eight yards for a second nutmeg in three seconds. Diouf wheels away in celebration at finishing his 70-yard dash so clinically and the Potters hold on for a first Premier League win at Manchester City, which pleases former Blues manager, Mark Hughes, now in charge at Stoke, hugely.

59

21 September 1946

Freddie Steele scores the second of two goals in two minutes against Matt Busby's league leaders. For his first, Steele outpaces Allenby Chilton to hammer home on the run from the edge of the box. A few seconds later he heads home 'Jock' Kirton's cross emphatically. Manchester United score two late goals, but cannot prevent Stoke taking the points 3-2.

26 December 1988

Amidst a carnival of inflatable bananas at the visitors' end and pink panthers in the Boothen End, Stoke have come from a 0-1 half-time deficit to lead Mel Machin's Manchester City 2-1 thanks to goals from Chris Kamara and Dave Bamber. The Potters' biggest crowd of the season, 24,056, celebrate a 3-1 victory when George Berry slots a penalty low, right-footed, to Andy Dibble's left, awarded after Bamber is upended.

24 October 2020

Tyrese Campbell has already provided two assists in a brilliant City performance against visiting Brentford, but this time he is the scorer as Stoke extend their lead to 3-0. It is a virtuoso goal as Campbell picks up the ball deep on the left wing, cuts inside, Fuller-esque, then sells three Bees defenders with a dip of the left shoulder before moving the ball into a position to shoot with his right foot. His curling shot from the left-hand corner of the D finds the very bottom-right corner of David Raya's net. Despite two late Marcus Forss goals, City hold on to win 3-2 and announce their credentials as play-off contenders under Michael O'Neill, with Campbell the creator and scorer.

60

25 April 1955

Stoke visit Vale Park for a league match for the first time and 41,674 are drawn to this Second Division encounter. A scrappy game, marred by a strong wind, is settled by a moment of genius when Frank Bowyer, reprising his role of goal hero from Stoke's previous visit to Vale's old Recreation Ground in Hanley in the FA Cup four years earlier, hooks home from an unlikely angle as the ball cannons around the penalty area. Bowyer's winner puts City top of the Second Division table on goal average with just one game remaining. But Birmingham, Luton and Leeds below them have games in hand and when City lose their final match at Plymouth 0-2 they will drop to finish a disappointing fifth in the tightest promotion race of all time.

3 January 2000

Peter Thorne grabs the first Stoke City goal of the new millennium when he slides in to nudge home after James O'Connor is tackled eight yards out and the ball breaks kindly for the striker six yards from goal, right in front of the massed Potters supporters.

6 November 2006

Andy Griffin, sold by Stoke for £1.5m nine years earlier to fund the Britannia Stadium, has returned on loan from Portsmouth via Newcastle and is filling in at left-back. In a fogbound game, which leaves Sky TV viewers barely able to see, Griff cuts in from the left side 40 yards out. With little happening in front of him, he nudges the ball on and, 35 yards from goal, unleashes a pearler of a right-foot drive which continues to rise, right into the top-left corner of Andy Marshall's net. Griffin just stands in awe at what he's just done, arms upraised, shaking his head in disbelief. Despite Ricardo Fuller's sending off just afterwards, Stoke hold on for a 1-0 win against Micky Adams's Coventry.

21 May 2017

Peter Crouch heads home Geoff Cameron's right-wing, far-post cross from three yards to clinch a final-day victory, a 1-0 win at Claude Puel's Southampton, which secures 13th position in the Premier League table for Mark Hughes's men, also bringing the manager his 150th Premier League win, becoming only the seventh man to achieve that feat. It is Crouch's tenth goal of the season, leaving him as top scorer, and also his 50th headed Premier League career goal, a record. More importantly, at the final whistle Crouch has to make good on a promise he made to supporter Tyrone Sidley, who has attended the game clad in only Speedos and a snorkel, in return for which Crouch donates his shirt, gives the fan a huge cuddle and blows up his snorkel tube.

61

23 March 1959

City win a pulsating match to secure a second-ever league victory at Anfield, and the last to date. Tony Allen roves forward from left-back, exchanges passes with Dennis Wilshaw on the left-hand side, then puts the striker through on goal with just Tommy Younger to beat. Wilshaw nets with a side-footed, rolling shot to silence the Kop. Victory is almost larger as City win a last-minute penalty, but Johnny King's spot kick, given for a trip on him by the keeper as he is about to score, rebounds to safety off the foot of the post.

12 September 1962

Left-winger Don Ratcliffe puts City ahead 3-2 as they search for their first victory of the 1962/63 season, against Charlton in their seventh game. He has already had two sizzling shots well saved by visiting keeper Wakeman, when he finishes off a wonderful move involving the sprightly Stan Matthews and eventual four-goal hero of the day Dennis Viollet, latching on to the latter's pass to finish low into the Boothen End net.

4 March 2000

Peter Thorne has already bagged a hat-trick, but he is hungry for more as he begins a scoring streak of 20 goals in 14 games at the back end of the season to propel City into the play-offs. His fourth against bottom-of-the-table Chesterfield arrives when Graham Kavanagh releases Mikael Hansson down the right and the speedy Icelandic full-back nudges the ball across for Thorne to prod home right-footed to complete a 'perfect' treble for the last three of his four goals. It is the only four-goal haul for a Stoke player at the Britannia/Bet365 Stadium and the first four goals in a match since Paul Maguire versus Wolves in May 1984. It is also the first four goals for a player from open play (not involving penalties) since John Ritchie's versus Northampton in February 1966.

15 December 2007

Ricardo Fuller has the bit between his teeth and a goal already at Bloomfield Road against Simon Grayson's Blackpool. He nets a third of the game for City when he races on to Liam Lawrence's through ball to outpace Ian Evatt and slot low into the bottom-right corner. That's four wins in five games for Stoke, who rise to fourth in the Championship. Promotion is very much on.

26 January 2015

Victor Moses, on a season-long loan from Chelsea, scores a wonderful individual goal to put City 3-0 ahead in a tricky FA Cup tie at Rochdale. Picking the ball up level with the penalty area on the left wing, he heads for the byline, then cuts inside to make just enough angle, 12 yards from goal, to curl the ball perfectly inside the far post, leaving Dale keeper Josh Lillis nonplussed at his near stick.

62

15 April 1964

In Stoke's first-ever major cup final, the 1964 League Cup Final, which is held over two legs, the Potters take the lead midway through the second half when Leicester and England keeper Gordon Banks saves Bill Asprey's 30-yard shot, but Keith Bebbington gets to the rebound first to give Stoke a deserved lead. Peter Dobing has already hit a post and John Ritchie, seeking an 11th goal in the competition, having already set a new record of ten, has had an effort cleared off the line. But Leicester deliver a sucker punch when Eric Skeels's clearance hits Terry Heath and rebounds to the edge of the penalty area, where Dave Gibson lobs Stoke keeper Lawrie Leslie perfectly to take a 1-1 draw back to Filbert Street.

26 September 1970

Terry Conroy collects the ball halfway inside the Arsenal half and looks around for support. It comes in the form of Peter Dobing, who shows himself to receive a pass five yards from the Gunners' D. Conroy slots the ball to Dobing with the outside of his right foot, then races on to the first-time return pass, which falls perfectly into his stride, to rocket a tremendous right-foot shot into the far-left side of Bob Wilson's net at the Town End. The goal is voted as *Match of the Day*'s Goal of the Month for September 1970 and is the third of Stoke's five that balmy afternoon.

27 March 1982

Lawrie McMenemy's high-flying Southampton lead 3-0 by the break against Richie Barker's relegation strugglers. In a classic game, City come back to level before losing 3-4. The best goal of the game is scored by Stoke's veteran centre-back Dave Watson, a former Saints player, who runs on to a layback by Alan Dodd 30 yards out and wallops it, right-footed, in off the bar of the motionless Ivan Katalinić's goal, where it bounces up and down satisfyingly and memorably.

30 March 1985

It's been an utterly miserable season for Stoke so far: only two wins and just 14 points. But the visit of Don Howe's Arsenal brings some light relief from the drudgery of being thrashed every week when first Phil Heath is tripped by David O'Leary and Ian Painter crashes the penalty past John Lukic, then Paul Dyson rises like a swan amidst the Victoria Ground mudbath to head Sammy McIlroy's cross into the Boothen End net from four yards. It's little consolation as these three points prove to be the last Stoke pick up this dreadful season, ending on just 17 to set a new record low, only beaten by Derby's 11 in 2007/08.

4 May 2004

Tony Pulis's new-look, youthful Stoke thrash already promoted West Brom in a rearranged Championship game at the Britannia Stadium. Left-winger Kris Commons runs the show in the second half, scoring his first goal from a 25-yard free kick, cracked left-footed, which slips through Russell Hoult's hands into the Boothen End net. His later goal is a calm right-foot finish from 15 yards from John Halls's pinpoint pullback. The 4-1 victory is rounded off when Albion's Jason Koumas is sent off for kicking Darel Russell on 87 minutes. Satisfying.

14 October 2006

City have just made it 2-0 against a Leeds team under the caretaker managership of John Carver as Tony Pulis's new-look side cut loose, and before you know it a third goal arrives. Danny Higginbotham rises at the far post to head home Lee Hendrie's corner from 12 yards into the top-left corner of the goal. Seven minutes later Steve Simonsen saves Robbie Blake's penalty low to his right and City lead 3-0, with the visiting fans in raptures in the corner of Elland Road.

14 May 2011

Stoke have been under the cosh since the first whistle of the FA Cup Final, but suddenly win the ball, when Glenn Whelan slides in to tackle David Silva, and break out. Matty Etherington plays a long ball forward down the left channel, which finds Kenwyne Jones, striding forward. He lets the ball bounce once as he outpaces Joleon Lescott, bursting into the penalty area on the left-hand side. About 14 yards out, after bouncing again, the ball hits him on the head and falls perfectly for him to hit a shot at goal. But he opts to adjust slightly to hit it with his stronger right foot, which means he can only poke it against the onrushing Joe Hart and the chance is gone. It will be Stoke's only shot on target in the eventual 0-1 defeat.

63

7 October 1967

City have been woeful defensively at Upton Park as Geoff Hurst with two close-range finishes and Martin Peters with an acrobatic scissors kick have put West Ham 3-0 up at half-time. But the most remarkable fightback in Stoke City's history begins when left-winger Harry Burrows pounces to fire into the roof of the net from a tight angle after keeper Bobby Ferguson parries Peter Dobing's shot.

14 February 1981

Lee Chapman completes his second hat-trick of the season, following his treble at home against Norwich, to hand City a 3-1 victory at Elland Road. His third goal arrives when he is sent clear by Adrian Heath and rounds John Lukic to slot home.

11 November 1995

Stoke are 1-2 behind at Southend when Lee Sandford plays a through ball from inside his own half for Simon Sturridge to run on to. 'Studger' still has 40 yards to go when he picks it up, but he drives into the right edge of the penalty area, beating two players in the process, then veers right to hammer a shot across keeper Simon Royce into the far-left bottom corner to equalise.

30 April 2006

Adam Rooney has already bagged two goals at Brighton's temporary home at the Withdean Stadium, when he curls his best goal of the game past Wayne Henderson into the far-right corner from 20 yards. This makes Rooney the youngest-ever scorer of a hat-trick for Stoke and City win 5-1 on the final day of the season to finish Johan Boskamp's reign in 13th position in the Championship.

13 March 2011

Controversy is reigning in the FA Cup quarter-final at the Britannia Stadium. First referee Mike Jones allows West Ham's 30th-minute equaliser, when Frédéric Piquionne appears to have handled a through ball before chipping Thomas Sørenson in the Stoke goal. Then Jones angers the Hammers when he seems to even things up, awarding a softish penalty for a Scott Parker foul on Matty Etherington 14 seconds into the second half. But the left-winger sees his spot kick saved by Rob Green. With the scores level at 1-1, City need inspiration and find it from left-back Danny Higginbotham, something of a dead-ball specialist. Awarded a free kick for handball, 19 yards out on the right edge of the D, City have three players over the ball. But Glenn Whelan and Rory Delap defer to Higgy, who slams it low past the left edge of the wall so fiercely that Rob Green can only palm the ball on to the post and then over the line, despite the keeper's desperate efforts to pretend it hasn't crossed the whitewash. Stoke are in their first FA Cup semi-final for 39 years. Wembley awaits.

19 September 2017

Eric Maxim Choupo-Moting rises at the far post to head home Xherdan Shaqiri's deep corner into the top-left corner of the tunnel-end net at the Bet365 Stadium from seven yards to secure a 2-2 draw against José Mourinho's Manchester United. The 2017/18 season would only go downhill from this point, though, ending in Mark Hughes's sacking and relegation after a decade in the top flight.

20 February 2021

Nick Powell is on fire against Nathan Jones's Luton, most likely because the former Stoke manager, who bought the 'Crewe Cantona' from Wigan to the Bet365 Stadium, made himself something of a pariah in his awful spell at the club. Having already tapped in the opening goal of this stroll of a 3-0 win, Powell steams on to Joe Allen's right-wing, far-post cross to power a header home from six yards into the top-left corner of the Boothen End net.

64

7 October 1967

A minute after Harry Burrows has made it 1-3 at West Ham, Peter Dobing runs on to a through ball from Roy Vernon to shake off Martin Peters's challenge and flick the ball left-footed past Bobby Ferguson. It's a soft goal, but City are now only one behind and the momentum is with them.

26 September 1970

Stoke are already 3-0 up against Bertie Mee's Arsenal at the Victoria Ground when John Farmer catches a cross and rolls the ball out to Terry Conroy, who sets off like a hare down the right wing. As he approaches the Arsenal penalty area, Conroy slots the ball through to Jimmy Greenhoff, at pace, down the right side of the penalty area. Bob Wilson races out to save at Greenhoff's feet, but he cannot hold on and Greenhoff picks up the loose ball to chip it over the keeper into the far-left corner of the Town End net and sets off down the length of the Butler Street Stand with both arms raised in celebration.

30 October 1993

In a crazy game which has seen two own goals and Stoke take the lead and lose it twice, City score a fifth goal for the first time in seven years, when a Barnsley back pass is left woefully short and Martin Carruthers steals in to round Lee Butler and run the ball into the Town End net. City win 5-4. Who needs Macari and Stein?

9 November 2019

Stoke lead 2-1 at Oakwell in a battle of the Championship's bottom two. In a tense game, City always have the upper hand and take full control when Sam Clucas slings over a left-wing, deep, outswinging corner for Danny Batth to head towards goal. The ball is controlled by Joe Allen with his back to goal in front of the stand containing thousands of eager Stokies. The 'Welsh Pirlo' swivels to shoot, but slightly loses his footing. He still manages to get his shot off, and because of the fall, it is directed into the far bottom-left corner. The stand behind the goal erupts and the congas, which lasted the entirety of the half-time break, begin again in celebration. Not least because it is the first time since December 2017, 88 games ago, that Stoke have scored more than two goals in a game.

65

12 September 1962

Dennis Viollet notches his first Stoke City hat-trick thanks to a lovely right-footed shot that nestles just inside the far post, from a perfectly weighted Matthews inside pass. But Viollet's goalscoring exploits for the day are not over yet as he will go on to get a fourth and City six in a win over visitors Charlton that sparks their 1962/63 season promotion push.

23 April 1968

Somehow Stoke have relinquished a two-goal lead, given to them by a Peter Dobing brace, thanks to goals by Leeds' Jimmy Greenhoff and veteran centre-half Jack Charlton. Tied at 2-2 under the lights in this vital, winner-takes-all game, Dobing seals his best-ever performance in a Potters shirt by grabbing a hat-trick to seal a crucial victory. Harry Burrows takes a near-post corner which is flicked on by John Mahoney. Charlton misses his clearance and Dobing steals in to fire high into the roof of the net. Don Revie's Leeds miss the chance to hit the top of the league with three games remaining, all of which they lose to capitulate to a fourth-place finish, while City, still second bottom but just a point off 18th place, now have four games left to save their First Division lives. But the momentum is with them following Dobing's superman display.

15 April 1972

Stoke square up to Arsenal again in the FA Cup semi-final, a year on from the pain of Hillsborough. This time the tie is at Villa Park and City ensure that Gunners keeper Bob Wilson is in the wars. First, he slams his face into a post in ensuring George Eastham's deep cross goes over the top, then he injures his knee collecting a cross and, before he can be replaced by striker John Radford, Denis Smith challenges Peter Simpson and the ball flies in off the Arsenal player to equalise Armstrong's opening goal. In a bruising encounter, Peter Storey's lunge on Mike Bernard sparks a ten-man brawl. Honours even. The replay will be at Goodison Park.

11 May 1977

Stoke are plummeting towards the First Division relegation zone when Tommy Docherty's Manchester United visit and hooligans run riot on the Victoria Ground terraces. City go 0-2 behind early on, but young local striker Garth Crooks slots in from three yards past Alex Stepney and Alan Bloor pokes home in a scramble to level. Gordon Hill pounces on Denis Smith's weak back pass to give United the lead again, but then Crooks strikes with a superb goal. Picking the ball up 20 yards out, the young striker weaves his way past three United defenders before firing past Stepney left-footed. The ground erupts, but it will prove to be the last point Stoke win in that season as they slump into the Second Division under the caretaker managership of George Eastham, following Tony Waddington's sacking 13 games before the season's end.

12 October 1984

Chris Maskery isn't a big name in Stoke City history. Those fans who do recall him probably remember that he had a heart defect, yet still made it as a First Division footballer and once punched Trevor Steven in the face right in front of the dugouts at the Victoria Ground to spark a massive brawl. But Maskery could play a bit as well. He filled every spot across the back four and also in central midfield, and it was from there that his most memorable goal is scored. Thirty yards out and with little else on, Maskery cracks a left-foot shot, which sails past Perry Digweed in the Brighton goal to secure a 1-1 home, Second Division draw.

16 May 1992

City are out for revenge in the Autoglass Trophy Final against Stockport after Danny Bergara's team dumped them out of the Third Division play-offs just three days earlier. Mark Stein proves the difference in the Wembley sunshine, twisting with a quicksilver burst of speed to latch on to a couple of flick-ons from Adrian Heath, then Lee Sandford, as the ball drops into the County box.

Stein lets it bounce twice, then soars with both feet off the floor to lash a vicious, right-footed volley across his body from 12 yards into the top-right corner of keeper Neil Edwards's net. Wembley resounds to the loudest 'Delilah' of all after skipper Vince Overson lifts the trophy.

6 December 2014

City lead Arsène Wenger's Arsenal 3-0 already and should have a fourth when Bojan cuts in from the left to slot inside the near post in the 65th minute. But Mame Diouf is controversially ruled offside, despite not seeming to be interfering with play. The scoreboard actually turns to show the score as 4-0 for a moment. Only Stoke could turn that position into a narrow, heart-stopping 3-2 victory in the end.

66

27 September 1972

It is all going wrong for Stoke. Defending a 3-1 first-leg lead in Kaiserslautern in their first-ever UEFA Cup match, the Potters have already conceded three times and need a goal. Manager Tony Waddington sends on John Ritchie as a substitute, but, before the game can restart, the new arrival tussles with Yugoslav international Idriz Hošić and is sent off by Hungarian referee Eksztazn after being on the pitch for just nine seconds. City lose 0-4 to go out 3-5 on aggregate, having led the first leg 3-0 at one point.

23 September 1989

In a feverish atmosphere in the first Potteries league derby for 32 years, City are behind to Robbie Earle's 50th-minute goal. Mick Mills brings on winger Gary Hackett, who makes a huge difference, and just a few minutes later his cross finds Dave Bamber. The big centre-forward's header finds on-loan Leigh Palin to shoot home via a deflection. The game ends 1-1, but the aftermath is marred by fighting as the modern rivalry between the two clubs is ignited both on and off the pitch.

6 April 1992

Stoke have been 2-0 ahead, but are now 2-3 behind to Chris Turner's Peterborough in the Autoglass Trophy semi-final first leg at the Victoria Ground. In driving rain, City pour forward seeking an equaliser which arrives when a deep cross from the right wing by Paul Ware finds an unmarked Lee Sandford, who bullets a header home at the Town End. Honours even going into the second leg.

22 October 1995

This First Division game against Jim Smith's Derby is goalless and little is happening as Nigel Gleghorn and Kevin Keen, Stoke's Brains trust in midfield, stand over a free kick 33 yards out from goal in the centre of the pitch. Almost unnoticed, Keen peels off to the right side of the area, as Gleghorn sets himself to launch the obvious ball into the mixer, but the pair have been busy on the training ground. Instead of lobbing the ball to where the giants like Overson and Sandford are waiting, Gleghorn cleverly disguises a chip out to the right-hand side of the box. It drops perfectly for Keen, running on to it as it arrives just five yards in from the goal line. From such an acute angle, surely all he can do is pull the ball back, but no: Keen slaps a perfectly executed volley with his right foot into the very top-right corner of Russell Hoult's net, in front of an adoring Boothen End. It is a stunning, van Basten-esque goal, which lives long in the memory, even though a late equaliser sees the game end 1-1.

14 November 1999

News has broken that the club is to be taken over by an Icelandic consortium and manager Gary Megson will be replaced by their man, Guðjón Thórdarson. Megson has one last swansong at home against Bristol City and in an emotional moment Nicky Mohan, captain of the team, heads an equaliser from eight yards from a right-wing corner at the Boothen End and then sets off, pursued by his team-mates, to celebrate with his manager, deluging him in the Britannia Stadium technical area. A victim of circumstance, Megson won eight of his 17 league games in charge and was widely seen to be unfortunate to be sacked.

22 December 2007

Having already scored both goals as City lead promotion rivals West Brom at the Britannia Stadium, Ricardo Fuller sniffs a hat-trick when Richard Cresswell plays a long ball up the left wing. Fuller has so much to do as he picks it up right on the touchline, faced down by right-back Boštjan Cesar, but he dribbles to level with the edge of the penalty area, then sparks into action with a left-footed stepover before cutting in on his right foot and dipping his shoulder to leave Cesar in a heap, having tripped over himself. Fuller leaves Paul Robinson for dead and, eight yards from goal, feints to go left, but instead shoots with his right foot, wrong-footing both facing defender Pedro Pelé and Dean Kiely in the Albion goal. The ball screams into the bottom-right corner of the Boothen End net and Stoke are three up, eventually going on to win 3-1 to assert their dominance over a West Brom team who will win promotion to the Premier League alongside the Potters at the end of the season.

27 February 2010

One of the most infamous red cards in Stoke history occurs at the Britannia Stadium when Ryan Shawcross is late in a challenge with Arsenal's Aaron Ramsey and unfortunately breaks the midfielder's leg. Recriminations ensue, but Sky analysis proves Shawcross's challenge was 0.15 of a second late, and that he had been fouled going into the tackle by the Gunners' Nicklas Bendtner. Those facts didn't stop Arsenal supporters vilifying Shawcross for the rest of his career, armed with the ammunition of Ramsey's refusal to accept Ryan's apology.

1 January 2020

It's 2-2 in a vital relegation tussle at the John Smith's Stadium when Tyrese Campbell produces a piece of inspired magic. Huddersfield keeper Kamil Grabara punches a long free kick clear of the penalty area, but it drops to the 20-year-old Campbell, who controls with one touch of his left foot, then sweetly half-volleys the ball back into the unguarded net from 26 yards, wide out on the right side of the penalty area. Four minutes later, Campbell drills in his second to set Stoke on the way to a wonderful 5-2 victory and eventual salvation under Michael O'Neill.

67

18 August 1973

Stoke win the first sponsored trophy in English football, the Watney Cup, a competition for the two top-scoring teams from each division who didn't win promotion or qualify for Europe, in its last running. The Potters defeat Hull City 2-0 in the final played at the Victoria Ground, with both goals coming from Jimmy Greenhoff. His first is a low shot to the bottom-left corner, but in the second half he soars to flick a perfect, near-post header into the left side of the Boothen End net from Jimmy Robertson's right-wing cross. The players parade the trophy around the ground in front of 18,000 excited fans. Silverware is becoming a habit.

19 January 1974

Alan Hudson shines on his debut, earning high praise from Liverpool manager Bill Shankly, but City only draw 1-1, despite taking the lead when Geoff Hurst nets from Huddy's pass. All the good work is undone when Stoke keeper John Farmer drops a cross and Tommy Smith prods home the equaliser in the last minute.

13 May 2000

Having gone 2-0 up, then conceded to Ty Gooden's dribbler of a shot, which wrong-foots the defender on the line, then weathered a huge storm thanks to a series of saves by keeper Gavin Ward, Stoke take the Second Division play-off semi-final at the Britannia Stadium against Gillingham by the scruff of the neck again. Striker Peter Thorne has already hit a post with a cutely angled header, but finally finds the back of the net when Graham Kavanagh's driven, right-foot cross from the left wing is headed towards goal by James O'Connor. Vince Bartram saves low to his left, but Thorne is on the spot to slot home into an empty net for his 30th goal of the season and his 20th since 4 March. City are 3-1 up. Surely nothing can go wrong now?

15 February 2008

Chasing promotion, Tony Pulis's men are dismal in the first half against Scunthorpe in a Friday-night game and go in 0-2 behind. But Pulis simply tells them they are a good team and to go out and show it. Halfway through the second half, the Potters are level thanks to goals by Liam Lawrence and Richard Cresswell. The winner, completing a tremendous comeback, and a second 3-2 home win of the week after the previous Tuesday's victory over Southampton, comes from Lawrence again, but the goal is made entirely by Ricardo Fuller. The Jamaican's jinking run down the left byline sees him beat three visiting defenders, spot Lawrence's dart to the near post, and release the ball at just the right moment to allow the winger to prod home right-footed from five yards.

9 November 2019

Already 3-1 ahead, Stoke make sure of victory in a crucial relegation battle when midfielder Sam Clucas, having his best game for the club thus far, rifles in a 25-yard low shot into the bottom-right corner. The goal comes after James McClean tackles Tykes midfielder Luke Thomas in the centre circle and drives forward to supply Clucas. Despite a late consolation which makes the final score 4-2, City leapfrog Barnsley to move off the bottom of the Championship into 23rd and the incredible survival battle, which will see O'Neill's Stoke win 48 points from 31 games before the end of the Covid-19-disrupted season, is on.

68

12 September 1962

Dennis Viollet scores his second goal in three minutes, with Charlton, remarkably, getting a goal in between, to notch his fourth of the game. He latches on to another Jackie Mudie through pass to slot home accurately into the far corner at the Boothen End. Keith Bebbington adds a sixth goal in the final minute as City record their first victory of the campaign in the seventh game, sparking an unbeaten run of 18 matches, propelling Stoke to top of the table, putting the club on course for promotion back to the top flight for the first time in a decade.

23 February 1974

In a classic encounter with Don Revie's seemingly unbeatable Leeds at the Victoria Ground, the titanic struggle swings Stoke's way when Jimmy Robertson slings over a right-wing corner, the third in a row in a spell of intense pressure, to the far edge of the six-yard box, slipping as he takes it. Denis Smith wins the header, but only directs it back the way it came. John Ritchie intervenes, heading the ball back to the far post, where Smith, continuing his momentum, rises to dive and head high into the top-left corner of the Boothen End net. It proves to be the clinching goal in a famous 3-2 win. Leeds' unbeaten run ends at 29 games, one short of Burnley's record. Smith scored many crucial goals and diving headers in his career, but few are so fondly remembered as this one.

1 February 1975

On a quagmire of a pitch, Alan Hudson performs balletically in midfield against Manchester City, defying the laws of physics with his movement and ability to find team-mates with accurate passes. He nets a stunning goal himself, starting the move by taking a throw-in, halfway inside the visitors' half on the right-hand side, going down the wing to Jimmy Greenhoff, then picking up the return and setting off towards goal. After hurdling Willie Donachie's lunging challenge, 30 yards out, Huddy slides a pass across the mud into Ian Moores on the edge of the penalty area, then runs on to take the young striker's back-heeled return in his stride on the left side of the D. Huddy then bamboozles four defenders by stopping, turning back on himself and firing into the bottom-right corner of the Boothen End net, right-footed from 18 yards. Huddy is then hoisted to the heavens by Jimmy Greenhoff in celebration of a stupendous goal.

17 April 2011

Stoke are already 3-0 up at Wembley in the FA Cup semi-final. Most Bolton fans have headed off, having admitted it isn't their day, but their pain is about to get deeper. Robert Huth steals the ball off Kevin Davies in the centre circle and feeds Jon Walters on halfway. The Irish international heads in a beeline for goal, drifting slightly left, then, as he reaches the edge of the penalty area, jags back on to his right foot, beating Mark Davies as he does so, and curls an absolute peach of a 28-yard shot into Jussi Jääskeläinen's bottom-right corner, where all four of Stoke's goals so far this afternoon have nestled.

69

12 June 1947

Stoke are behind 1-2 in the biggest game in the club's history, the title decider at Bramall Lane. George Mountford takes aim and fires in a superb, dipping shot, but Jack Smith in the Sheffield United goal rises out of the mud and tips it on to the bar. Two Stoke attackers fall over each other trying to get to the rebound and it is somehow smuggled clear by the home side. Time is running out for the Potters.

1 October 1988

Bournemouth have a right-wing corner at the Town End of the Victoria Ground. It is played in to the near post and a melee ensues, leaving several players on the ground. The ball is dug out of the ruck, 15 yards from his own goal, by Peter Beagrie's right foot, which will play a significant role in the next 14 seconds. Stoke's new winger, signed from Sheffield United the previous summer for £210,000, accelerates down the left side of the pitch to full speed within four paces, beating the first visiting defender on the edge of the box, the ball glued to that right foot. He reaches the halfway line in a flash. There are now only two defenders, plus another trying to tackle him from behind, between Beagrie and the goal. He veers inside, meaning the chasing player stumbles in trying to tackle him and falls over, jags back to the left to beat one of the others, then finally transfers the ball to his preferred left foot on the edge of the box and hits a superb drive low past Gerry Peyton into the bottom-right corner of the Boothen End net. Absolute genius. When he throws in a backflip in front of the Butler Street Stand for good measure to celebrate his first Stoke goal the moment passes into club legend.

24 October 1992

In an epic season in which the Potteries derby is competed for in the most heated fashion on five occasions, the series kicks off with City's home league game in front of the third-highest league crowd across England's leagues that day: 24,344. City trail when Paul Kerr neatly curls home from the edge of the area into the top corner from Taylor's pass, but within a minute the Valiants' fans are silenced as Ian Cranson, on this occasion not wearing his trademark headband, rises highest at the far post to powerfully head a Kevin Russell free kick into the roof of the net via a defender's head on the line. At 1-1 and with both teams already on long unbeaten runs and just one place apart in the formative table, and only three points off top spot, the game is very much afoot.

23 January 1993

The Stoke City juggernaut arrives at the Hawthorns, 18 league games unbeaten since September under Lou Macari. After Nigel Gleghorn heads in a corner early on to give City the lead, Albion's Bob Taylor equalises, but the Potters seal the points and another chapter in the 'We always beat West Brom' bible that is the 1990s, when Kevin Russell hits a low, right-footed drive from the right side of the penalty area, which Mark Stein deliberately deflects past Stuart Naylor into the bottom-right corner of the net.

5 May 1997

It's carnival time as Stoke say farewell to the Victoria Ground, their home for 119 years and the oldest league football ground in the world. In front of a capacity crowd, now only 22,500, City clinch victory when Graham Kavanagh runs on to Gerry McMahon's through ball, which leaves the entire Albion defence static, to flick a cheeky, right-footed lob over the advancing Alan Miller from the edge of the D to put City 2-0 ahead.

27 March 2010

Substitute Ricardo Fuller has only been on the Upton Park pitch for two minutes, but he brings down Danny Collins's high ball on the left side of the pitch, 25 yards from goal, facing the touchline and tightly marked by Manuel da Costa. There seems little danger, but Stoke fans know that, when the Jamaican has the ball in tight spaces, danger lurks just around the corner for opposing defenders. Da Costa commits the cardinal error of letting Fuller turn. With the ball glued to his right foot, Fuller shuffles into the left corner of the penalty area, then dips his shoulder and accelerates towards goal on his right, between Scott Parker and da Costa, who lunges in to tackle thin air. Now 12 yards out and with Matthew Upson still between him and Rob Green, Fuller twists left then right to leave both bewildered, before slamming a right-foot shot high past the keeper's right hand from six yards to send the supporters behind that goal wild with frenzy at a stupendous solo goal.

20 January 2018

It is new manager Paul Lambert's first game in charge of the Potters, who have sacked Mark Hughes with the club in disarray: in the relegation zone with just five league wins all season and knocked out of the FA Cup ignominiously by League Two Coventry. Lambert is animated on the touchline in this crucial game with David Wagner's newly promoted strugglers. Joe Allen has already put City in the lead, but hope that the drop can be averted arrives when Mame Diouf, netting his 22nd goal in the Premier League for Stoke, making him City's third-highest scorer in the competition, level with Marko Arnautović, takes Xherdan Shaqiri's deft back-heel in his stride and slides a right-foot shot past Huddersfield keeper Jonas Lössl from 16 yards, off the left post and into the Boothen End net. The hope is false. City will not win again until the last game of the season when their fate is already sealed and Lambert departs in the summer.

22 April 2019

Stoke are behind again to Daniel Farke's Premier League-bound Norwich in a meaningless end-of-season game at the Britannia Stadium. Meaningless that is unless you are Tom Edwards, the Potters' young, local right-back, who is desperate to notch his first goal for the club in his breakthrough season. It arrives at the Boothen End when Norwich's Abel Hernández falls over himself when trying to run the ball clear and hands it to Edwards, 25 yards out on the right side of the box. He takes one touch to move in closer, then lashes it first time, low into the far bottom-left corner from 22 yards and celebrates wildly. Perhaps there is hope for the new season under manager Nathan Jones after all?

In the same, crazy game against David Pleat's Hatters, Paul Bracewell makes it 3-2 with a 50th-minute header which skews into the bottom left corner, despite the efforts of Luton's Kirk Stephens.

Flying right-winger Mark Chamberlain produced a devastating display against soon-to-be European champions and treble winners Liverpool on 14 May 1984 as Stoke sought to clamber free of the First Division relegation zone. In the 21st minute, he beat left-back Alan Kennedy to fire a shot at Bruce Grobbelaar in the Liverpool goal, with Ian Painter following up the rebound to score.

Paul Maguire scored all four goals in a 4-0 win against already-relegated Wolves in May 1984 to complete Stoke's incredible escape from relegation in superb fashion.

In brilliant Wembley sunshine, in the 65th minute, Mark Stein catches the ball perfectly on the volley to lash it high into the Stockport net to win the 1992 Autoglass Trophy Final.

The most controversial penalty in Potteries derby history flies into the bottom corner of Port Vale keeper Paul Musselwhite's net in the 86th minute to clinch a 2-1 victory. Mark Stein scores it, after going down in instalments in the Boothen End penalty area under the keeper's challenge to be awarded it.

Captain Vince Overson has escaped the celebrating hordes on the Victoria Ground pitch to take the acclaim for leading his team to promotion from Division Two in 1992/93 after securing the title with a 1-0 victory over Plymouth.

In the 64th minute against Burnley, Mark Stein heads his 30th goal, and the club's 92nd and final one, of the Second Division championship-winning 1992/93 season under manager Lou Macari.

Stein lashes the first of his two goals past Peter Schmeichel in the 32nd minute of the League Cup second round first leg tie at the Victoria Ground, leaving Manchester United defender Gary Pallister floundering as the ball flies into the net.

Mike Sheron arrived at Stoke as part of a swap deal for misfit striker Keith Scott, which proved to be another managerial masterstroke by Lou Macari. Sheron notched 39 goals in 76 games across his two seasons at the club.

Gerry McMahon scores Stoke's penultimate goal at the Victoria Ground in the 33rd minute against West Brom as the club bade farewell to the then oldest league ground in the world in May 1997.

Striker Peter Thorne celebrates scoring the winning goal against Bradford in the 42nd minute in a crucial Division One match in front of Sky TV's cameras in January 1998. Thorne scored 80 goals in 189 games for Stoke, 30 of them in the 1999/2000 season.

Midfielder Graham Kavanagh takes the plaudits after notching a wonderful, slaloming solo goal to open the scoring in the 32nd minute of the Auto Windscreens Shield Final at Wembley in April 2000. He would also supply the cross for Peter Thorne's winning goal in the 82nd minute.

Deon Burton fires home the opening goal in the 16th minute of the 2002 Second Division Play-off Final at the Millennium Stadium. Stoke defeated Brentford 2-0 to win promotion, then sacked manager Gudjon Thordarson shortly afterwards.

Gerry Taggart and Millwall's Dennis Wise get to grips with each other in the 35th minute of the Championship game at the Britannia Stadium on 30 October 2004.

Talismanic striker Ricardo Fuller celebrates putting away the penalty in the 55th minute of the Championship game at Coventry's Ricoh Arena which makes the score 1-1. City's victory is secured by Liam Lawrence, who nets in the 79th minute to put Stoke within touching distance of promotion to the Premier League.

Free-kick and penalty specialist Danny Higginbotham celebrates scoring the winning goal, from a set piece 19 yards out, hit with his piledriver of a left foot in the 63rd minute of the FA Cup quarter-final against West Ham at the Britannia Stadium.

Left-winger Matthew Etherington sets the ball rolling in the FA Cup semi-final thrashing of Bolton at Wembley in April 2011 with a left-footed shot from 22 yards in the 11th minute and leaps in celebration.

Incredibly, Stoke lead the FA Cup semi-final at Wembley 5-0 against Bolton after Jon Walters' second goal of the game, scored in the 81st minute.

Potters fans sing one last 'Delilah' as the team goes out of the Europa League at the last 32 stage on a balmy night in Valencia's Mestalla Stadium.

In the 58th minute of the home Premier League game against leaders Manchester City, Peter Crouch hits an unstoppable volley into the far corner of Joe Hart's net, then sets off to celebrate, slightly disbelievingly at what he has done, while the home fans take the Mickey out of the visiting ones by doing the 'Poznan'.

In the sixth minute, Nick Powell picks himself up off the deck to celebrate a classic diving header which wins the Championship home game against visitors Blackburn 1-0 in December 2020, in a match played behind closed doors due to COVID-19.

70

16 September 1959

New signing from Port Vale, Dickie Cunliffe, runs riot on the left wing against Lincoln City in the Second Division, scoring one of the first-half goals himself, then smashing a drive against the bar, before cutting the ball back for veteran striker Dennis Wilshaw to stroke home. It is the former England international's second and Stoke's fifth goal in a 6-1 victory at the Victoria Ground.

8 March 1975

Stoke are in third place in the First Division and challenging for the title after a win at Derby four days earlier, but under the Victoria Ground lights it all starts to go wrong when visitors Ipswich, managed by future England boss Bobby Robson, score twice. Jimmy Greenhoff pulls one back, but then disaster strikes when Denis Smith suffers a leg break, the fifth of his career, in a fierce challenge with Mick Lambert. Ten-man Stoke cannot pull it back and sink to sixth place.

23 October 1976

John Tudor scored twice on his debut to win a First Division game against Ipswich; now he's at it again, throwing himself to dive in and nod Jimmy Greenhoff's cross past Derby keeper Graham Moseley to sneak a 1-0 win against Dave Mackay's Derby at the Victoria Ground. It's such a classic diving header it has kids all over the Potteries trying to replicate it for weeks.

1 October 1983

City are level with top-of-the-table West Ham when Paul Dyson lofts a free kick into the Hammers' penalty area. Alvin Martin wins the header, but in the driving Potteries rain it skims off his head and proves to be the perfect flick-on for Ian Painter, steaming in five yards out. Phil Parkes saves his header, but the rebound falls to Dave McAughtrie. His lunging, right-footed effort is completely miscued, but falls for Mark Chamberlain, stealing in six yards out, to hammer home left-footed high into the Boothen End net. A splendid finish after a series of woeful errors.

2 November 2005

Stoke lead 2-1 at Coventry's brand-new Ricoh stadium, but that isn't the full story. With 20 minutes to go, and after watching the Sky Blues' right-back Richard Duffy tearing down the wing, director of football John Rudge makes his way down from the directors' box to the dugout. He whispers a tactical change to assistant manager Jan de Koning, as manager Johan Boskamp is on the edge of the technical area, and de Koning implements the switch. When he learns of it, Boskamp goes crazy as he feels undermined, despite it extinguishing the threat and allowing Stoke to hold on to win. Boskamp issues a 'they go or I do' ultimatum to the Icelandic board and de Koning and Rudge are put on gardening leave until the Dutchman himself departs after a bonkers season in charge, which sees Stoke finish 13th in the Championship, but with ten away wins.

23 August 2016

In 261 appearances, talismanic striker Peter Crouch netted 62 goals for Stoke, but only one hat-trick amongst them. He completes it on City's only ever visit to Stevenage's Broadhall Way in the League Cup second round to complete a comfortable 4-0 win for Mark Hughes's men. Crouch rounds off his treble with a clever scissor kick from Joe Allen's deep cross, which bounces into the top of keeper Jamie Jones's net from six yards.

71

22 February 1946

With snow falling heavily, Stoke destroy struggling Arsenal at the Victoria Ground. Frank Baker opens the scoring on 23 minutes, with George Jackson netting on 64, then Johnny Sellars completes the scoring when he pounces on George Swindin's mishandling of a cross to fire home from eight yards. The eventual 3-1 scoreline doesn't do Stoke's superiority justice, but does take the Potters into third place in the First Division with just 13 games remaining.

24 April 1963

Stoke City FC celebrate their centenary as the second-oldest league club in the world, after Notts County, with a glittering friendly match under the Victoria Ground lights against glamorous Real Madrid. Level at 1-1, Jimmy McIlroy puts City 2-1 ahead as he latches on to Don Ratcliffe's clever cutback from the left wing to control and shoot home via a deflection off a Madrid defender. Four minutes later Ron Andrew trips Ferenc Puskás and the Hungarian slams the resultant penalty into the corner to make the final score 2-2.

20 May 1982

Brendan O'Callaghan secures First Division safety for Stoke by powering home a header from a corner past Tony Godden to net a third goal to clinch a 3-0 win over West Brom in front of a buoyant Victoria Ground crowd. It contains hundreds of Leeds fans, who depart, shoulders slumped, as their side's relegation is confirmed by the night's events. At the final whistle the Stoke fans invade and hoist their heroes high on shoulders. Key amongst them is long-time servant Denis Smith, whose last game this is for the club.

26 March 1988

Mick Mills's City secure a famous win at Villa Park when first debutant David Puckett hooks Alan McInally's shot off the line heroically, and then Graham Shaw cuts the ball back to the near post for Phil Heath to bobble the only goal of the game over Nigel Spink's body from five yards. Stoke had only 12 fit professionals at kick-off, with Gerry Daly going off after 15 minutes, and produce a brilliant, backs-to-the-wall defensive display to hold on.

9 November 2010

Ricardo Fuller picks the ball up on the halfway line on the right-hand side of the Britannia Stadium pitch. The pressure is on as Tony Pulis's men have lost the previous four Premier League games, so inspiration is needed as Stoke lead the visitors narrowly 1-0. Fuller edges Barry Ferguson towards the left corner flag, then bursts into life when he reaches the touchline, level with the Blues' penalty area, cutting the ball back with his right foot and leaving his marker for dead. He swerves around Craig Gardner as he enters the penalty area and unleashes a curling, left-foot shot from 20 yards, which flashes past Ben Foster just inside the far post of the Boothen End net. It is yet another stunning individual goal from the Jamaican international.

25 August 2011

City complete the scoring against their Swiss visitors in this Europa League play-off round second leg, when Ricardo Fuller is fed in down the right-hand side of FC Thun's penalty area, beats Thomas Reinmann for pace, and chips an inviting cross back to the penalty spot for Kenwyne Jones to rise and power his second impressive header of the night past Dragan Djukić from six yards into the top-left corner. The group stages await.

23 September 2014

Stoke are level at the Stadium of Light in this League Cup third-round tie. Marc Muniesa, the Spanish defender come midfielder, who arrived from Barcelona on a free transfer in July 2013, has already netted his first Potters goal, but he then wins the tie with another left-foot shot. This time he picks up a cleared corner on the left corner of the penalty area, takes it on one touch and lashes a wonderful strike high into the top-left corner of Costel Pantilimon's goal. They are the first two first-team goals of Muniesa's career and he will only score one more in his four-year stay at the Potteries.

72

25 December 1950

Stoke already lead 1-0 at Highbury, when centre-forward Roy Brown pops up on the wing to cross into the Arsenal penalty area. Centre-half and sometime cricketer, 38-year-old Leslie Compton, makes a hash of his clearance, which falls to Stoke left-winger Alec Ormston. His shot crashes against a post, but is followed in by inside-left Les Johnston, with keeper George Swindin still prone on the ground.

6 September 1967

With Stoke leading visitors Leicester 2-1, flame-haired Irish winger Terry Conroy, on his debut, produces a memorable spark to cut inside and drive a right-footed shot past keeper Williamson and into the far corner, with his marker, Graham Cross, struggling in his wake. The goal proves to be the winner as Leicester's late fightback, which sees John Sjoberg head home on 85 minutes, is not enough. Conroy, who signed from Glentoran in March 1967 for £8,000, after being recommended to Tony Waddington by a cattle merchant, has also played a key part in Stoke's second, harassing left-back Richie Norman so much that he handles the ball to keep it away from the flying winger. City win 3-2 and Conroy has embarked upon one of the great Potters careers.

7 October 1967

City are on the warpath after falling 0-3 behind to Ron Greenwood's team at the interval at Upton Park and draw level thanks to a comedy of errors. Eastham pings a pass to Burrows 25 yards out in the centre of the pitch, but the left-winger's left-foot shot, normally so unerring and accurate, is so wildly off target when he shoots that it falls directly to Peter Dobing, on the right side of the area. The skipper controls and shoots in one movement, but as it's his right, not his favoured left, it bobbles straight at Ferguson, who goes down too early, fumbles and compounds the error by trying to kick the ball away with his feet, only serving to nudge it further right, with his defence completely wrong-footed. Burrows, though, has continued his momentum into the penalty area and makes up for his initial mishit shot by haring in to slot the ball right-footed past the despairing keeper, who has barely got up off the floor. Stoke are level just ten minutes after being 0-3 down and the momentum is only going one way.

13 September 1972

Geoff Hurst gives Stoke a 2-0 lead over Kaiserslautern in City's first-ever European tie when he prods home the rebound after Josef Elting saves his initial shot.

15 December 1972

The Potters are 1-2 down after the first leg of the League Cup semi-final at the Victoria Ground, but are giving as good as they get at Upton Park against Ron Greenwood's West Ham. Terry Conroy skips away from Frank Lampard on the right wing, crosses to beyond the far post and John Ritchie controls adroitly, then turns to fire low, right-footed from six yards past Bobby Ferguson to level the tie. But the drama is only just beginning.

27 December 1982

Mark Chamberlain has been a devastating weapon for Richie Barker's Stoke since signing from Port Vale in the summer. Against Howard Kendall's Everton, Chambo turns from provider to goalscorer. City are up against it as George Berry has been sent off 15 minutes earlier for a bad foul, but the newly capped England winger turns on a sixpence to fire a low, right-footed drive from the edge of the penalty area past a startled Jim Arnold. It's as quick as a flash: 1-0 Stoke. Three points sealed.

21 December 1986

Nicky Morgan completes a hat-trick of snap shots inside Leeds' box to become the second Stoke striker to bag a treble in the last three home games, after Keith Bertschin against Reading. It is City's seventh goal against visitors Leeds, whose keeper Mervyn Day had promised his supporters prematch that he wouldn't concede six again, like he did last season. Mick Mills's Stoke are magnificent and will end an incredible Christmas and new year period in fifth position, well placed for a push for the play-offs after languishing in the relegation zone up until the start of November.

16 February 2010

Stoke are up against it when Abdoulaye Faye is sent off for dragging down the clean-through Emmanuel Adebayor, but Glenn Whelan pounces on a poor clearance to hammer a 28-yard, right-foot drive low past visiting Manchester City keeper Shay Given, who should do better with the shot, into the bottom-left corner of the Boothen End net. It secures Stoke's second successive draw against Roberto Mancini's men, following the FA Cup tie at Eastlands three days earlier.

2 December 2020

Tyrese Campbell spreads the ball wide to the left, where James McClean takes it on and crosses deep for Nick Powell to head past Wycombe's Ryan Allsop from six yards at the far post. Powell then cups his ears in celebration as this goal is scored on the first night of having supporters back after nine months following the Covid-19 lockdown, so there are 1,000 home fans present as the restrictions are lifted in certain parts of the country. The goal gives the Potters a 1-0 victory at Adams Park over Gareth Ainsworth's Chairboys.

73

23 February 1957

Tim Coleman nets a sixth goal to set a new club record for any player in a single game. The right-winger scores a carbon copy of his fifth and City's sixth goal, when Johnny King finds him with a pass and Coleman fires home from 15 yards right-footed. Coleman's six goals beat the previous record of five scored by Freddie Steele against West Brom in February 1937. But he isn't finished yet. This record will only last 11 minutes.

6 February 1965

It is Sir Stanley Matthews's final appearance in his glittering career, almost a year since his last first-team game, an FA Cup tie against Swansea in which he scored Stoke's opening goal. Fulham are the opponents for the 50-year-old, recently knighted winger to make dance to his tune. Veteran left-back Jim Langley, a sprightly 36 years of age, has the task of keeping Matthews quiet, but he can't. With the score tied at 1-1, proving it is no token farewell game, Matthews drifts unmarked across to the inside-left position, just outside the penalty area. He receives the ball from Jimmy McIlroy and turns to slot through for John Ritchie to run on to and fire home, left-footed, past visiting keeper Tony Macedo. A fitting way to end the arch-provider's career. Dennis Viollet makes the game safe with a late solo clincher. Matthews became the oldest player ever to play top-flight football, at 50 years and five days, breaking a 40-year-old bar held by Billy Meredith (49 years 245 days), a record he still holds today.

7 October 1967

Just a minute after drawing level, City's remarkable comeback stuns Upton Park into silence when Peter Dobing scores a fourth goal in 11 minutes. West Ham crumble as Harry Burrows picks up a loose pass in his own half, then speeds forward to thread a ball into Dobing, who controls on the run with his left foot and steers home with his right from the edge of the box past the onrushing Bobby Ferguson. It caps the most incredible comeback in Potters history. Hammers fans end up slow handclapping their own team as City play keep ball at the end to see the game out. Even more remarkably, one of the driving forces of the incredible turnaround, midfielder Calvin Palmer, plays this day in the knowledge that his family are in a Northampton hospital after being caught up in an M1 crash the night before the game, when their car was blown off the road whilst returning from a holiday on Jersey.

4 March 1972

With the scores locked at 1-1 in the 1972 League Cup Final, City drive forward in attack once again. Mike Bernard feeds Jimmy Greenhoff halfway inside the Chelsea half and City appear to be going down the right when he finds Jackie Marsh on the touchline. But the right-back passes inside to Peter Dobing and the skipper instantly clips a long ball out to the far-left wing where Terry Conroy has found acres of space as most of the Chelsea side have funnelled across. The flame-haired Irishman controls superbly with his left foot, then takes on temporary right-back David Webb, deputising for Paddy Mulligan who has had to go off injured. He jags the ball left towards the byline, speeds forward and arcs a perfect left-footed cross to the far post. Big John Ritchie is there to cushion the ball back to the waiting Jimmy Greenhoff with a perfectly judged header and the striker lashes a waist-high volley, right-footed, low to Peter Bonetti's right from the penalty spot. The keeper makes a save, but cannot hold on to the ball, and in rushes old stager, evergreen 35-year-old George Eastham to slot the ball home left-footed from five yards with Bonetti still on the floor. Stoke hang on amidst huge fervour in the stands and a first, and so far only, major trophy can take pride of place in the Potters' cabinet. What a time to score your only goal of the season and the last of a distinguished career. 'The old man has done it!' says Brian Moore on ITV's classic coverage of the final.

22 February 1975

Stoke are in the league title hunt and put soon-to-be-relegated Carlisle to the sword 5-2 at the Victoria Ground. Irish winger

Terry Conroy bags a hat-trick against Alan Ashman's Cumbrians, completing it when he deflects Ian Moores's shot deliberately past keeper Allan Ross.

1 November 2008

Already having scored once from a Rory Delap throw, City bag the quintessential long-throw goal to annoy Arsène Wenger when Ryan Shawcross flicks on another Delap howitzer, this time from the left wing. What follows is the scruffiest goal football has ever seen. The Gunners' defence is transfixed as midfielder Seyi Olofinjana connects with the ball with his chest in the centre of the goal three yards out, then falls over and, in doing so, connects again, breasting the ball over the line, nutmegging keeper Manuel Almunia in the process. It is untidy, it is unique and it is not 'football', according to Wenger, but only once he has retreated to the safety of London to renounce Stoke and Pulis as the Antichrist, sparking a decade's worth of Premier League rivalry. Incidentally, in a game which Wenger claims shows Stoke's 'brutality', it is his striker Robin van Persie who is sent off for assaulting Stoke keeper Thomas Sørenson late on, and only after Emmanuel Adebayor has escaped a red card for kicking Ryan Shawcross in the throat earlier.

9 May 2009

The Potters hordes are sent into ecstasy when Liam Lawrence picks up the ball 35 yards out on the right from Ricardo Fuller's square pass, advances a few yards, then hits a dipping, swerving right-foot shot into the far top-left corner of Boaz Myhill's goal. The keeper remains static, watching the ball sail over him, to put Stoke 2-0 up at the KCOM Stadium and secure Premier League safety after an epic season. Five thousand travelling supporters rejoice in the sunshine.

3 May 2014

City relegate Felix Magath's Fulham when Oussama Assaidi, who has had left-back Dan Burn on toast all game, prompting the American to ask him to 'please switch wings', taps in Marko Arnautović's pullback, left-footed, from four yards after Steven Nzonzi leads a devastating breakaway to release the Austrian down the right.

74

12 October 1946

Left-winger Alec Ormston completes his hat-trick with a low, left-footed shot in off the far post of Chelsea keeper Bill Robertson's goal. His two previous goals, on 50 and 58 minutes, were also both scored left-footed from inside the Stamford Bridge penalty area. Ormston's treble turns the First Division game around as City trailed 1-2 after Tommy Lawton's double either side of half-time and the Potters will go on to win 5-2.

12 June 1947

Time is short as Stoke are trying desperately to claw themselves back into the game which could win them the league championship at Sheffield United, when Freddie Steele gets his head to an Alec Ormston cross. Even with the centre-forward's customary power on his header, the ball gets stuck in the mud on the line, when it seems to be heading into the net, and the grateful Blades keeper Jack Smith dives on it to smother. City's chances have run out and the league title passes them by as they cannot find the win that would clinch the ultimate prize.

22 March 1972

Denis Smith, Stoke's inspirational centre-half, has only come down to the Victoria Ground to wish his team-mates luck against Manchester United, driven there by his wife, Kate. Due to the huge swarms of supporters heading to the game, he has to get dropped off half a mile from the ground and walk, back bent, to the stadium, as he has badly ricked it in the previous weekend's game. But the act of getting out of the car and then that walk improves things and, when he reaches the dressing room, manager Tony Waddington persuades him to play. The next thing Kate knows, she is watching her husband run out, kitted up, instead of sitting on the vacant seat next to her. Smithy responds typically bravely by flying in to head home the equaliser in this pulsating FA Cup quarter-final replay.

22 September 1993

Attacking the Boothen End, with the scores locked at 1-1 in this League Cup second-round first leg, Stoke are pressuring a full-strength Manchester United team, who will go on to win the double this season under Alex Ferguson. From a right-wing throw-in, Toddy Örlygsson plays in Mickey Gynn on the left-hand side. Gynn turns the ball inside to Steve Foley, but, as the midfielder lines up a shot, he is tackled by Bryan Robson. The ball breaks for Mark Stein, 24 yards out just to the left of the D. The little striker tricks his way past two challenges on the edge of the area, until he is right in the middle of the goal, 18 yards out, then pulls the trigger and smashes the ball, right-footed into the bottom-right corner of Peter Schmeichel's net. The Boothen End, behind that goal, go berserk, while Alan Parry, on commentary, simply says, 'This man is magic.'

2 March 2019

After Peter Etebo's 18-yard opener, City seal a vital 2-0 victory, one of only three at the Bet365 Stadium in Nathan Jones's reign, when Nottingham Forest's João Carvalho loses possession, allowing Tom Ince to pick out the run of Benik Afobe, who races through to smash home past Costel Pantilimon to bag his ninth goal of the season, right-footed into the far-left side of the Boothen End net from 14 yards. The clean sheet sparks a run of six consecutive shutouts, leading to the team setting a club record of 1,131 minutes without conceding.

75

3 May 1945

Stoke's title challenge is wilting at Elland Road against relegation-threatened Leeds, but Freddie Steele sparks into life, equalising Short's opener, with a header from Stan Matthews's corner. Can the Potters grab a vital victory?

21 January 1950

George Mountford, deputising for the first time at centre-forward for Freddie Steele, out for the season, nets his second goal of the top-flight game against league leaders Manchester United when right-back Cyril Watkin crosses for him to head home. United players complain to the referee that Mountford had fouled keeper Feehan in flying in to nod home, but their appeals are brushed aside by Mr J. Pickles of Bradford.

25 April 1953

Injury-ravaged Stoke need a point to survive another relegation struggle in the top flight, but visitors and already relegated Derby lead 2-1. With time running out, Harry Oscroft's shot is handled on the line and referee Mr R. Burgess of Berkshire awards a spot kick. Amidst high tension, up steps captain Ken Thomson, a centre-half signed from Aberdeen early in the campaign, to take the vital kick, but he fails to strike the ball properly and Derby keeper Middleton stops the ball on the line. Stoke cannot find an equaliser and drop out of the top flight for the first time in 20 years. Had the penalty gone in City would have survived to finish 18th on goal average. Instead, Frank Taylor suffered relegation in his first season as Stoke City manager.

15 October 1966

Stoke rise to the top of the First Division for the first time in 19 years, with 18 points from 12 games, when John Ritchie bags a third goal against Ted Bates's newly promoted Southampton. His shot hits White and deflects past keeper Maclaren to put City 3-1 up. The other two goals are both left-footed beauties from Peter Dobing and Calvin Palmer. A late Saints goal, a second header from big Ron Davies, cannot prevent the Potters from topping the table. But by the time the return game is played three weeks later at the Dell, Stoke have lost at Sunderland to fall away. Not only that, but, despite Ritchie scoring again in a 2-3 defeat, manager Tony Waddington inexplicably accepts an £80,000 offer from Sheffield Wednesday for the 25-year-old's services, selling him in the belief that his ageing forward line of Dobing, Roy Vernon (£40,000 from Everton in 1965) and George Eastham (£35,000 from Arsenal in August 1966) can keep City in the championship hunt. They can't and Stoke end the season 12th. Oddly only 25,554 fans are in attendance to watch Stoke hit top spot, while in the Second Division 32,522 watch Hull rise to first place.

2 March 1983

Mickey Thomas scurries down the left side of Manchester United's penalty area, steers a cross towards the near post and 'Big' Brendan O'Callaghan dives, full length, to power home a header into the bottom-left corner of the Boothen End net to earn Stoke a famous 1-0 victory under the Victoria Ground floodlights. United's keeper Gary Bailey has been superb, thwarting Bren with two previous world-class saves before the classic diving header wins it.

26 December 1984

Ron Atkinson's Manchester United lead thanks to Frank Stapleton's first-half goal, but City rouse themselves and equalise thanks to an Ian Painter penalty, after Arthur Albiston handles on the line. Stoke go on to win only their second game of the awful 1984/85 season when young striker Carl Saunders pounces to prod home high into the net from close range after Brendan O'Callaghan flicks on Mark Chamberlain's near-post corner. It's some small relief in an otherwise dark time.

26 August 1985

Stoke cut loose in their second home game following relegation to the Second Division when Eddie Gray's Leeds fall apart. City score six times, the most memorable of which comes after midfielder Chris Maskery loses two teeth in a challenge, but steels himself to continue and then flies in to head home Keith Bertschin's cross. That comes in the middle of a devastating four-goal 16-minute spell in which Mark Chamberlain bags two brilliant goals. But within a month the mercurial winger will be sold to Sheffield Wednesday.

12 December 1992

Stoke are struggling to break down Ian Ross's Huddersfield when Johnny Butler launches a long, curling ball forwards from the right wing on the halfway line. It tempts visiting keeper Tim Clarke out of his goal, but then dips to land inside the D, where midfielder Paul Ware nips in to head past the onrushing custodian and into the empty Boothen End net, much to the delight of the hordes on the terraces, who suck the ball in, just in case it gets stuck on the wet Victoria Ground turf.

4 October 1995

After a goalless draw at the Victoria Ground in the first leg, City ride their luck against Glenn Hoddle's Chelsea in this League Cup second-round second-leg tie. The vital goal arrives when Mark Hughes dallies on the ball inside his own half and Ray Wallace slides around him to poke the ball away, much to the striker's chagrin. The ball runs through to Paul Peschisolido, 28 yards out, who uses his low centre of gravity to beat two defenders, leaving Frank Sinclair fully prone, and then fires high from eight yards past goalkeeper Dmitri Kharine. Pesch then dances a jig in front of 2,500 Stoke fans on the temporary stand, in place while the Shed End is being turned into a hotel, which bounces around like a trampoline under the celebrations – a famous win at Stamford Bridge.

11 November 1995

Simon Sturridge completes his hat-trick and a first-ever win at Roots Hall when a long ball from defence catches the Southend defence flat-footed and Sturridge races on to it on the right edge of the penalty area before cutting inside, leaving Mick Bodley on his backside, then beating Phil Gridelet and slotting home from six yards into the bottom-left corner. It is a superb individual goal which seals a 4-2 victory and, when Sturridge scores at Portsmouth in the following game, he will have bagged six of Stoke's 12 goals in the past three First Division games.

1 December 2015

City are in control of the League Cup quarter-final against Carlos Carvalhal's Sheffield Wednesday, but make sure of progress to a semi-final tie with Liverpool when substitute Phil Bardsley lashes a free kick, rolled to him by Marko van Ginkel, right-footed past rookie keeper Joe Wildsmith into the Boothen End net, off the foot of the left post, from 32 yards.

76

21 January 1950

Frank Bowyer scores Stoke's second goal in a minute to put paid to any thoughts visitors Manchester United may have of an unlikely comeback. Stoke's inside-right finishes Matt Busby's league leaders off by turning home right-winger Johnny Malkin's cross. United's Charlie Mitten grabs a late consolation, but only due to Stoke's Frank Mountford, hobbling due to injury, being unable to tackle him; 38,901 fans go home mostly very happy.

25 December 1950

Within four minutes of making it 2-0 at Highbury, right-winger Johnny Malkin threads a pass inside to Frank Bowyer and the inside-right crashes home a drive from the edge of the penalty area to give City only their second-ever win at Arsenal. Memories of the 11-2 aggregate hammerings the previous season are laid fully to rest when the following day, Boxing Day, City also win the return match at home, this time 1-0. Mostly local lads, costing just their £10 signing-on fee, Bowyer is the shining light of manager Bob McGrory's post-Matthews team. He was renowned as a brilliant volleyer of the ball and had timing and grace. He made 436 appearances and scored 149 goals for the Potters in a 13-year league career, before being moved on to Macclesfield Town in the summer of 1960, aged 38, when assistant coach Tony Waddington took over from Frank Taylor. But if you add in the 56 goals he scored throughout the war, which ruined the early years of his career, Bowyer would easily be the leading scorer in a Stoke shirt, topping 200 goals.

18 April 1964

Young striker John Ritchie finishes off visitors Manchester United as he takes advantage of a defensive mix-up to net the clinching third goal in a 3-1 victory. Matt Busby's men are already struggling when Harry Gregg and Pat Crerand mess up a clearance, which ends up being closed down by Ritchie. The striker simply slots the rebound off his own block into the empty net with the keeper and defender stranded, arguing, on the edge of the area.

19 April 1972

Stoke are clad in all white in this FA Cup semi-final replay, but the kit works against them when the linesman mistakes a white-coated ice-cream seller on the far side of the Goodison Park pitch as a City defender. It allows Charlie George to race through, despite being ten yards offside, and pull the ball back for John Radford to slam home the winner in a 2-1 victory at the near post from three yards. Bedlam ensues as Bertie Mee's Gunners celebrate and Stoke remonstrate with the officials. In the days after the game, linesman Bob Matthewson is awarded a special trophy by the Stoke Supporters Club: a horse's backside.

18 September 1974

'Total Football' comes to Stoke in the form of legendary Dutch club Ajax, who, after three successive European Cup triumphs from 1971 to 1973, have been pipped to the title by Feyenoord and end up at the Victoria Ground in the UEFA Cup first round. Ruud Krol lashes a superb shot from distance past John Farmer just before half-time, but a jam-packed 37,398 see Denis Smith earn City a first-leg draw and the chance to nick something in Amsterdam, heading home at the near post from six yards.

19 September 1992

Stoke were 2-1 up, now they are 2-3 down against Ossie Ardiles's West Brom. But bald winger Kevin 'Rooster' Russell nips in to collect a short back pass, round keeper Stuart Naylor and slot home right-footed from eight yards into an empty Boothen End net. At 3-3 it's been a topsy-turvy, feverish clash of styles, but Lou Macari's men are about to send the home fans home very happy indeed.

77

5 January 1980

One of the most infamous red cards in Stoke's history is shown by the preening extrovert that is referee Kevin McInally, a man who once found it in his soul to send off a brass band before kick-off. On this occasion, Denis Smith, already on a booking, but clearly badly crocked, limps off the field to be substituted, but receives a second booking from the power-crazed official for stopping the restart of play by being too slow to depart. Stoke become even more enraged when first the referee awards a penalty to Brian Miller's Burnley, currently in the relegation zone in the Second Division, and then dismisses Ray Evans for arguing over the award. City lose this third-round FA Cup tie 0-1 at Turf Moor. Ignominious.

2 September 1981

Stoke lead 3-0 and are heading to the top of the formative First Division, but Adrian 'Inchy' Heath completes the rout with another clinical finish, this time low to Coventry keeper Jim Blyth's right. Heath has a hat-trick goal ruled out shortly afterwards when referee Mr D. Richardson awards him a free kick for a foul before he fires home. The fervour at being top after just two matches is short-lived; in Stoke's next game, at home to Manchester City, they are well beaten 1-3 at the Victoria Ground.

21 February 1987

Lee Dixon roams forward down the right side towards the Town End goal at the Victoria Ground. Stoke are trying to find a way back into this fifth-round FA Cup tie against Coventry following Mickey Gynn's goal and seem to have found it when the right-back is upended by Dave Phillips just inside the penalty area. But referee Nixon is unmoved, waving away Stoke protests and later stating, 'It was a good tackle, he just didn't get the ball', which in the opinion of most of the 31,255 in attendance is the very definition of a penalty! The eventual 0-1 defeat means the Potters have lost in each of the season's three cup competitions to the eventual winners.

13 May 2012

Stoke have let a lead slip at home to Owen Coyle's Bolton in a crucial final-day clash, which Wanderers must win to have any hope of staying up. When Peter Crouch is tripped by keeper Ádám Bogdán to give City a penalty, up steps Jon Walters, scorer of the controversial opening goal, to make the score 2-2. He slams the ball low into the bottom-left corner of the Boothen End net to condemn his former club to relegation. Even worse for Wanderers is the fact that Manchester City's two injury-time goals against QPR, which win them the Premier League title, would have meant Bolton's survival had they clung on to win. Stoke fans don't care. They are too busy saying farewell to favourite son Ricardo Fuller, who makes his last appearance for the club.

78

5 May 1945

After John Sellars has scored to put Stoke 4-0 ahead against Port Vale in this War League North game, George Mountford notches his fourth goal of the game, while a few minutes later Tommy Sale completes the rout with a typical rocket left-foot drive. Mountford has now scored nine goals against Stoke's neighbours in the last three games against them, five in an 8-1 hammering on 17 February and now another four. Just four days later, he would be rested for the hastily arranged Staffordshire Victory Cup match, the day after the VE Day armistice is signed ending the Second World War. Instead, Johnny Sellars, with two goals, Jock Kirton and John Jackson secure a 4-2 triumph for Stoke in what proves to be the last Potteries derby played at Vale's Hanley Recreation Ground.

12 October 1946

Stoke have been imperious in the second half at Stamford Bridge, with Alec Ormston's hat-trick clinching the game, but left-half Jock Kirton roams forward to set the seal on the victory with a sensational, curling, left-footed drive into the top corner from 35 yards. And all that without the injured Stan Matthews. That goal was Kirton's first for Stoke, and one of only two in his 249-game Potters career.

8 March 1978

Stoke are struggling to break down Wilf McGuinness's Hull at the Victoria Ground. Needing something different, new manager Alan Durban, who has been in the job all of three weeks, turns to his bench where his first signing, 6ft 2in Brendan O'Callaghan, a £40,000 arrival from Doncaster Rovers a week earlier, pipes up saying, 'Put me on boss, I'll score you a goal.' Durban opts to throw 'Big Bren' on to replace Viv Busby after Stoke win a left-wing corner and he jogs on to take up a position at the near post. Paul Richardson slings the ball into that area and O'Callaghan rises highest, amidst a ruck of players, to nod the ball into the Boothen End net just 11 seconds after taking the field. Not a bad way to start your Stoke City career. O'Callaghan would spend seven years at the Victoria Ground, playing both as a striker and as a central defender, scoring 47 goals in 294 appearances. He also won six caps for the Republic of Ireland and, after retiring early due to an adductor muscle injury, worked in the club's community development department and later moved on to work for Save the Children.

8 December 1979

Ron Atkinson's West Brom have fought back to level at 2-2 from two goals down at the Victoria Ground, but City's Garth Crooks completes his hat-trick when strike partner Viv Busby delivers a cheeky back-heel to put the youngster through on Tony Godden's goal. Crooks ghosts around the keeper to score and clinch a 3-2 victory on the way to an 18th-place finish in City's first season back in the First Division following last season's promotion.

31 August 1998

Stoke have won Brian Little's first four games in charge to top the formative Second Division table, but Colchester are proving a tough nut to crack at Layer Road. Inspiration is needed and it comes in the form of City midfielder Graham Kavanagh. Seizing on a dropping ball, 27 yards out, after it loops clear from the edge of the box, Kav steadies himself and unleashes a powerful, right-foot volley which sizzles into the top-left corner of Carl Emberson's net, right in front of the massed Stokies. Five wins in a row for Little's men have blown away the relegation cobwebs, but can it last?

21 October 2001

A sweeping Stoke move from the back, then down the left-hand side, sees two substitutes, only on the pitch for a minute, combine to bag an equaliser in the Potteries derby with their first touches of the game. Lewis Neal plays the ball in from the left wing towards Andy Cooke, but the striker opens his legs to dummy the ball, which rolls through to Neal's sub partner Chris Iwelumo. Anticipating the move, he takes the ball in his stride on the penalty spot right-footed, jinks to the left to round Mark Goodlad in the Vale goal and slides the ball home left-footed in front of the packed away end, several of whom spill on to the pitch to celebrate with the players, bear-hugging 'Big Chris'. The 1-1 draw is Stoke's last point in this most passionate of fixtures and Iwelumo's goal the last scored for the Potters in a Potteries derby.

9 December 2005

Madcap manager Johan Boskamp seems to have hit on a winning formula in the run-up to Christmas, bringing in previously unknown striker Sammy Bangoura for a club-record £950,000 from Standard Liège in Belgium, where Boskamp has been managing. The Guinean international has made quite an impression, scoring in five league games in a row, closing in on Mike Sheron's club record of seven. Stoke are hosting Leicester at the Britannia Stadium, but are behind 1-2 in a Friday-night Sky TV game and need a dramatic comeback. It comes when first Mama Sidibé flicks home a header and then, three minutes later, Bangoura makes it seven goals in six consecutive games when he rises to head a curling, left-footed Dave Brammer cross past keeper Rob Douglas from eight yards to give Stoke the three points. Bangoura, who played with a piece of white tape on his left ear to protect his earring, couldn't make it seven games in a row in the next match at Luton and his form waned, notably after he began to go AWOL after going on international breaks. In the end everyone gave up on him and his manager took to calling him names, putting it mildly, in interviews.

24 January 2010

Stoke are level 1-1 with a youthful Arsenal side in the FA Cup fourth round at the Britannia Stadium when Mama Sidibé latches on to a pass down the right wing and, in a passable impression of Stanley Matthews in his heyday, beats Francis Coquelin for pace, before outwitting Mikaël Silvestre to cross perfectly for Ricardo Fuller to dive like a swan to nod home his second goal of the game. For his dribble, acceleration and cross, 'Big Mama' earns a second terrace nickname, 'Sir Stanley Sidibé'.

29 September 2011

Stoke produce a rousing display in their first home Europa League group match, which owes much to their lauded prowess from set pieces, despite UEFA regulations meaning the pitch has had to be widened and, in the process, the run-up area for Rory Delap's long throws reduced. City win the game from a corner, with Jermaine Pennant's delivery being headed goalwards by Matthew Upson and Tomáš Sivok pulls down Peter Crouch inside the six-yard box as he goes for the ball. Jon Walters steps up and smashes the spot kick high into the left side of veteran Rüştü Reçber's net to secure the 2-1 victory. After drawing their first game in Kiev, the Potters are now top of Europa League group E ahead of back-to-back games with Maccabi Tel Aviv.

79

22 November 1986

Potters striker Keith Bertschin completes a rare hat-trick of headed goals when he pounces after Gary Westwood in the Reading goal saves Nicky Morgan's shot and Bertschin is on the spot to nod the rebound home from six yards. It is the highlight of Bertschin's Potters career, as he plays second fiddle to 19-goal Carl Saunders and 12-goal Morgan for most of the season, bagging just eight goals himself before being sold to Sunderland in March.

24 November 1992

City are 1-2 behind at Vale Park in a pulsating FA Cup first-round replay, with conditions torrential and the pitch boggy with puddles and sticky like glue. Dave Regis, a 65th-minute substitute for Graham Shaw, makes an immediate impact when he latches on to a loose ball, with keeper Musselwhite outside his area, to fire the ball home ... except the ball never makes it into the net or even to the goal line as it sticks, defying the laws of motion, in the mud on the edge of the six-yard box and is cleared away. City's chance is gone and try as they might they cannot equalise. Instead, Martin Foyle rounds Sinclair to clinch the tie in the last minute. Stoke would not lose a game again until 27 February, as the team was on a run of 23 league games without defeat, to set a new club record.

1 April 2000

Despite opening the scoring and then equalising at 2-2, City need Peter Thorne to rescue them again at third-placed promotion rivals Bristol Rovers in a vital Second Division match. His second goal was a superb, near-post header into the top corner, but his hat-trick goal arrives when Bjarni Guðjónsson's long ball towards the edge of the penalty area is headed backwards by Rovers' centre-half Andy Tillson, only for him to watch in horror as Thorne romps in to fire past Jones left-footed from 15 yards to complete a 'perfect' hat-trick.

12 April 2008

Liam Lawrence has only just made the subs bench after passing a late fitness test on his injured groin, but Tony Pulis throws him on, desperate to halt a run of only one win in eight games as the club seek promotion to the Premier League. Level at 1-1 at Coventry, Mama Sidibé flicks on a goal kick for Ricardo Fuller to nudge the ball onwards to Richard Cresswell, haring in off the left side, to run through. Coventry keeper Kasper Schmeichel is quickly out of his goal and smothers Cresswell's shot on the edge of the area, but it pops up to Lawrence, 20 yards out, but on his weaker left foot. The right-winger coolly half-volleys the ball back towards goal, beating two despairing defenders to slot home the winner, then rips his shirt off and celebrates with the 3,000 travelling supporters. Stoke go top with three games remaining. Nerves steadied, promotion is very much on.

80

16 September 1959

City score a sixth goal against Lincoln in a Second Division encounter, with forward and former England star Dennis Wilshaw completing his hat-trick with a cracking drive, after recent £15,000 signing from Burnley Doug Newlands's pullback to the edge of the area. The Imps, who have beaten Stoke 3-0 at home the previous Saturday, are put to the sword in front of just 13,453.

27 September 1969

John Ritchie secures the points for Stoke as visitors Manchester City are undone when their determination to push up as a free kick is taken in order to catch Stoke offside fails. George Eastham's quick set piece sees them leave Ritchie unmarked and the big striker nets his sixth goal since his return from Sheffield Wednesday in the summer with a powerful header from ten yards. Stoke are fifth in the formative table and playing some lovely football under manager Tony Waddington.

7 May 1971

City atone for losing the FA Cup semi-final to Arsenal by becoming only the second club ever to finish third in the competition. Oddly, the powers that be have instituted a short-lived third/fourth play-off which takes place at Selhurst Park the night before the big Wembley showpiece. City go 0-2 down early on to Harry Catterick's Everton, but Mike Bernard and then John Ritchie bring Stoke level, before the big striker runs on to John Mahoney's pass to fire low past Andy Rankin to complete the comeback and win City's 56th competitive game of the season with his 19th goal.

27 January 1974

Alan Hudson runs the show against his former team-mates in only his second Stoke appearance. Chelsea finally succumb when Gary Locke trips Hudson, and Geoff Hurst slams the penalty triumphantly past Gary Phillips to earn a deserved First Division victory.

16 March 1974

John Ritchie has had his goat well and truly got by Southampton's star striker Peter Osgood mouthing off in the papers in the lead-up to their visit to the Victoria Ground for this First Division game. Ritchie responds with a superb second-half hat-trick, the last goal of which lives on in legend. Rounding keeper Eric Martin, Ritchie responds to Osgood's allegations that all Ritchie can do these days is head the ball by stopping it on the Boothen End goal line, kneeling down and heading it over the line. Point well and truly made. City humble Saints 4-1. Osgood is rather more humble as he trundles off.

25 April 1981

New England under-21 cap Adrian Heath fires in, right-footed from 28 yards, to give Stoke a first win at Goodison Park since 1969, beating Jim McDonagh all ends up.

23 August 2008

City are level with Martin O'Neill's Aston Villa in their first Premier League home game and giving as good as they get. Gareth Barry misplaces a pass in midfield, straight to Liam Lawrence, who turns and threads a pass through to the mercurial Ricardo Fuller, who has his back to goal and Martin Laursen breathing down his neck. What happens next is sheer brilliance. Fuller flicks the ball up and over his head, swivels and sets off into the Villa box. Laursen is momentarily stunned and cannot keep up. Fuller does a little stutter as he sets himself to hit the ball just outside the right edge of the six-yard box as the Boothen End rise in anticipation and then lashes it low into the far-bottom corner, beating Brad Friedel low to his right. It is a stunning, inspirational goal.

31 January 2009

If any minute and any moment sums up Stoke City's first season in the Premier League and survival against all the odds, then it is the 80th minute against billionaire club Manchester City at the

Britannia Stadium. Down to ten men after Rory Delap's red card, but ahead thanks to James Beattie's header, Stoke are manfully tackling, blocking and stifling the visitors, much to the frustration of their manager Mark Hughes. In the stands, the Potters fans are going ballistic in support. Hackles were raised by the Delap red card and injustice of Shaun Wright-Phillips not being sent off as well. Then, as the players seem to take a breather amidst wave after wave of blue attacks, the crowd gives them a lift. It starts seemingly in the East Stand with a chant of 'Go'arn Stoke!' and spreads like wildfire. It is a guttural, urging sound which reaches over 125 decibels and makes the hairs on the back of your neck stand on end. It visibly makes the Stoke players grow and the visitors wilt just a little and the energy continues through the last few minutes to carry Stoke to a remarkable victory. Never was a team more at one with its supporters.

13 September 2010

On a balmy late summer's evening, new signing Kenwyne Jones's industry is finally rewarded with his first goal for Stoke, against Aston Villa. Matty Etherington follows up his own blocked shot to dig out a far-post cross that the Trinidad and Tobago forward, an £8m arrival from Sunderland, gets ahead of Richard Dunne to nod past a helpless Brad Friedel. City are level and the fans noisy, hungry for a first win of the season.

1 December 2011

City are desperate for the equaliser which will bring them qualification from the group stage of the Europa League into its knockout stages, but visitors Dynamo Kiev are tough opponents and lead 1-0. Their defence is finally unlocked when Matty Etherington launches a ball from the left wing to the far post which Kenwyne Jones can only help on to the far side, where Jermaine Pennant picks it up. The winger hits the byline then chips a cross to the near post where Jones rises, swan-like, to guide a firm, downward header low to the bottom-right corner of the Boothen End net, past keeper Oleksandr Shovkovskyi. It will bring the draw that Stoke need to knock out the Ukrainians and go through as the first English club to qualify for the last 32, to be drawn against Valencia.

28 December 2015

Stoke are 2-3 behind in a topsy-turvy match at Goodison Park when Marko Arnautović races down the left and crosses left-footed to the far post where everyone goes for it, but no one connects, except keeper Tim Howard, who fingertips it away left-handed. The ball bounces out to where City's substitute Joselu is lurking, eight yards out on a tight angle on the right side of the box. But no matter; the Spaniard cracks a crisp, right-footed volley inside the near post to make it 3-3. The hurly-burly of this tumultuous game continues.

15 April 2017

Having scored both goals at the KCOM Stadium in a 2-0 win earlier in the campaign, including a 25-yarder into the top-right corner, Xherdan Shaqiri ensures Hull never want to see him again when he picks up a short pass from Marko Arnautović, looks up, then smashes a 30-yarder into the other top corner of Eldin Jakupović's net at the Boothen End. Spectacular.

81

30 November 1957

Stoke complete a brilliant victory at Second Division promotion rivals Fulham when right-winger Tim Coleman nets his hat-trick goal. After Coleman's opening brace, dogged Fulham have netted three quick goals, while Johnny King has bagged for Stoke, and the scores are tied at 3-3 with only ten minutes left in a breathless game. Coleman completes the win after Fulham keeper Hewkins mishandles a high cross, which hits the bar and bounces out for Coleman to slot home from a narrow angle.

15 May 1968

Stoke round off a disappointing season with First Division survival confirmed thanks to a cracking victory over Bill Shankly's Liverpool. The 2-1 win is sealed when Harry Burrows, after swapping wings with Terry Conroy, cuts in on the right and curls a deep cross left-footed for John Mahoney to head deftly home, securing 18th place for the Potters.

6 March 1971

John Ritchie has already equalised against Hull with a tap-in from two yards, but now he seals Stoke's first FA Cup semi-final appearance in 72 years, when he heads in a perfect cross to the far post from four yards. It all comes from a controversial throw-in, which the officials are undecided which way to give. John Mahoney just decides for them, picking the ball up down by the right corner flag, throwing it to Terry Conroy, inside the penalty area, to turn and chip the ball across for the winning goal. A thrilling comeback from 0-2 down is complete.

28 January 1987

Stoke have struggled to dispose of Mick Lyons's Grimsby Town in the FA Cup third round, but in this second replay the Potters overwhelm the visitors. Leading 4-0 by half-time, Carl Saunders scores his second of the night to complete a 6-0 thrashing when Phil Heath hares down the left wing, then cuts the ball back from the byline to find Saunders, eight yards out at the near post. The lanky striker side-foots neatly into the far bottom-right corner of the Boothen End net. That's now 12 goals in the last 12 games for 'Spider', who, three days later in the fourth-round match against Cardiff, will net the first goal in a comeback 2-1 win and help Stoke reach the fifth round for the first time in 11 years, where they will face Coventry.

3 May 2000

Since hitting a hot streak on 4 March, striker Peter Thorne has netted 12 league goals in 11 games, including a four and a three. He has now bagged another brace against Andy Preece's Bury and completes his hat-trick when Kyle Lightbourne wins a deep, left-wing corner and powers a header towards goal. Thorne stoops, with his back to goal, to redirect the ball high into the roof of the Boothen End net, past three defenders and the keeper on the line.

24 October 2010

With Stoke behind 0-1 to Javier Hernández's improvised back-header, Tony Pulis introduces substitutes Tuncay and Eiður Guðjohnsen in a bid to add more quality in the final third and the two combine to deliver a stunning equaliser. Tuncay's moment of magic sees him cut in from the right-hand side, just inside the area, then curl the ball into the far top-right corner of Edwin van der Sar's net. This was the first goal Stoke had managed to score past Manchester United since Mark Stein's double in a League Cup tie in 1993 and was well worth the wait, sending the Boothen End fans behind that goal ballistic. The joy would only last a few minutes, though, as Hernández contrived to bag a winning goal just four minutes later.

30 January 2011

Stoke have a free kick right on the byline on the right wing with the score goalless at Molineux in the FA Cup fourth round. Matty Etherington swings it in and Robert Huth rises high, shaven head standing out in the south Staffordshire sunshine, to nod into the top-left corner of Marcus Hahnemann's goal from four yards. City are on their way to Wembley with a 1-0 victory.

17 April 2011

One end of Wembley is almost empty, while City's end is ablaze with colour, fervour and general disbelief at the perfection of the Potters performance they have witnessed, as City head for the first FA Cup Final in their 148-year history. Already 4-0 ahead in the FA Cup semi-final against Owen Coyle's Bolton, the cherry is put on top of the cake when Jon Walters bags his second goal of the afternoon and City's fifth. But the striker owes everything to right-back Andy Wilkinson, who is determined to get in on the goalscoring act. He plays in Kenwyne Jones down the right, then races forward to receive the cross in the middle of the goal. But at this point Wilko remembers he is a full-back who has never scored a professional goal and miscontrols the ball with his left foot, with the goal at his mercy. No matter, it falls for Walters to control and score with his right foot from six yards at the far post with a cheeky chip past Gary Cahill, who has had a hapless afternoon, and Jussi Jääskeläinen, who has had a personal nightmare. Five-nil is the biggest win at the new Wembley in a club match (since eclipsed by Manchester City's 6-0 thrashing of Watford in 2019) and is the biggest FA Cup semi-final victory since Wolves defeated Grimsby by the same score in 1939. Potters fans leave the stadium singing about 'going on a European tour', as the runners-up will receive qualification to the following season's Europa League.

82

3 May 1952

With Stoke desperate for a victory on the final day of the First Division season to avert relegation, the score is tied at 2-2 against visitors Middlesbrough and the supporters are anxious and letting their players know what they think. Who can be the Stoke hero? None of the usual suspects. Instead, up steps ever-present left-back John 'Jock' McCue. Stoke's record appearance holder (if wartime games are taken into account) scored just two goals in his entire Potters career. One comes just when City are desperate for it. McCue picks up an injury which sees him despatched to the left wing as a passenger. But he turns up trumps when he gets on to the end of a cross from Alan Martin (a club-record signing nine months earlier at £10,000 from Port Vale) from the other wing to hobble in and head home from close range, sparking celebrations on the pitch and in the stands, for those remaining fans who have stayed to the bitter end amongst the 10,993 crowd. Stoke are safe by the skin of their teeth. After the game, manager Bob McGrory announces he is to retire after 31 years' service at the club, 17 of those as manager, having taken Stoke to their highest-ever finishing position of fourth in the top flight in both 1935/36 and 1946/47.

28 December 1953

Johnny King bags a brilliant hat-trick against Swansea Town on a bitterly cold December afternoon at the Victoria Ground. Having scored early in the first half, he nets on 69 minutes when he turns the ball past his namesake John King in the Swansea goal to crown a glorious move, begun by Frank Bowyer's inch-perfect pass out to the right wing for Johnny Malkin to cross. King completes his treble late on by latching on to a Malkin pass through the middle, rounding the keeper and slotting home to complete a superb personal and team display. Not surprisingly the headlines all run along the theme of 'King of Kings'.

23 September 1972

Stoke have annihilated Malcolm Allison's Blues, with Terry Conroy, Geoff Hurst and Jimmy Greenhoff, with two, scoring as the Potters lead 4-1. Greenhoff completes a 5-1 victory when he starts a move in the middle of the opposition half, sweeping the ball out to the left. Conroy, repaying the compliment for Greenhoff setting him up for the opener, tricks his way down the wing, then crosses for the blond striker, arriving late into the area to lose his marker, to finish from six yards. It is the first hat-trick by a Stoke player for four years.

27 December 1986

Carl Saunders completes a superb hat-trick with an exultant header from Tony 'Zico' Kelly's cross. His earlier two strikes saw him break the shaky Sheffield United offside trap to speed through and round John Burridge. That is now 28 goals in nine games for Mick Mills's rampant Stoke as they thrash the Blades 5-2.

20 January 1993

Midfielder Steve Foley bags one of the more unexpected hat-tricks in Stoke's history against visitors Barnet in the Autoglass Trophy southern-section second round. His first sees him race clear on to Paul Ware's pass to fire home from 12 yards. His second is a firm, right-footed drive into the far-right side of the goal from eight yards and his hat-trick is sealed when Mark Stein sets him clear again. Foley takes the ball on by flicking it with his heel into his stride and then guides a shot with the outside of his boot into the bottom-right corner and takes the applause with a raised right arm in front of the Boothen End.

16 April 2000

After Paul Holland's headed equaliser, Stoke go hunting for the winning goal in the Auto Windscreens Shield Final at Wembley. Attacking the tunnel end, where the Potters fans are gathered, right-back Mikael Hansson launches a long, cross-field pass towards Bjarni Guðjónsson on the left wing. Bjarni is pushed over by Louis Carey near the corner flag and referee Kevin Lynch awards a free kick. As Bristol City argue with the referee over the decision, Stoke think quickly. Guðjónsson, the son of the Stoke manager Guðjón Thórðarson, slides a pass through to Graham Kavanagh, who races down the left side of the Robins penalty area to flick a cross to the far post. It takes a slight deflection which sees it fly beyond keeper Billy Mercer, but means Stoke striker Peter Thorne has to stretch his right boot to its very tip to poke the ball into the unguarded net, sending the Potters hordes ballistic and earning Stoke a third straight Wembley win and trophy lift.

8 May 2011

Arsenal have just pulled a goal back, but Stoke make it 3-1 almost immediately when Andy Wilkinson shoots from the edge of the area, low and hard. The ball is blocked poorly by Johan Djourou, on the edge of the six-yard box, only as far as Jon Walters, who takes one touch, then toe-pokes it into the Boothen End net past the onrushing Wojciech Szczęsny and despairing Djourou. Arsène Wenger holds his head in his hands on the bench in the Potteries sunshine, while Walters high fives the front row of the entire Boothen End in celebration. What a way to head to Wembley for the following week's FA Cup Final!

2 October 2016

José Mourinho's Manchester United dominate at Old Trafford, but can only score once, mostly thanks to Stoke's emergency loan keeper Lee Grant delivering a stupendous performance. Mark Hughes's Potters come back into the game late on and force an equaliser. Glen Johnson cuts in from the right to hit a weak-looking, left-foot shot from 23 yards which David de Gea, having one of his moments, spills. Jon Walters nips in and hits the ball off the sliding challenge of Eric Bailly four yards out at the near post. The ball flies up and hits the bar at the Stretford End, and, despite Peter Crouch waiting on the line for the ball to drop, Joe Allen, a summer £13m signing from Liverpool, darts in to prod home, left-footed from two yards, to secure a point. It is the first time the Potters have avoided defeat at Old Trafford in the Premier League, and overall since 1981.

83

17 December 1960

Stoke score five goals in the last 16 minutes to complete their record 9-0 victory over Plymouth. The Potters' eighth arrives when centre-forward Johnny King latches on to Bill Asprey's right-wing cross to fire high into Argyle's net to complete his hat-trick. But the man of the match is wing dynamo Don Ratcliffe, who nets a brace either side of King's third with a superb 35-yard run and shot from 18 yards, followed by a lunging prod to send King's spinning shot over the line with the goalkeeper stranded. Bizarrely, City's goal spree comes as they have sunk to being the lowest scorers in the 1960/61 season across all four divisions. Consequently, Stoke's lowest crowd of the season, just 6,479, is at the Victoria Ground to witness the avalanche of goals in gathering fog.

16 March 1963

Bill Asprey rounds off a superb performance, coming back from 0-1 down to Grimsby to win 4-1 at the Victoria Ground to keep City's Second Division promotion challenge going in the right direction. The right-back shoots home as the ball ricochets out to the edge of the area after yet another heavy spell of Stoke pressure. That adds to Dennis Viollet's second goal of the game 20 minutes earlier, forced home after a ping-pong session around the six-yard box. The win sparks a run of six consecutive wins, ten games unbeaten in total, which puts Stoke in pole position to lift the championship come the end of the campaign.

28 January 1989

Stoke are on the comeback from being 1-3 down to Barnsley in the FA Cup fourth round. Mick Mills's team need some inspiration to find the equaliser after George Berry hits a left-foot shot from ten yards in off the Boothen End bar. It arrives from Peter Beagrie. The mercurial winger picks the ball up 25 yards out on the corner of the box, drives into the Tykes penalty area, outpacing three defenders, and then sidesteps to his left before unleashing a powerful left-foot shot which flies past Clive Baker high into the net from 15 yards. Another special goal, from a special player.

19 September 1992

It's been a pulsating Staffordshire derby with Ossie Ardiles's West Brom and it's tied at 3-3 when City win a right-wing corner, which is sent over, right-footed, by man of the match Kevin Russell. The ball flies to the middle of the goal, where centre-half Ian Cranson rises highest, head resplendent in his trademark headband, to hammer a header home which flies into the top-left corner of the Boothen End net, off the underside of the bar from six yards. Bedlam ensues and City are on their way to three points, a club-record unbeaten run of 23 league games and eventual promotion back into the second tier as champions.

19 October 2008

Stoke lead Juande Ramos's ten-man Spurs 2-1 at a windy Britannia Stadium. The visitors' goalkeeper has been struggling to deal with Rory Delap's long throws all afternoon and Heurelho Gomes finally cracks, bursting into tears, caught on Sky's cameras, after attempting to punch the latest Exocet missile into his penalty area clear, instead connecting with his team-mate Vedran Ćorluka, knocking the Croatian international clean out. Gomes is simultaneously flattened by City's Tom Soares, taking a whack in the ribs in the process. Ćorluka leaves the stadium on a stretcher and it proves all too much for Gomes, who has already thwacked his defender once before in trying to clear, and is caught by the watching cameras crying on Jonathan Woodgate's shoulder. In injury time Ricardo Fuller hits a penalty off both posts, with Rory Delap slamming the rebound off the bar, before Michael Dawson joins Gareth Bale in taking an early bath for a dreadful challenge on Mama Sidibé. Spurs just can't cope with the Britannia Stadium experience. City's second win of the season catapults them into a run of form which will see them down Arsenal and Manchester City and draw with Liverpool in forthcoming matches.

84

23 February 1957

Neville 'Tim' Coleman completes the scoring in Stoke's 8-0 win over Lincoln in the Second Division with his seventh goal of the game, setting a world record for any winger in a professional game (yes, even Cristiano Ronaldo) and a club record which stands today. Additionally, this eight-goal margin of victory has only been bettered once since. Coleman's seventh is the best of the lot, as he flies in to dive headlong and bullet George Kelly's cross into the back of keeper Downie's net. Coleman injures himself in the process, but is dragged up by his team-mates to take the adulation of the meagre 10,790 crowd and is chaired off shoulder high at the final whistle. That seventh goal was also Coleman's 26th of the 1956/57 season, but, bizarrely, despite there being ten games remaining, Coleman did not score again that campaign.

26 September 1970

Denis Smith blocks Eddie Kelly's shot on the edge of the area and it rebounds almost to the halfway line where Jimmy Greenhoff finds Harry Burrows, who releases Jackie Marsh, City's right-back, to fly down the right wing. Marsh cuts inside when he reaches the right side of the penalty area and hits a left-foot shot low to Bob Wilson's right. The Scotland keeper saves, but the ball pops up invitingly, six yards out, right in the middle of the goal, for Alan Bloor, who has raced unnoticed from City's penalty area to get in on the goalscoring fun. The defender leathers it, left-footed, into the roof of the Town End net. Stoke have thrashed Bertie Mee's Arsenal, who will go on to win the double this season, 5-0.

25 September 1982

Ten-man Stoke are 3-4 down at home to free-scoring Luton, but this team never knows when it is beaten. George Berry plays a long ball forward from halfway and left-back Peter Hampton, for some reason up in attack, nods the ball across into the centre of the pitch, 25 yards out, for Brendan O'Callaghan to run on to and lash home a superb half-volley with the outside of his right foot that curls into the bottom-right corner of Alan Judge's goal. It's 4-4, but this frantic game isn't over yet. There is more drama to come.

31 March 1993

With a narrow lead late in the fifth Potteries derby of a wonderful 1992/93 Second Division championship-winning season, Stoke pile on the pressure and Nigel Gleghorn hammers a free kick, left-footed, from 30 yards which Paul Musselwhite fingertips over the bar. But from the resulting corner the cultured midfielder gets his head to the ball six yards out to score a rare headed goal to seal victory. City move ten points clear at the top of the table ahead of second-placed Vale, who will eventually miss out on automatic promotion by a point and then lose in the play-off final to West Brom. Shame.

26 December 2007

Liam Lawrence is on fire. He has already scored a penalty and hit the bar at Oakwell, but City are 1-2 behind to Barnsley when the right-winger finishes a brilliantly worked free-kick move. Lawrence runs over the ball, 30 yards out, slightly to the right of the D, and Danny Pugh plays it in left-footed to Ricardo Fuller. The Jamaican striker has his back to goal, but just flicks the ball nonchalantly, right-footed, into Lawrence's path and the Irish international steadies himself and fires home right-footed from six yards. But the drama is by no means over yet as Barnsley go straight up the other end and score from the kick-off. Stoke need Lawrence to complete his superhero act.

21 March 2009

Rory Delap winds up yet another long throw, this time into the Middlesbrough box. It is tense, towards the end of a tight, crucial relegation battle with Gareth Southgate's visitors, but a hero is about to emerge. It is young Ryan Shawcross, who races from the blindside of a host of defenders, including his future partner Robert Huth, to leap to connect with the near-post throw, eight yards out, and steer it with a flick of his neck into the left side of Brad Jones's goal at the tunnel end. Shawcross pumps the air with his right fist in celebration and the shaven-headed centre-back has just written himself another piece of folklore as the 1-0 victory means Stoke just need two more wins to be safe.

85

13 September 1972

John Ritchie bags City's third in their first-ever European tie, in the UEFA Cup against Kaiserslautern. He has already had one header ruled out when he finally nets, nodding in Terry Conroy's cross. At 3-0 up Stoke should be through, but just before the end of the game Idric Hošić heads in for the West Germans to score a vital away goal and put them back in the tie.

17 August 1974

Billy Bremner's long ball into the Stoke penalty area is headed away by Jackie Marsh and Alan Hudson picks up the loose ball. He lets new signing Geoff Salmons, on debut after his £160,000 move from Sheffield United, take over. The left-winger feeds Mike Pejic, who crosses into the Leeds area. John Ritchie dummies the ball, allowing it to run through for Jimmy Greenhoff, who controls right-footed, then slams the ball towards David Harvey's goal. The ball beats the keeper's dive, deflecting off Trevor Cherry's knee, into the back of the Boothen End net. It is a flowing move from one end of the Victoria Ground to the other, which typifies the football played by Tony Waddington's team. Brian Clough's Leeds are humbled 3-0 when Ritchie drives into the same bottom-right corner of the goal from 15 yards just two minutes later, following Alan Hudson's forceful run and inch-perfect pass.

14 October 1995

City are 3-1 up at Molineux and Wolves centre-half Dean Richards has had to go in goal due to an injury to keeper Mike Stowell, picked up in a horrible clash of heads with his own defender, Eric Young. City pile misery on when Ray Wallace's 23-yard, right-foot shot squirms through the replacement keeper's hands into the bottom-left corner.

It's a goal at complete odds with Stoke's opener, a corkscrew of a 30-yarder from Nigel Gleghorn's sweet left foot into the top-right corner. The 4-1 triumph secures the Potters' first win at Wolves since 1967.

22 September 1996

On live TV Stoke come back brilliantly from a horrible start, going behind 0-2 to Brian Horton's Huddersfield. The 3-2 victory is sealed by Mike Sheron's second goal of the game, following his six-yard header into the top-left corner. His winner is prodded home from six yards after Ray Wallace's 28-yard effort bangs back off the left post at the Town End.

20 April 1997

City are leading Port Vale 1-0 in the last Potteries derby at the Vic, the penultimate home match of the 1996/97 season. Mike Sheron, having already netted just before half-time, scores a clinching second goal when Carl Beeston charges down a clearance on the edge of the box which falls perfectly for Sheron to fire home first time, right-footed, into the bottom-right corner from 16 yards. It proves to be Sheron's last goal for the club as he is sold to Queens Park Rangers in the summer for £2.75m in order to fund the new stadium, the Britannia, high up on the hill above the Vic. To complete Stoke fans' misery, despite the joy of victory over their neighbours, this derby is played the day after manager Lou Macari has announced that he will be leaving the club at the end of the season, ending his second tenure and a total of five and a half years in charge, most of which were glorious.

27 August 1997

Amidst all the excitement of the first game at the new Britannia Stadium, Stoke are comfortable after a 3-1 first-leg victory over Rochdale in the League Cup first round. This second leg is not a great game, but it is crowned by a great goal, which arrives when new signing Paul Stewart cuts along the left edge of the penalty area, but is tackled and the ball breaks to Graham Kavanagh, 26 yards out. The Irish international simply takes two steps up to the rolling ball and leathers it, right-footed, into the top-left corner of Lance Key's net at the Boothen End. City are up and running at the new ground.

22 August 1998

In a pulsating game, played in brilliant sunshine, Stoke have fought back from 0-2 and 1-3 down to level, thanks to two goals from Graham Kavanagh and one from Dean Crowe. The diminutive forward is about to make a real name for himself, though, as City go route one to snatch it. Bryan Small whacks the ball from inside Stoke's penalty area to the halfway line, then Kavanagh prods it on for Crowe to run through and beat Preston's keeper Tepi Moilanen with a low right-foot side-foot into the bottom-right corner from eight yards to secure a famous 4-3 away win. Could new manager Brian Little be about to return the Potters to the second tier at the first time of asking? Three wins in the opening three games suggest there is great cause for optimism.

28 April 2002

Stoke have been a let-down in the Second Division play-offs yet again, for the third season in succession. Two goals down at home to a Cardiff team featuring former Stokies Peter Thorne and Graham Kavanagh, the atmosphere is depressed at the Britannia Stadium. But it is pepped up when Stoke lay siege to the Cardiff penalty area, pinging crosses in. One lands 12 yards out at the feet of loanee striker Deon Burton, who controls right-footed and then lashes in a right-foot shot high into the top-right corner, beating Cardiff keeper Neil Alexander to bring Stoke back into the tie. Just one goal behind now, there is renewed vigour to the Potters. It still could happen.

14 September 2004

In front of Stoke's biggest crowd of the season, 23,029, City overcome John Halls's red card to topple Joe Royle's Ipswich. The game is tied at 2-2 when the right-back receives his marching orders for picking up two cautions. But Stoke secure the 3-2 win when a defensive mix-up leaves Ade Akinbiyi through on goal and he beats Kelvin Davis to slide the ball home to much jubilation in the stands. The visitors were the leaders at kick-off. Defeat sees them replaced by Stoke at the top of the formative Championship table.

24 January 2010

City seal progress to the FA Cup fifth round with a 3-1 victory over Arsène Wenger's insipid Arsenal when Matty Etherington is fed down the left by Mama Sidibé and crosses to the far post for Dean Whitehead to side-foot home. Sol Campbell's first game back after a return to top-flight football is ruined by City's verve and attacking play.

9 November 2010

Stoke have been pegged back by visitors Birmingham, having been 2-0 up, thanks to two goals in three minutes. Confidence is hit, but the Potters clinch a crucial win when Dean Whitehead runs on to a deflected Matthew Etherington cross, which squirms through Scott Dann's legs, to clip the ball over the onrushing Ben Foster from eight yards to secure a 3-2 Premier League home victory.

5 March 2016

Stoke have lost every Premier League visit to Stamford Bridge thus far, so when Mame Diouf pounces to head home Thibaut Courtois's palm-out of a Xherdan Shaqiri right-wing cross from 12 yards out to equalise at 1-1, Potters fans are ecstatic to avoid defeat for once.

29 September 2018

Gary Rowett's Stoke are 0-2 behind at Rotherham on their first visit to their new New York Stadium. City's tag as preseason Championship promotion favourites is not weighing well on the players' shoulders and the football has been dour. But there is still some joy around in the form of Bojan. The Spanish attacking midfielder surprises everyone, including himself, by ghosting in at the near post to flick home Benik Afobe's inswinging left-wing cross past Marek Rodák into the top-left corner from ten yards to level things up, after Tom Ince's earlier left-foot finish pulled one goal back. The little man's huge smile as he is deluged by team-mates, and some Potters fans running on to the pitch from the stands, is plain for everyone to see. Sadly, this will be his last goal for the club as he departs for Montreal Impact, but not until a rift with his manager gets Rowett the sack.

86

19 September 1946

Left-winger Alec Ormston runs on to a well-judged through ball on the edge of the box to fire a characteristic, left-footed shot low into the far corner to clinch City's first win of the 1946/47 season at the fifth time of asking. The goal gives City a 3-2 victory over Stuart McMillan's reigning FA Cup holders, Derby County, and Stoke's epic title challenge is up and running.

3 May 1947

With time running out and Stoke's title challenge hanging in the balance, Freddie Steele flings himself at a deep Jock Kirton cross to head powerfully past Leeds' Toomery and secure a vital win. After the game it is announced that Stan Matthews has played his final match for the club and, despite City having three more matches remaining in a season in which they can win the league title, he has, astonishingly, been sold to Blackpool for £11,500. The Potters miss out on the championship when they lose their final game. What if Matthews had stayed to play?

13 January 1958

As Stoke are looking to hang on for a famous victory over top-flight opponents Aston Villa in an FA Cup third-round second replay, forward Dennis Wilshaw, back on his old stomping ground of Molineux, having signed from Wolves less than two months previously, ghosts into the area and cuts the ball back from the byline. Neville 'Tim' Coleman races in from the right wing to slot the ball home and confirm that Stoke have knocked out the holders of the FA Cup for the first, and so far only, time in their history.

14 April 1979

It's the sharp end of the season and Alan Durban's City are sitting in the final promotion position in the Second Division. On a visit to the Valley, tension mounts when Charlton win a dubious penalty and Kevin Hales beats Roger Jones. It galvanises Stoke into action and the Potters overpower the Addicks, scoring four goals without further reply. The last goal is rattled in by little Sammy Irvine, the barrel-chested Scottish midfielder, who hammers in a right-foot shot on the run from 16 yards. In the final five games City keep five clean sheets, winning three of them, to clinch that precious last promotion place by one point from Sunderland.

24 October 1992

As time ebbs away and the first Potteries derby of an epic season seems to be heading towards a draw, and with debutant Nigel Gleghorn's prompting getting City ever closer, striker Mark Stein hares through on to Kevin Russell's precise through ball. But controversy reigns. Firstly, because everyone thinks Stein, only just inside Vale's half when the ball is played, is offside, even Stein himself stopping momentarily before running on to the pass with no defender in sight. But then, even more controversially, he slightly stumbles as he rounds Paul Musselwhite on the right-hand side of the Vale penalty area, only to be tripped by the keeper's dangling left hand. Referee John Watson points to the spot as bedlam lets loose in the stands. Musselwhite's lengthy protests earn him a booking, but that doesn't put Stein off and the 'Golden One' picks himself up to slam the spot kick home right-footed, into the bottom-left corner. The Potters see the game out to claim a famous derby 2-1 victory.

9 April 1996

Lou Macari's Stoke are a goal down at Luton in their quest for the First Division play-offs. It's tense, but enter the Stoke-on-Trent version of the SAS; not Sutton and Shearer of Blackburn and England fame, but Sheron and Sturridge. Between them the pair bag 29 goals across the season. City's path to victory at Kenilworth Road is laid when Simon Sturridge races into the left side of the Hatters box, outpacing Darren Patterson, and fires a cross shot, left-footed, past Iain Feuer from nine yards. He then celebrates by running right along the front of the Stoke fans behind the goal, arm upraised.

20 September 2000

Top-half Premier League side Charlton field a weakened side, but seem to have got away with it in this League Cup second-round first-leg tie at the Britannia Stadium. That is until teenage substitute winger Mark Goodfellow enters to race clear on to Graham Kavanagh's pass on the left side, takes two touches as he gallops into the box and then slams a left-foot shot into the far-bottom corner from 12 yards. It's a memorable winner on his 19th birthday, earning Goodfellow the nickname 'Freezer' in the process.

24 October 2009

Stoke haven't won at White Hart Lane for 34 years, but Tony Pulis's well-drilled defence is stubbornly holding on to a clean sheet thanks to a fantastic display by reserve keeper Steve Simonsen, the post and a goal-line clearance by James Beattie. Hearts are in mouths when Salif Diao seems to have tripped Spurs' Niko Kranjčar in the penalty area, but he has just got a toe end on the ball and referee Lee Probert waves play on. Victory is secured when Ricardo Fuller weaves his way down the right side, cuts into the Tottenham area and pulls the ball back perfectly for Glenn Whelan to fire a right-foot shot, high into the top-left corner from 15 yards. It is a rare goal for the Irish midfielder, who will go on to become Stoke's most-capped international of all time, accumulating 91 in total, 81 whilst with the Potters. Whelan only scored eight goals for Stoke in 338 games as the mainstay anchor in midfield under both Tony Pulis and Mark Hughes. Indeed, it was only after he moved on to Aston Villa in 2017 that the team lost its renowned steel in the middle of the park and succumbed to relegation.

24 May 2015

Peter Crouch puts the seal on Stoke's biggest Premier League victory, a 6-1 thumping of his former club Liverpool, to ruin Steven Gerrard's final appearance for the Reds, his 710th. Gerrard has at least managed to score, prompting an impromptu standing ovation from all four sides of the ground, but the Stoke fans really let rip when Crouch nods home Mame Diouf's pinpoint left-foot cross from the left wing from seven yards, low into the bottom-left corner. It is the first time Stoke have scored six goals since 1987 and the first time Liverpool have let in six since 1963. Stoke finish ninth for a second season in a row under Mark Hughes, notching up 54 points, the most ever collected by the club in the Premier League.

7 March 2020

Stoke are swarming all over hapless Hull and already lead 4-1 in a vital relegation tussle at the foot of the Championship. City wrap things up when Tom Ince feeds debutant substitute Tashan Oakley-Boothe, a new arrival from Spurs, who tricks his way down the left side of the penalty area and pulls the ball back neatly for Nick Powell to flick a near-post, left-footed shot high into the roof of the net from four yards. The stadium is jubilant, but little does everyone know that this will be the last goal witnessed by Stoke fans in the Bet365 Stadium for well over a year due to the coronavirus pandemic.

17 September 2020

Michael O'Neill has turned Stoke from one of the most porous defences in the country to one of the best. Indeed, no English club delivers more clean sheets in the calendar year of 2020, with 24 across all competitions. One of these arrives at Molineux in the League Cup second round, when a makeshift back three of youngsters Nathan Collins, Harry Souttar and skipper Bruno Martins Indi keep Wolves' £35m new striker Fábio Silva at bay. City take their chance when James McClean barrels down the left wing, cuts in, finds Sam Vokes on the edge of the box and, instead of taking the return pass, dummies it to allow it to run through to Jacob Brown. The new arrival from Barnsley fires right-footed, first time from 12 yards, and home keeper John Ruddy makes something of a hash of his attempt to save, misjudging its curl, only deflecting the ball into the net. As there are no fans in the stadium, it falls to those watching on streams to jump around living rooms, kitchens and bedrooms to celebrate a rare cup victory over a team from a higher division.

87

15 April 1974

Having scored his 200th league goal against Southampton the previous month, former England striker Geoff Hurst bags his 201st to seal a vital home win against Leicester. It's a special goal, a 25-yard piledriver, hit with the left foot that scored that famous, clinching, World Cup Final hat-trick goal eight years earlier. It keeps the Potters on course for a European place, maintaining their astonishing run of having lost just twice since Alan Hudson's arrival from Chelsea in January. Hurst may be most famous for his England and West Ham exploits, but he spent a great three years at Stoke in the twilight of his career, netting 39 goals in 130 appearances, and he was crucial in settling in Hudson so quickly.

Manager Tony Waddington persuaded the Hurst family to have Huddy as a lodger and the pair got on famously, inspiring the midfielder's incredible form; a fifth-place finish this season and league title challenge the next.

5 April 1975

Terry Conroy bags his second of this game, and his ninth in the last five, when he is set up by John Mahoney to finish past John Phillips in the visitor's net to complete a comfortable 3-0 win. Chelsea are heading down, while Stoke will finish fifth in the closest championship race in years, despite ending this game in third position, level on points with the top two, with just three games remaining.

21 April 1976

A youthful City team, featuring John Lumsden, Alan Dodd, Kevin Sheldon, Sean Haslegrave and Danny Bowers, offer stern resistance at Old Trafford. A tight game is won when, on the break, Jimmy Greenhoff heads low and keeper Alex Stepney manages to pull off a blinding reflex save, but stalwart defender Alan Bloor is there to head home Sheldon's cross from the rebound and clinch Stoke's last-ever victory at Manchester United.

28 October 1981

The Potters have already pulled one goal back of the first-leg 0-2 deficit against Manchester City in this League Cup second-round second leg, and are pummelling the visitors, when full-back and captain Ray Evans, a free-transfer signing after returning from a spell in the MLS playing for California Surf, latches on to a loose ball, 16 yards out, to rifle a right-foot shot past Joe Corrigan at the Boothen End to send the tie into extra time. It is a very rare strike from Evans; his only other goal for Stoke was a penalty two seasons earlier and he won't score for the club again as he returns to the MLS to play for Seattle Sounders the following summer.

10 October 1992

Stoke's nascent revival under Lou Macari is nearly cut off before it starts as table-topping Leyton Orient take the lead thanks to flying winger Ricky Otto. With time running out, enter the magic man, Mark Stein. Carl Beeston slams a 20-yard volley against the corner of post and bar and the rebound is nodded back goalwards by Ian Cranson. Stein cleverly twists to flick the ball over keeper Chris Turner with a looping header that finds the bottom-left corner of the Town End net.

12 December 1992

Ian Cranson, a man far better known for towering headers, roves forward in the dying embers of a home Second Division game against Huddersfield. From 30 yards, he takes aim and leathers a left-footed piledriver high into the top-right corner of the Boothen End net. A superb strike, which seals a 3-0 victory and keeps Stoke at the top of the table.

7 May 1995

The name Keith Scott is often taken in vain by Stoke fans, but the, mostly, lumbering striker did find the net occasionally, four times to be precise. The last of these is at Kenilworth Road to win an otherwise meaningless last-day-of-the-season game in the

Bedfordshire sunshine. Typically, Scott heads against the bar from two yards to the dismay of the fancy-dress-clad, travelling Stokies. But then he makes amends by nodding home Nigel Gleghorn's cross to win the game 3-2. Scott, though, is mainly remembered for being the makeweight in a swap deal which brings Mike Sheron to the Victoria Ground in one of manager Lou Macari's brilliant pieces of transfer business.

3 May 1998

It's all kicking off in the stands as thousands of visiting Manchester City fans have somehow nabbed tickets in home sections of the Britannia Stadium amongst the 26,664 then record crowd watching this crucial final-day game between two sides who both need to win to have any chance of staying in the First Division. Joe Royle's Blues have already won the match, netting four goals to Stoke's one, but results elsewhere are going to condemn both clubs to the drop. The most pointless of all consolation goals arrives from striker Peter Thorne with a flying header back across keeper Martyn Margetson from six yards from Graham Kavanagh's chip. Stoke concede a fifth straight afterwards and a disastrous day all round ends with a 2-5 defeat. What a way to end your first season in a new stadium.

13 December 2003

City have already secured victory against Steve Coppell's Reading, but left-winger Peter Hoekstra wants a hat-trick. Having scored two superb goals in the first half, the Dutch winger despatches a penalty, after being rugby tackled to the floor by Nicky Shorey, who he has tormented after switching to the right wing. The spot kick is a cheeky 'Panenka' chip, which leaves keeper Marcus Hahnemann prone and hits the back of the Boothen End net just under the crossbar as the supporters rise to acclaim a wonderful individual performance.

11 August 2007

Stoke lead 1-0 at the Cardiff City Stadium on the opening day of the season, when debutant loanee Ryan Shawcross, who has already scored the only goal of the game at the other end, pulls Steven

MacLean's shirt to give away a penalty. MacLean dusts himself off to take the spot kick, but the striker sees Simonsen dive full length to his right to save his penalty. Even better, the keeper then recovers brilliantly back to his left to somehow get off the ground and throw his arms up to miraculously parry MacLean's follow-up to safety. The superb double save secures the win and sends Stoke on their way to an incredible season and eventual promotion back to the top flight for the first time in 23 years.

11 May 2014

Scottish midfielder Charlie Adam seals a final-day victory at the Hawthorns when he runs unchallenged at the West Brom defence and fires in a low, left-footed drive from the edge of the area to give Stoke a fifth successive win at the Hawthorns. It also seals ninth place in the top flight, the club's best finish since 1975. Adam almost tops it, though, as his shot from inside his own half hits the back of the net, but after referee Lee Probert has blown the final whistle, robbing him of a wonderful end to manager Mark Hughes's first season in charge.

88

8 January 1951

First Division Stoke visit Third Division (South) Port Vale's new Vale Park for the first time for an FA Cup third-round replay, following a slightly embarrassing 2-2 draw at the Victoria Ground in front of 49,500 just two days earlier. A huge 40,977 cram into the Valiants' new home, nicknamed the 'Wembley of the North', to see a tight, chanceless affair appear to be heading towards extra time. Just before the end, Stoke's inside-right Frank Bowyer cuts in from the right, jinks into the penalty area and slots an incisive, accurate shot past King in the Vale goal. Late saves by Dennis Herod keep Stoke's noses in front and they progress to meet West Ham at home in the fourth round.

28 October 1961

After Tommy Thompson has converted a flimsy penalty award ten minutes earlier, Stan Matthews ends his second debut a 3-0 winner over Huddersfield Town in this Second Division encounter at a packed Victoria Ground. The third goal arrives to seal victory when Thompson takes advantage of Huddersfield's determination to triple mark Matthews to slip through unmarked and shoot past keeper Fearnley.

At the final whistle, Matthews is royally cheered from the pitch by the Stoke fans with *The Sentinel* journalist N.G. writing, 'It was a moving demonstration of mingled sentiment and emotion on the occasion, the likes of which may not happen again for 100 years.' Manager Tony Waddington, having seen the success the likes of Matthews and Jackie Mudie brought at the twilight of their careers, continues to recruit older players such as Jimmy McIlroy and Dennis Viollet for their experience. Stoke win six of the next nine games to revive fortunes, beginning the Waddington era in earnest and ending with a return to the big time.

10 April 1965

Stoke lead high-flying Sheffield Wednesday 2-1 thanks to a John Ritchie brace and the big striker makes the game safe by grabbing his hat-trick goal, following up another Jimmy McIlroy shot to fire home. It is his first hat-trick since a treble against the same opponents in the equivalent fixture last season. Within two minutes, Ritchie repeats the trick to notch his fourth and complete a 4-1 victory. This time his goal follows centre-half George Kinnell slaloming from the halfway line through the centre of the Wednesday team, leaving players in his wake, before drawing the keeper and teeing up Ritchie with an open net to bag a fourth. A year and a half later the Owls make one of the most controversial signings in Stoke City's history when they prize then 25-year-old Ritchie from Tony Waddington's grasp for £80,000 in November 1966. Thankfully, Ritchie would make the return journey in 1969 after scoring 45 goals in three seasons at Hillsborough.

15 November 1971

In the League Cup fourth round Stoke have already drawn twice with Frank O'Farrell's Manchester United. The second replay is at the Victoria Ground and the score is level again at 1-1 when George Eastham, a half-time substitute, arrows a cross into the penalty area with his cultured left foot and John Ritchie, who has stayed on despite injuring his back, rises to head home the dramatic winning goal, sending most of the 42,233 present home happy. Stoke go through to meet Third Division Bristol Rovers in the quarter-final.

5 May 1979

Stoke have to win to secure promotion back to the top flight or Sunderland, who are leading at Wrexham, will pip the Potters. With time running out, in front of around 10,000 visiting frantic fans, strewn all around Meadow Lane, Brendan O'Callaghan knocks a cross back across goal to find Paul Richardson, stooping low, four yards out, throwing his whole body behind his header to get power into it, to nod past Eric McManus and score a famous promotion-clinching goal. At the final whistle, the Stokies spill on to the turf in celebration in their thousands, mobbing Alan Durban's men.

26 August 1985

Stoke have had a poor start to life after relegation down in the Second Division. Mick Mills is still adjusting to being player-manager and nothing has clicked so far. But when Leeds come to visit, that all changes. City lash six goals past keeper Mervyn Day, the last of which is bagged by star man, right-winger Mark Chamberlain. The England winger drops his shoulder, sets himself, then curls home a beauty from 15 yards. Sadly, Chambo will move on to Sheffield Wednesday, in the First Division, where he belongs, just a fortnight later, after scoring 18 goals in 123 games, but more importantly exciting Stoke fans with his electric pace and swashbuckling wing play.

25 September 1991

Third Division City have performed superbly and are only one goal behind Graeme Souness's Liverpool at Anfield in this League Cup second-round first-leg match. The impossible comes true when Lee Sandford hits a long ball down the left-hand touchline and Gary Ablett and Steve Nicol commit the cardinal sin of letting it bounce. Ablett then miskicks his back pass, leaving it short, and Tony Kelly nips in to bear down on goal. Bruce Grobbelaar comes out and Kelly slots home between his legs, performing the perfect nutmeg to equalise at 2-2; 6,000 Stokies behind the goal go absolutely berserk, celebrating a famous equaliser at Anfield..

1 February 2003

Tony Pulis's Stoke are hunting points in their relegation battle against Norwich, but go 0-2 behind after 23 minutes at Carrow Road and the game seems up. But gradually City get back into the game and after Brynjar Gunnarsson nods in Peter Hoekstra's chipped cross, ex-Port Vale man Lee Mills, on loan from Derby, gets in on the act. The striker turns and lashes a 22-yard right-foot rocket into the top-right corner of Rob Green's net to earn a precious point.

14 October 2006

The game is already dead and buried at Elland Road as Stoke lead managerless Leeds 3-0, but City have saved the best til last. Darel

Russell drives forward in midfield and feeds Ricardo Fuller on the left touchline, 35 yards out. The Jamaican jinks inside, dribbles into the corner of the penalty area, standing his frightened defender up, and then curls a beautiful, right-foot shot into the far bottom-right corner to complete a 4-0 victory that is Stoke's biggest-ever win at Leeds. It turns City's form around and within two months the Potters will be in the play-off positions. Leeds drop to the foot of the table, where they will finish the season.

15 May 2016

Mame Diouf secures a 2-1 last-day win for Stoke over visitors West Ham and a third successive ninth-place finish in the Premier League with a flashing header from Glenn Whelan's corner. The Senegalese striker celebrates by doing a double backflip, taking his shirt off and stage-diving into the Boothen End crowd to rejoice in the glorious Staffordshire sunshine.

19 January 2019

Welsh midfielder Joe Allen slides in to prod James McClean's left-wing cross home from five yards at the far post to secure victory in Nathan Jones's first home game as manager. Despite Leeds pulling a very late goal back, Jones has outwitted his opposite number, Marcelo Bielsa, the wily Argentine coach. The Welshman celebrates victory by striding on to the Bet365 Stadium pitch and beating his chest in front of the Boothen End. It gets a mixed reaction and, as it proves to be one of only three victories at home in Jones's entire nine-month tenure, any cheers soon fade away.

89

6 October 1973

Stoke are behind at Elland Road against Don Revie's all-conquering Leeds. But City steal a late equaliser when Terry Conroy escapes down the right and crosses, right-footed, deep to the far post, where Denis Smith, leaping high above his marker, hammers a header home from two yards, which keeper David Harvey cannot keep out.

15 February 1975

Stoke lose yet another player with a broken leg when Mike Pejic goes into a challenge with Wolves' Steve Kindon. Pej being Pej, he limps through the remaining minutes of the game, only discovering the true extent of his injury when he returns to the dressing room. The terrible luck with injuries is derailing City's title challenge, but the stirring fightback, inspired by Pejic's grit, which has seen first Terry Conroy and then record appearance holder Eric Skeels slot home amidst goalmouth scrambles in each of the preceding two minutes, keeps it very much alive for now. The equaliser is Skeels's seventh goal for the club in 597 games. He retires a year later, spending some time in America before returning to make five appearances for Port Vale in 1977. Skeels went on to work for Staffordshire University's security department and returned to watch his club as often as he could. Unassuming in person off and, seemingly, on the pitch, Skeels was the kind of player who could fill in every position, deliver a solid performance and be happy to let others take the glory – a tremendous club servant.

15 March 1975

Jimmy Greenhoff throws himself at Geoff Salmons's left-wing cross to head home from nine yards into the bottom-right corner of Colin Boulton's net. The winner secures a vital 2-1 victory at Derby, the club that will eventually lift the First Division trophy, in this top-of-the-table clash. It is Greenhoff's second goal of the game, after his superb far-post volley from another Salmons cross, amidst the mudbath that is the Baseball Ground pitch. The former Leeds and Birmingham striker, signed in the summer of 1969 to partner John Ritchie for £100,000, a then club record, will score another three goals during the title run-in, which sees City finish fifth, just four points behind Derby. Although Greenhoff finishes as the leading scorer this season, with 15 goals, the following season with 13, after his 20 goals made him top scorer in 1972/73, he then has to be sold after the collapse of the Butler Street Stand roof in January 1976. After being told of his sale, Greenhoff cried in the Victoria Ground tunnel before departing to Manchester United, where he ended up scoring the FA Cup Final-winning goal in 1977. A Stoke legend, Greenhoff netted 103 goals in 346 games for the Potters in a glittering eight-year career.

12 May 1984

Paul Maguire nets his second right-footed penalty of the match at the Boothen End, high to the left side of the net, to give Stoke a resounding 4-0 victory over Wolves. The convincing win secures Stoke's First Division survival, which seemed unlikely until the return of Alan Hudson sparked a run of ten wins in 18 games, winning 33 points in that spell. City finish 18th, while Wolves are bottom by miles. Manager Bill Asprey takes all the plaudits himself and bizarrely thanks Maguire by releasing the four-goal hero on a free transfer a few days later.

29 February 1992

All hell breaks loose when Stoke striker Paul Barnes is the beneficiary of strike partner Wayne Biggins's diving into a tackle with Birmingham keeper Alan Miller. Barnes prods the loose ball home to ignite mayhem, as the whole of St Andrew's expects a free kick to be given, but referee Roger Wiseman awards the goal. The home fans riot in response and then stage a full pitch invasion when Stoke keeper Ronnie Sinclair makes a save on the line that they think has gone over. During the ensuing scenes, 15 fans are evicted from the ground, 18 arrested and one man charged with assaulting the referee. When it has all calmed down, St Andrew's is emptied and the final few moments played out in silence. A dreadful day.

10 October 1992

Having drawn level just two minutes earlier against table-topping Leyton Orient in a crucial Second Division clash, Mark Stein nets again to give City a vital win and huge boost in their promotion bid. This time, two forward headers in midfield find Graham Shaw, racing towards the penalty area with the O's defence looking for the offside flag. It doesn't come and Shaw squares for Stein to tap into an empty net from three yards.

28 August 2011

Ryan Shotton poaches a late winner to keep Stoke's record against West Brom going. This time, at the Hawthorns, Shotton outpaces Albion centre-back Gabriel Tamaş and pips Ben Foster to a long through ball to tap home, with the West Brom keeper claiming he had both hands on it and that Shotton's foot was up at chest height, arguably with studs showing. Referee Mike Dean is unmoved. That's now 28 league games in which Stoke have lost just once against Albion. 'We only beat West Brom,' the away fans sing.

90

15 April 1963

As a tempestuous, explosive, uproarious and sometimes unruly struggle between two clubs vying for promotion at the top of the Second Division table heads towards the final whistle tied at 1-1, left-back Tony Allen sticks out a boot to tackle Sunderland's Andy Kerr in the Stoke penalty area and the Boothen End holds its breath as all eyes turn to referee Mr J. Thacker, who, controversially, waves play on. City take advantage to break while confusion reigns as Sunderland berate the official. A sweeping move down the right wing sees Don Ratcliffe cross for Dennis Viollet to stoop to head home past Jim Montgomery in the Rokerites goal. The late winner means City have now won 17 of 18 points since a 0-6 thrashing at Norwich in March, scoring 19 goals and conceding just three in that run. It sends the Stoke fans into total raptures, having been 'very much in ferment', according to *The Sentinel* scribe N.G., throughout the game due to the visitors' physical tactics. Stoke, though, give as good as they get and come out on top, much to the disgust of Alan Brown's men, who surround the referee again and then harangue him from the field when he blows the final whistle seconds later. Sunderland, who had lost 24-goal centre-forward Brian Clough to a career-ending injury on Boxing Day, would eventually miss out on promotion on goal difference, despite finishing only a point behind champions Stoke, so the penalty decision and Viollet's crucial late winner made all the difference.

21 March 1964

Winger Keith Bebbington slots home to complete City's record home top-flight victory of 9-1 over hapless Ipswich Town. It is the 100th goal the visitors have now conceded, out of a final total of 121 this season. City had knocked Ipswich out of the FA Cup the previous month, but only by a rather more humble 1-0 margin of victory. Stoke are well on the way to a 17th-place finish in their first season back in the First Division, but only 16,166 are at the Victoria Ground to see it, partly because of the recent poor run of form, but also partly due to the game being scheduled for the same afternoon as the 118th running of the Grand National, won by a head after a strong late run by 18/1 shot, 12-year-old Team Spirit, ridden by Willie Robinson.

26 October 1974

Leading 3-2 at Stamford Bridge, Tony Waddington's team look to have the game wrapped up. As Ian Britton sends a hopeful cross into the Stoke penalty area, goalkeeper John Farmer runs out to collect the ball. It seems a straightforward take, but the ball balloons slightly off the turf near the penalty spot, bounces off Farmer's fingertips, goes over his head and is nodded into the net by the grateful Ian Hutchinson from five yards. Frustrated at a number of such fluffs, the manager spends a world-record £325,000 for a goalkeeper on Leicester and England's Peter Shilton shortly afterwards. Arguments rage over the wisdom of that expenditure as, just a couple of weeks earlier, John Ritchie's career had been ended by a Kevin Beattie challenge at Ipswich and a school of thought says the money would have been better spent on a replacement striker.

26 December 1989

Stoke are plumb bottom of the Second Division, Mick Mills has been sacked and the early optimism of new manager Alan Ball's opening victory has been allayed by just one point from the next four games. High-flying Newcastle arrive at the Victoria Ground for a Christmas cracker and take an early lead, but City hit back with Wayne 'Bertie' Biggins sliding the ball under John Burridge to level. Debutants Tony Ellis and Lee Sandford impress, but it is left-back Cliff Carr's strong tackle on Newcastle's Ray Ranson which sees the ball break for midfielder Carl Beeston to leather an unstoppable right-foot shot home to clinch a vital three points.

9 February 2008

Leon Cort has put Stoke 3-2 up at Molineux, but Mick McCarthy's Wolves are pressing for the equaliser when a remarkable ten seconds swings the game in City's favour. Salif Diao appears to trip Andy Keogh in the Potters penalty area, but referee Andre Marriner waves play on. As Wolves complain, incensed, Diao clears to Ricardo Fuller, who picks the ball up 15 yards outside his own penalty area on the right side of the field. The Jamaican turns and sets off on a beeline for the Wolves goal. Thirty yards out, Fuller dips left then right to unsteady Rob Edwards and then, with a burst of speed, makes space to the right to fire a shot across Wayne Hennessy and into the far-left corner of the goal from ten yards. Stoke win 4-2 and promotion is well and truly on as this is the second of five wins in a row to take City to the top of the table by the end of February.

23 August 2008

Tied at 2-2 and entering injury time, Rory Delap picks up the ball level with the edge of the Aston Villa penalty area and steadies himself to hurl one last howitzer of a throw into the melee. It arrows in and finds the head of Mama Sidibé, ten yards out, jumping higher than both Martin Laursen and John Carew. As Sidibé arches his back to get his head down to the ball, it glances off near his right temple into the unguarded bottom-right corner of the Boothen End net. The Britannia Stadium goes ballistic as a first Premier League win is secured, but no one's smile is wider than the heroic Malian's.

6 December 2008

Struggling, 2-0 down at half-time and seemingly sinking on their return to the Premier League, Tony Pulis's Potters find the gumption to mount a great comeback at St James' Park. First, Mamady Sidibé converts Ricardo Fuller's cutback from the right byline to pull one back. Then, as time runs out, Danny Higginbotham flicks Glenn Whelan's right-wing free kick on for Abdoulaye Faye, signed by Stoke from the Magpies the previous summer for £2.25m, to control on his thigh, then fire into the bottom-left corner past Shay Given. Newcastle boss Joe Kinnear is so unhappy he is sent to the stands by referee Mike Riley.

1 March 2009

Stoke are 0-2 down at Villa Park in the search for points to avoid relegation in their first season in the Premier League. Martin O'Neill's Villa seem to be cruising, but then on 87 minutes Ryan Shawcross heads home from a right-wing corner. As the tide turns, the ball drops to Glenn Whelan on the edge of the penalty area and the Irish midfielder hammers his volley low, right-footed, into the bottom-left corner of Brad Friedel's net from 25 yards. Bedlam in the stands. Villa must be sick of the sight of Tony Pulis's Stoke this season.

16 January 2010

At the death, Robert Huth sticks out his massive right boot to deflect Danny Higginbotham's flick header, which was going wide of Pepe Reina's net, into the goal to secure a 1-1 draw against Rafa Benítez's Liverpool. It's the least Stoke deserve in this lunchtime TV encounter, played at breathtaking pace.

30 January 2011

Stoke are 1-0 up at Wolves in the FA Cup fourth round with time ticking away, when they hand the home side a lifeline to keep themselves in the competition as Robert Huth slides in and Nenad Milijaš tumbles in the penalty area. Referee Mike Jones awards the spot kick, but Thomas Sørenson, as so often, guesses correctly and saves the Serbian's penalty, low to his right, with the ball bouncing back to Huth to clear. The big German then double high fives his keeper in gratitude and Stoke are on their way to Wembley.

19 January 2013

It's a consolation goal of little consequence in a 1-3 defeat, but Michael Owen did score once for Stoke. Coming off the bench at Swansea's Liberty Stadium, Owen latches on to Steven Nzonzi's left-wing, inswinging cross to head home from six yards.

7 December 2013

If you think of late Stoke City winners in the modern era then you probably think of on-loan winger Oussama Assaidi, cutting inside Branislav Ivanović, then slamming the ball into Chelsea's net before swinging his red and white striped shirt around his head as he sets off down the length of the main stand in celebration, amidst a tumult of sound, as City seal a 3-2 victory over José Mourinho's Chelsea. The goal, a right-foot rocket from 22 yards wide out on the left corner of the penalty area at the Boothen End, which flies into Petr Čech's far top-right corner, seals Stoke's first league win over the Blues since 1975. Absolute monster classic.

23 March 2014

Stoke wrap up an impressive 4-1 victory at Villa Park when Marko Arnautović is released down the left, then leaves Leandro Bacuna for dead with a stepover and turn of speed, before pulling the ball back for Geoff Cameron to side-foot home right-footed from 14 yards.

10 February 2018

Stoke are desperately seeking a late winner against fellow strugglers Brighton in this crucial Premier League battle at the Bet365 Stadium and hope seems to be given to them when Jesé Rodriguez goes down under a Dale Stephens challenge in the penalty area. Referee Bobby Madley awards a spot kick, despite it being a touch-and-go foul. What then ensues is an utter shambles as first Jesé, Xherdan Shaqiri and Charlie Adam have a fight over who is going to take the penalty, with Adam winning out. And then, amidst huge tension, Adam mishits his spot kick to Mat Ryan's right and the keeper saves well, but the ball rebounds and Adam moves far too slowly to it to slot home and he is clattered out of the way and over the dead-ball line by an almighty challenge by Lewis Dunk, which arguably was a foul and another penalty, but it's not given. The chance is spurned and City fail to win at home again all season, falling to relegation and dropping out of the Premier League after a decade. The Potters have now missed their past three penalties in the Premier League, with each taken by a different player – Adam, Saido Berahino and Marko Arnautović.

5 October 2019

The Potters have not yet won a game all season under Nathan Jones, and it seems unlikely they will at the Liberty Stadium against top-of-the-Championship Swansea. Amazingly, Stoke's ten-game winless run ends when Swans keeper Freddie Woodman makes a terrific save, low to his left, on the line, from Sam Vokes's 11-yard header, but on-loan striker Scott Hogan is on hand to slot home the rebound from three yards. Crazy scenes ensue in the away end as Hogan is buried under a mountain of his team-mates, but it only reprieves the manager for a couple of weeks.

90+1

22 April 1964

With Stoke 1-3 down and heading for defeat in the 1964 two-legged League Cup Final, skipper Calvin Palmer crosses and centre-half George Kinnell side-foots home to give Stoke hope in the dying embers of the game. In the very final minute, England keeper Gordon Banks tips John Ritchie's drive around the post with his fingertips. Leicester lift the cup, presented to them by league president Joe Richards.

2 October 1974

Stoke are visiting the De Meer Stadion in Amsterdam to play Ajax and are still in the tie as the game is goalless, following a 1-1 draw at the Victoria Ground a fortnight earlier. Tony Waddington's men come agonisingly close to putting out the Dutch masters, who have won every league game so far this season, when Geoff Salmons skips down the left wing and crosses from near the corner flag. The ball lands, six yards out, at the left foot of substitute Jimmy Robertson, who connects well enough on the turn and hits it low. But Dutch international keeper Piet Schrijvers flicks out his left boot in response and the ball deflects away just past the right-hand post, leaving Jimmy Greenhoff inches away from being able to apply the finishing touch. Agonisingly close to immortality.

11 April 1998

Former boss Alan Durban has temporarily taken over desperate Stoke after Chic Bates and then Chris Kamara have been sacked with the Potters in the relegation zone. Misfit striker Kyle Lightbourne, a £500,000 signing from Coventry three months earlier, has yet to score a goal, but Durban brings the Bermudan on, despite the fans chanting 'Bring on the Hippo', noting their preference for the entry of Pottermus, the club mascot, as City are searching for a winner with the score tied at 1-1 against fellow strugglers Portsmouth. Lightbourne proves the better option, however, as he runs on to

Peter Thorne's pass, which leaves him with just the defender on the line to beat, to bag his first goal for the club from ten yards. The victory lifts City out of the relegation zone. Can they save their skins in the final four matches?

9 August 2003

Lewis Neal lashes in a triumphant, left-footed volley from a Chris Iwelumo cross to complete a remarkable 3-0 opening-day-of-the-season win at Derby. It comes as a massive surprise to the Potters fans basking in the sunshine as the Rams had been preseason favourites for promotion, while Tony Pulis's City had just avoided relegation by the skin of their teeth. It is Stoke's first win at the new Pride Park and the first at Derby since 1975.

13 November 2010

Stoke lead 1-0 and are withstanding Liverpool pressure when Jermaine Pennant breaks forward on the right and threads a pass through to Kenwyne Jones, despite being fouled in the process. Jones runs on and slots past Pepe Reina comfortably, low into the Boothen End net from 12 yards, to secure Stoke's first victory over Liverpool in 26 years.

28 December 2015

At the end of a crazy game in which Stoke have led twice and just come back from behind to level at 3-3, City are probing for a dramatic winner at Everton. Marko Arnautović drives into the penalty area and comes together with John Stones. Referee Mark Clattenburg thinks about it for a second before awarding City a debatable penalty, for which the ref is rewarded with a cuddle by City's Joselu. In nerve-shredding tension, Arnie puts the ball on the spot, but as he strikes it the Austrian slips, sending the ball down the middle, just under the bar. Thankfully, Toffees keeper Tim Howard has dived to his right and the goal clinches a famous 4-3 victory at Goodison Park. The superb game comes in the midst of the Potters' peak 'Stokelona' period under Mark Hughes. City move two places above their hosts into ninth place in the Premier League.

90+2

10 April 1965

Stoke's John Ritchie has already scored at either end of the first half against visitors Sheffield Wednesday, but now he swoops to strike twice more, once in the 88th minute and then again in injury time. Both goals are carbon copies, seizing on loose balls to make space 14 yards out to smash home right-footed, leaving his marker, Vic Mobley, an England under-23 international, in his wake. Ritchie's four goals are the first time a Potters striker has bagged four times in the top flight since Freddie Steele against Birmingham in January 1939 and he will do it again, against Northampton, the following year. Alan Brown's Owls are so fed up with facing the 6ft 2in striker that they end up buying him in November 1966, when Tony Waddington, for some bizarre reason, decides to sell him for £80,000.

14 April 1984

Stoke are 2-0 up against Bob Paisley's all-conquering Liverpool, who will win the treble of league, League Cup and European Cup this season. But City have won this game comfortably 2-0 and take to taunting the opposition. The Potters are so in control that 'Big Bren' O'Callaghan stands on the ball on the edge of his own area, goading and beckoning Liverpool captain, and infamous grump, Graeme Souness to come and get it. Bren is mocking Souness's mickey-taking earlier in the season when Stoke had put ten men behind the ball at Anfield, but the Scot is not amused. As he goes to tackle O'Callaghan, Bren simply back-heels the ball to Peter Fox. Souness is so annoyed he smashes a pane of glass in the tunnel as he storms off the field at full time and then picks up a post-match booking after making remarks to referee Eric Read that earn him a ban for Liverpool's next match. Stoke's win earns a full team strip and cheque for £250 for a local youth club when a panel chaired by England boss Bobby Robson selects the Potters as performance of the week under a Fiat sponsorship scheme.

26 December 2001

Guðjón Thorðarson's Stoke are 1-2 behind, but win a last-minute penalty at Tranmere when Mark Goodfellow's volley is stopped by a defender's hand. The manager's son, right-winger Bjarni Guðjónsson, has the ball, but, in an effort to intimidate him, the Rovers players are crowding around him, barging him, doing anything they can to put him off. All their efforts are in vain, however, as, once the furore has died down, Bjarni has a simple answer. He calmly hands the ball to striker Rikhadur Dadason, who slams the penalty past John Achterberg, low, left-footed. The looks on the Tranmere players' faces are hilarious!

20 August 2005

At a sunlit Britannia Stadium, City are struggling to break down Mike Newell's resilient Luton, despite them being down to ten men since the 26th minute after striker Steve Howard was sent off for spitting. In injury time, keeper Steve Simonsen launches a free kick to the edge of the penalty area, which is won by Michael Duberry. His header is cleared out of the box to the waiting Luke Chadwick, midway inside the Hatters half. He squares inside to Karl Henry, who in turn moves the ball further right to Dave Brammer, who hurtles forward and catches a right-footed drive perfectly. It flies 40 yards into the far top-left corner of Marlon Beresford's net to give City a late, exhilarating victory that kicks off Johan Boskamp's managerial season in typical madcap fashion.

28 October 2006

Loan signing Lee Hendrie inspires revamped Stoke to a five-goal haul against new manager Peter Grant's struggling Canaries in the Championship. He nets the first and makes two of the other goals, while Luke Chadwick is also causing mayhem on the other wing, so much so that the Canaries boss will sign the winger within three weeks, first on loan, then for £270,000 in the January transfer window, with Tony Pulis replacing him with Liam Lawrence from Sunderland for £450,000. The scorer of City's fifth goal is former Norwich midfielder Darel Russell, who controls a defensive header 22 yards out on his right thigh, then lashes the ball low past substitute goalkeeper Paul Gallacher, on because Jamie Ashdown has been sent off for bringing down Chadwick. The new keeper gets fingertips to it, but sees the ball go into the Boothen End net off the left post. Sublime attacking football.

20 February 2010

Stoke have been up against it at struggling Portsmouth ever since right-back Andy Wilkinson has been rather harshly sent off by referee Mike Dean for two yellow cards in three minutes. Level at 1-1, City are hanging on for a point against the Premier League's bottom club, destined for relegation and facing a winding-up order in the High Court the following week. But the Potters pile misery on to Pompey when the ten men break out from their penalty area and Ricardo Fuller runs the length of Fratton Park to pull the ball back from the right byline, finding veteran midfielder Salif Diao, who hammers it from ten yards into the roof of the net, right in front of the visiting fans. It is wonderfully unexpected as this is Diao's first goal in eight years, which secures a first league double over Portsmouth for 67 years.

19 March 2011

Already 3-0 up, City finish off Alan Pardew's Newcastle with a classic route-one goal. Asmir Begović whacks a long kick upfield, and Jon Walters wins the flick-on to put substitute Ricardo Fuller through on the right side of the penalty area. Fuller lets the ball bounce, then hammers it, right-footed on the volley, into the far-left corner of Steve Harper's goal.

1 December 2011

City are hanging on to a crucial 1-1 draw at the Britannia Stadium in their last home Europa League group game against Dynamo Kiev. A point will see City through, but the visitors, managed by Yuri Semin and with stars like Andriy Shevchenko and Andriy Yarmolenko in their team, are pressing hard. Into injury time, Yarmolenko steals forward and hits a right-foot shot which seems destined for the bottom-right corner. But City's Bosnian keeper Asmir Begović produces a magnificent fingertip save to tip the ball around the post and secure the vital point.

31 January 2015

Jon Walters completes his 'perfect' hat-trick, having already scored with his right and left foot, netting a header against Harry Redknapp's QPR, reacting first to reach a bouncing cross at the far post to head in from eight yards. His goals have completely changed the mood in the stadium, which began much more sombrely as the club celebrated the life of its greatest son, Stanley Matthews, who would have been 100 years old the following day, with a video tribute before kick-off. Walters is Stoke's second-highest Premier League scorer, with 43 top-flight goals out of his total of 62 for the Potters (just two goals behind Peter Crouch). He joined the club from Ipswich Town in August 2010 for £2.75m, signed by Tony Pulis, who loved a striker who worked hard and Walters fitted the bill perfectly. He could also find the back of the net regularly and dovetailed brilliantly with Crouch. He would play through any injury too, famously sporting bloodstained headbands on a regular basis after picking up an injury, and he was consistent enough to become one of the few Stoke players ever to start over 100 consecutive games for the club. Walters also made 54 appearances for the Republic of Ireland, scoring 14 goals and appearing at Euro 2012.

90+3

9 April 1996

Nigel Gleghorn floats a free kick from the left-hand side deep to the edge of the six-yard box, finding the head of the unmarked Mike Sheron. His glancing header into the bottom-right corner sparks wild celebrations amongst the supporters at Kenilworth Road as City are on the charge to the First Division play-offs under manager Lou Macari, thanks to this superb turnaround victory with two goals in seven minutes against Luton.

1 November 2000

Icelandic striker Rikhadur Dadason has finally joined from Norwegian club Viking FK Stavanger the day before this League Cup third-round tie, after signing a pre-contract with Stoke months earlier. The hype has been huge, with manager Guðjón Thorðarson building him up to be some kind of Norse god. Dadason is on the bench, having only just flown in, but is introduced to great cheers in the final minute of normal time, with the game against First Division Barnsley tied at 2-2. With his first touch, the striker piles in to leap and fiercely head home an inswinging right-wing corner from four yards to win the tie and set pulses racing. Is this the new Peter Thorne, Mike Sheron or John Ritchie?

1 May 2002

Time is running out for Stoke. They need a goal to send this Second Division play-off semi-final into extra time at Ninian Park after the 1-2 first-leg home defeat. Cardiff are so confident the tannoy announcer has asked fans to stay off the pitch at the final whistle. But they reckon without James O'Connor. The diminutive, Duracell Bunny Irishman makes a run into the Cardiff penalty area one last time. As Clive Clarke's cross sails over him to the far post, Bjarni Guðjónsson reaches it to knock it back across goal first time. O'Connor picks himself up quickly from contesting the initial cross to steer the ball, right-footed,

265

through his former team-mate Graham Kavanagh's legs, into the bottom-left corner from eight yards. There are only 800 Stoke fans in attendance at Ninian Park, but over 7,000 watching back at the Britannia Stadium on a big screen also go ballistic. The dream of promotion is back on.

13 September 2010

Visitors Aston Villa fail to clear Jermaine Pennant's free kick and the ball ricochets out to Matt Etherington, in space on the left edge of the penalty area. The left-winger takes one touch, then hits a cross come shot across goal through a crowd of players. Amongst them, Robert Huth's reflexes are fast enough to flick out a right boot to steer home, high into the top-right corner of the Boothen End as the shot flashes past him. City have come back to win their first game of the season 2-1, on an emotional night which has seen manager Tony Pulis attend the game despite his mother dying earlier that day.

5 February 2011

Robert Huth was, according to the terrace song, 'a big German youth'. His size certainly came in handy at set pieces. Never more so than on this occasion when City are 1-2 down at home to Steve Bruce's Sunderland. Two copycat goals sink the visitors. Both come from Jermaine Pennant left-wing free kicks, swung in, right-footed, from 35 yards. The first finds Huth storming through to poke the ball past Craig Gordon from four yards. The winner arrives when the German slides in to force home from even closer in.

4 August 2011

Stoke are holding on to a slender 1-0 first-leg lead in this Europa League third-round away game against Hajduk Split. In a white-hot atmosphere, the defence holds out brilliantly and victory is assured when Dean Whitehead breaks down the right wing and crosses into the middle from near the corner flag. Six yards out, Ryan Shotton is tussling with centre-half Ljubo Milicevic. The pair seem more intent on grappling with each other, but it pays off for Stoke when the ball hits Milicevic on the rear and rebounds past Danijel Subašić to give the Potters a famous 1-0 win. It is not only

City's first-ever European away win, but the first time they have won a tie in Europe to progress to the next round.

26 December 2019

City are struggling 1-2 behind at home to Garry Monk's Sheffield Wednesday in a classic Boxing Day atmosphere. Desperate for points, and having lost the lead they had at half-time, Michael O'Neill's men need a spark. It comes after intense pressure in and around the penalty area sees the ball break up and out to Sam Clucas on the edge of the box. As it falls, he nods it back towards goal, where it is seized on by Tyrese Campbell. The young striker leaps, with both feet off the ground kung fu-style, and lashes the ball with his left, high into the roof of the Boothen End net from seven yards so hard that keeper Cameron Dawson can only watch it fly past his shoulder. The stadium goes ballistic, but better is to come.

90+4

25 September 1982

Deep into injury time in this incredible First Division match against Luton, City find themselves in trouble at the back. Clinging on for a 4-4 draw, despite having been without keeper Peter Fox since the 28th minute, Stoke allow Brian Stein to escape down the left, having beaten the offside trap. George Berry tries to trip him before he enters the penalty area, but fails. Paul Bracewell manages to halt Stein, but illegally. And within the box. It's a penalty at the death and Luton's David Moss never misses ... until today, when he hits his right-foot shot against the foot of stand-in keeper Derek Parkin's left post. It is cleared to safety by Peter Hampton and the final whistle goes on this crazy game, with the Boothen End, behind that goal, going ballistic. A game for the ages.

28 December 2002

It is Tony Pulis's tenth game in charge of Stoke and he hasn't won one yet, as Stoke languish in the relegation zone. The pressure is on as visitors Sheffield Wednesday twice quickly peg back Chris Iwelumo goals. Deep into injury time, Iwelumo flicks on, then Chris Greenacre dummies on the edge of the area to cleverly release Brynjar Gunnarsson, and the Icelandic international runs on to fire past Chris Stringer, low into the bottom-right corner of the Boothen End net, to send the crowd wild and spark a remarkable second half of the season which sees the club survive on the final day.

21 August 2011

It looks like one of those days at Carrow Road as Jon Walters has already missed a penalty, saved by John Ruddy, as Stoke try to peg back Norwich's lead. But Kenwyne Jones, an £8m signing from Sunderland, saves the day. Matty Etherington pulls back a ball for Glenn Whelan to chip a curling right-footed cross into the box, and Jones beats Roberto Ayala to leap and head past Ruddy. This Tony Pulis team was made of stiff, special stuff.

28 April 2012

The game is drifting to a 1-1 draw when Dean Whitehead goes down under the faintest of touches by Arsenal's Laurent Koscielny right in front of the technical areas, and referee Chris Foy gives Stoke a soft free kick. Coupled with having turned down a penalty shout for a challenge by Glenn Whelan on Yossi Benayoun moments earlier, Foy has now enraged visiting manager Arsène Wenger so much that the Frenchman charges out of the dugout, arms flapping and famous long coat flailing in protest. Within seconds, the entire stadium is singing 'let's all do the Wenger', jumping up and down in mockery of the beleaguered boss, arms flapping like helicopters. It is a moment which goes down in history and is replayed on *Match of the Day* and Sky Sports ad infinitum for years, quintessentially summing up the feelings Potters fans have for the harrumphing Wenger and his hoity-toity Gunners.

90+5

27 March 1971

In their first FA Cup semi-final since 1899, even after Peter Storey's thunderbolt has pulled a goal back for Arsenal, Stoke are hanging on successfully under intense Gunners pressure, seemingly Wembley-bound. With five minutes of injury time played, referee Pat Partridge awards a controversial free kick against Mike Pejic, 40 yards out on the right. It is lofted into the penalty area, where Arsenal's John Radford barges Gordon Banks in the back, but the referee misses it. In the melee which follows Banks dropping the ball, Denis Smith punches the ball away with his elbow, which Partridge also misses. The ball is then blocked away for a corner. After the inevitable stormy inquest following that passage of play, the corner comes in from the right wing, right-footed, and Ray Kennedy rises eight yards out to head the ball towards the far-left bottom corner. It is saved by a flying fist, but sadly it belongs to midfielder John Mahoney, not Gordon Banks. Even Partridge cannot miss that and awards the penalty, which Storey then slides past a dispirited Banks. City have been pegged back to 2-2 and Wembley suddenly seems a distant dream.

19 October 2008

With City 2-1 up against ten men and deep into 11 minutes of injury time added on for Vedrun Ćorluka's awful head injury, incurred when his own keeper Heurelho Gomes punches him in trying to clear a Rory Delap long throw, causing the Croatia international to leave the stadium on a stretcher with an oxygen mask on, Tom Soares drives forward again and is felled by Tottenham's Jonathan Woodgate. Ricardo Fuller insists on taking the spot kick at the Boothen End, despite Danny Higginbotham already having scored one at the other end in the first half. Fuller's right-footed penalty hits the right post, then bounces across to hit the left post and Delap hammers the follow-up against the bar from eight yards. But the action isn't yet over and Michael Dawson sees red for an awful lunge on Mama Sidibé moments later as Stoke win a second Premier League game 2-1, beginning the creation of the Britannia Stadium as 'Fortress Britannia'.

29 December 2012

The white-hot Brit atmosphere has been stoked up by Steven Nzonzi's unjust red card when City were 2-3 down to Southampton and then a blatant penalty for handball not awarded by referee Mark Clattenburg. But Stoke are never better than when the odds are stacked against them and a very special goal earns a point. Glenn Whelan chips a ball forward to Kenwyne Jones. The big striker flicks it inside to Peter Crouch, who chests it down, but slightly miscontrols it. It sits up perfectly, though, for fellow substitute Cameron Jerome to run on to it and lash it, right-footed, from 30 yards, straight as an arrow into the top-right corner of the Boothen End net. It is a super hit, which sends the stadium into wild celebrations.

10 November 2013

A dramatic game has seen new manager Mark Hughes's Potters go from 2-0 ahead at half-time to 2-3 behind at the Liberty Stadium. Stoke's dreadful second half seems to have left them in the relegation zone, but a point is stolen when Robert Huth wins a far-post header from a left-wing corner and the ball deflects off two Swansea defenders, seemingly for a corner. But referee Bobby Madley awards a penalty for handball, which seems harsh and sends the Swans players and fans into meltdown. Up steps substitute Charlie Adam to keep his head and fire his left-footed spot kick into the bottom-left corner, sending Gerhard Tremmel the wrong way. Phew.

11 April 2015

Marko Arnautović is on fire. He has already had two goals frustratingly disallowed for offside, one just two minutes ago, while Mame Diouf has headed against the inside of a post. It seems City are destined to lose at Upton Park, but salvation arrives in the depths of injury time. Steven Ireland deceives the West Ham defence with a deft touch in midfield, which is flicked on by Peter Crouch, releasing Arnautović to race in on goal. The Austrian winger runs 25 yards, then hits a low, right-footed drive from 16 yards past Adrian into the bottom-left corner from the right side of the penalty area. Relief at last, after a frustrating day in front of goal.

7 November 2020

Early-season Championship pace setters Reading are thrashed at the Madejski Stadium when Jacob Brown, a £2m summer 2020 signing from Barnsley, nets his first league goal for Stoke to wrap up a 3-0 win. Brown capitalises on a weak back pass by Lewis Gibson to round keeper Rafael Cabral before slotting in. It caps Stoke's first win in 16 league trips to Reading, a run stretching back to December 1992 at Elm Park, lifting Michael O'Neill's men up to eighth in the table, a point off the top six. Is a promotion challenge materialising in O'Neill's first full season in charge?

90+6

26 December 2007

Liam Lawrence is already a two-goal hero at Barnsley, but City are 2-3 behind, so need him to complete his hat-trick. Referee Trevor Kettle has already given each side a penalty in this pulsating game in south Yorkshire, when Lawrence's free kick is handled by a desperate Barnsley defender. Up steps the hat-trick hero to calmly fire home, right-footed, into the opposite corner that he netted his first penalty in, bottom left, with Heinz Müller again diving the wrong way. Bedlam in the away end at the other end of Oakwell in celebration of the kind of spirit which will see this Potters team promoted to the Premier League at the end of the season.

22 September 2009

Stoke were 0-2 down, missed a penalty, but have still come back to lead 3-2 in this League Cup third-round tie. However, Ben Burgess has just headed an equaliser for Championship visitors Blackpool to tie this topsy-turvy game at 3-3. Extra time looks nailed on, but up steps Potters skipper Andy Griffin to win the tie. He picks the ball up on the left wing, cuts inside on to his favoured right foot, dips his shoulder left then veers to the right as he enters the penalty area to commit a defender, before slamming a low shot into the far-right corner. Keeper Matt Gilks gets his fingertips to it, but it sneaks in to send City through to the last 16.

90+7

28 August 2018

The 7,290 fans who have bothered to show up to watch this League Cup second-round tie against Premier League Huddersfield at the Bet365 Stadium have already seen one remarkable goal, Saido Berahino's first for Stoke. But an equally memorable one follows to seal City's progress through to the next round. It comes as Darren Fletcher whacks a clearance into the visitors' half and Huddersfield debutant Juninho Bacuna flails his right foot at it, sending it spiralling up into the Staffordshire night sky. Unfortunately for him it's heading towards his own goal, at the Boothen End, and it is so late in the game that his goalkeeper Jonas Lössl has gone up for the free kick which precedes Fletcher's clearance. The ball sails over the desperate keeper's head as he races back and takes five bounces before rolling into the bottom-left corner, allowing fans to celebrate well before the ball crosses the line. It's a bizarre own goal from 50 yards that sets the seal on one of the oddest evenings in recent memory.

26 December 2019

James McClean is hobbling around, having injured his knee in an earlier challenge, but still finds the energy and guts to fly into two tackles on the left wing, winning a corner in the process. It's a selfless act of commitment to the Stoke cause, and the fans in the Boothen End behind that goal rise to applaud him as he takes the flag kick. The ball curls to the six-yard line, where Sheffield Wednesday's Dominic Iorfa crumbles under the heavy pressure of bodies flying in and heads it down, not away. It falls for Sam Vokes, three yards out, to control on his left thigh, then lunge to prod, right-footed, under keeper Cameron Dawson. The goal brings the house down as it seals a 3-2 victory when, three minutes earlier, City were staring defeat in the face. Delirious fans screech yet more choruses of the Michael O'Neill song, in honour of the new manager who is in the process of turning Stoke's fortunes around spectacularly.

Extra time first half

94

26 August 2009

In a downpour, Dave Kitson is on a one-man mission to break his 15-month goal drought. Having signed for Stoke in summer 2008, he has yet to find the net over a year later. But the ginger striker has already come incredibly close at Brisbane Road in this League Cup second-round tie. His header from six yards was deflected up on to the bar by Orient defender John Melligan, came down on to the defender's head again and then bounced, crazily, clear. It seems Kitson is destined never to score for Stoke. But then in extra time his moment arrives. As the ball bobbles around outside the Orient penalty area, it falls for Kitson, who swivels and hits a hip-high volley high into the top-left corner from 30 yards. Three days later Kitson nets the winner in the Premier League against Sunderland and his hoodoo is broken.

29 October 2013

In a bonkers game, Stoke have been 1-0 and 3-1 up at Championship Birmingham in the League Cup fourth round, yet find themselves pegged back to 3-3 and taken to extra time, despite Birmingham having only had ten men since Wade Elliott's dismissal just before half-time. Now, substitute Kenwyne Jones nets a fourth for Stoke, rounding keeper Colin Doyle after being picked out by Stephen Ireland, and sliding home from five yards out on the right. But the nonsense continues as Olly Lee equalises at the death to send the tie to penalties, which see the Potters finally win 4-2.

95

26 August 1992

After Mark Stein's last-minute equaliser takes the tie to extra time, and Vince Overson's header puts City ahead, Wayne Biggins settles things against Preston in this League Cup first-round tie with two goals in three minutes. His first is a header from a corner, but his second is a lovely, cultured chip over North End keeper Simon Farnworth from 15 yards. Sumptuous.

24 February 2010

Just eight days after having a last-gasp winner ruled out against Manchester City, Ryan Shawcross is in the visitors' penalty area again, causing havoc and getting on the end of a cross. This time it's actually a long Rory Delap throw, which travels fully 50 yards, that Ryan beats Shay Given to and heads into the empty net. Ten-man Manchester City's resistance is broken. Stoke seal the win with a Tuncay goal four minutes later, with first Glenn Whelan and then the Turkish international beating two men to create a tap-in for 3-1.

102

22 March 1972

A pulsating FA Cup quarter-final is tied at 1-1 with visitors Manchester United, but Terry Conroy wins it with a right-footed half-volley that flies past visiting keeper Alex Stepney. Gordon Banks produces two world-class saves to seal progress to a second successive FA Cup semi-final against Arsenal.

104

26 January 2016

Peter Crouch rises to flick on Erik Pieters's long ball for on-loan midfielder Marco van Ginkel to run on to. The Dutch international from Chelsea powers on to the ball, brushing aside the challenge of Lucas Leiva, to turn and fire, right-footed from 12 yards, against the foot of Simon Mignolet's left-hand post. Stoke end up winning 1-0 at Anfield for the first time since 1959, but go out 5-6 on penalties after the tie ends 1-1 on aggregate. So near, yet so far.

Extra time second half

107

26 September 2000

Stefán Thórðarson is a little-talked-about, underrated member of Stoke City's Icelandic clan. Amongst his 11 goals in 63 games is this peach of a left-foot shot from 30 yards, out on the left side of the Charlton half, after a run from inside his own half, which flies into the very top-right corner of the Addicks net. Charlton keeper Dean Kiely has a look of bemusement on his face as he watches the ball sail over his head that says, 'you can't do that ... oh, you have'. The goal sees Stoke qualify for the next round of the League Cup after losing the second leg of the tie at the Valley 3-4, but going through on away goals after a 2-1 home win.

114

1 May 2002

It's incredibly tense as Stoke and Cardiff tussle it out in the Second Division play-off semi-final. The Potters need inspiration, but the opposite is what wins the game and sends Stoke through to the final. A free kick is awarded, controversially, by referee Mike Dean, two yards outside the Bluebirds penalty area. James O'Connor, Stoke's industrious midfielder, steps up to take it. Will he shoot, will he cross, will he set up someone else for a shot? He opts for the former, side-footing a shot, which is heading for the bottom-right corner, but then the ball, having gone past the wall, strikes Guinean striker Souleymane Oularé on the backside and deflects past Neil Alexander into the opposite side of the Cardiff net. It is a scruffy goal, but neither the 800 Stoke fans at Ninian Park nor the gathered throng of 7,000 for the beam-back at the Britannia Stadium care. It will prove to be Oularé's only Stoke goal, as he had suffered major health problems, including a worrying blood clot, since signing for the club from Las Palmas. But he thankfully fully recovered to be in the right place at the right time. At least his bum did. His memory could be questioned, though; Oularé later claimed he headed his famous goal home!

115

18 January 2011

Jon Walters has already powered home a near-post header from Michael Tonge's corner to give Stoke the lead in extra time at Cardiff's swanky new Cardiff City Stadium. He seals progress to the fourth round in this replay when he takes Glenn Whelan's cute through ball in his stride, bears down on Tom Heaton in the Cardiff goal and slots home at the second attempt at the near post, under the keeper. Little do the few travelling fans know it, but they are witnessing the first victory on the road to the FA Cup Final.

117

15 December 1971

It is extra time in the League Cup semi-final second leg with the aggregate score tied at 2-2 – and Geoff Hurst, having smashed a penalty home to Gordon Banks's right in the first leg, has another spot kick, after Banks has brought down Harry Redknapp, to put Stoke in danger of going out. The tension is unbearable and various players cannot watch amidst a tumult of noise. But the genius keeper is more than capable of dealing with all that, his England team-mate's psyche-out techniques and the need to redeem himself. Banks takes up the story: 'Geoff was setting himself up to take the same sort of long run-up and I thought: "He's not going to change here, I'll gamble."' The England keeper hurls himself to his right as Hurst thumps his shot to that side. 'I was flying through the air with both my arms pointing towards the sky. Geoff had hit the ball so hard that when my left hand made contact, I had to tense the muscles in my arm and wrist or it would have knocked my hand aside. To my great relief it ricocheted up into the murky gloom and over the bar.' It is an incredible save, with the rigidity of that left wrist astonishing. It keeps City in the tie and they will finally reach Wembley after two more replays, all thanks to Banks's determination to right his own wrong.

120

24 January 1955

Neville 'Tim' Coleman, making his professional debut after leaving the RAF, comes in off the right wing to become the hero by heading home the winning goal for Frank Taylor's Potters from Johnny Malkin's cross, ending up in a crumpled heap in the mud of Old Trafford as he does so. Coleman had also sent the game into extra time by scoring in the 85th minute to make it 2-2, netting from Frank Bowyer's short pass. This last-gasp goal finally defeats Bury 3-2 in an FA Cup third-round fourth replay, after a record nine hours and 22 minutes of play, and four games ending 1-1, 1-1, 3-3 and 2-2. Exhausting.

Post-match

18 May 1963

The final whistle signals that Stoke City have won promotion back into the top flight after a decade away, thanks to goals from Jackie Mudie and 48-year-old Stan Matthews that have defeated Luton, whose relegation has been confirmed, to clinch the vital two points that get City over the line. Fans pour on to the pitch from all four sides of the Victoria Ground to mob the players. Presented to the buoyant crowd from the directors' box after being smuggled up into the Boothen Stand, the heroes are greeted with huge cheers. Matthews raises both hands in acclamation when he is announced, to the delight of the throng, and a speech by the Lord Mayor proclaims, 'Dreams have come true. Stoke City are back where they belong.' Back in the dressing room, with supporters still swarming in exaltation across the mud, teetotaller Matthews takes a rain check on the champagne, but says, 'This is one of the greatest moments of my life. It's what I came back here to Stoke for.'

28 April 1965

After 19 years of faithful service split across two stints, Stoke City lay on an extraordinary extravaganza of a farewell testimonial for the club's most famous son, 50-year-old, newly knighted Sir Stanley Matthews, on his retirement. As well as the 35,000 fans in attendance at the Victoria Ground, the stadium is chock full of Eurovision television cameras and radio services from around the world. All in all, around 112 million people tune in to watch 'The Wizard of Dribble' weave his silken magic one final time. An incredible array of talent turn out for his XI versus the Rest of the World, including Ferenc Puskás, Lev Yashin, Alfredo di Stéfano, Eusébio, Bobby Moore, Denis Law and John Charles. For the record, the result was a 6-4 victory for the Rest of the World. The momentous day ends with Matthews being carried off the Victoria Ground pitch on the shoulders of Yashin and Puskás to a standing ovation and a rousing chorus of 'Auld Lang Syne' all around the ground. What a way to end a glittering career. Super trivia for you:

Matthews suffered knee cartilage damage during the game, which he later described in his autobiography as 'a promising career cut tragically short'.

26 January 1972

As the final whistle sounds, England World Cup-winning goalkeeper Gordon Banks, covered from head to toe in sludge following a heroic performance in a mudbath amidst a storm, turns to the Stoke fans massed behind his goal in the Stretford End at Manchester United's Old Trafford and raises both fists to them. Stoke City have made it to their first-ever major cup final at Wembley, the League Cup Final of 1972. After four action-packed, tense matches they have finally edged past West Ham in a second replay of the semi-final, which eventually leads to the Potters claiming their first, and so far only, major trophy.

4 March 1972

Captain Peter Dobing climbs the famous old Wembley steps to accept the 1972 League Cup from Dr Gustav Wiederkehr, president of UEFA. Scarves and banners wave as the trophy is lifted aloft and proudly displayed to the Potters fans, who are making a tremendous noise singing new anthem 'We'll Be With You', penned by Tony Hatch and Jackie Trent, writers of the *Neighbours* and *Crossroads* theme tunes, ecstatic at finally having won a major trophy in the club's 109th year.

16 May 1992

Stoke City captain Vince Overson leads his team up the famous 39 Wembley steps to the Royal Box to receive the Autoglass Trophy from England legend Bobby Moore. The skipper lifts it high towards the Potters fans, bathed in sunlight at the tunnel end. Oddly, it is the second successive season Overson has made this walk to lift this trophy for a team managed by Lou Macari as both were with Birmingham 12 months before when they beat Tranmere. When the trophy is held aloft, former Stoke defender George Berry, amongst the fans, bursts into tears in pride and a huge 'Delilah' is led by Overson, later described by a Wembley spokesman as the 'loudest noise I have ever heard fans make here'.

28 April 1993

With tension rising to a nerve-shredding level, City are seeking to hold out for a narrow 1-0 victory over Plymouth in order to clinch promotion. Fans from the Boothen End are already on the edge of the pitch behind Peter Fox's goal in anticipation of referee David Elleray's whistle. Skipper Vince Overson is channelling his inner and outer Terry Butcher after smashing his head in a challenge with Mickey Evans – a wound that will need three stitches – but he's carrying on in a bloodied head bandage to marshal the Stoke rearguard. With five minutes to go Fox keeps out Paul Dalton's deflected shot with a superb save low to his left to seal his hero status. Then the whistle goes and the supporters stream on to the pitch in jubilation, with flags waving, to hail their heroes, who have returned the club to the First Division after three seasons in the third tier. Kevin Russell is hoisted shoulder high, but also has his shirt ripped from his back in enthusiastic celebration.

10 January 1998

Sixteen supporters are arrested after fans invade the Britannia Stadium pitch to protest at the state of the club. City have just lost 0-7 at home to Birmingham to notch up a new unwanted record home defeat, which still remains as Stoke's record home league loss. But it wasn't just the result on the day which supporters were angry about: earlier that week there had been unrest amongst players who had been told by managing director Jez Moxey that the club had financial issues and they might struggle to be paid – hardly motivational. With a handful of fans invading the Waddington Suite in the main stand and causing minor damage, added to some who had been ejected earlier during the game for encroaching on to the pitch after one of the goals, in the end 16 supporters appeared in court for various offences of affray following the post-match events, including one youth who was cautioned for stealing the match ball. Manager Chic Bates departs shortly afterwards as City spiral to relegation in their first season at the Britannia Stadium.